A HISTORY OF
THE KIKUYU
1500–1900

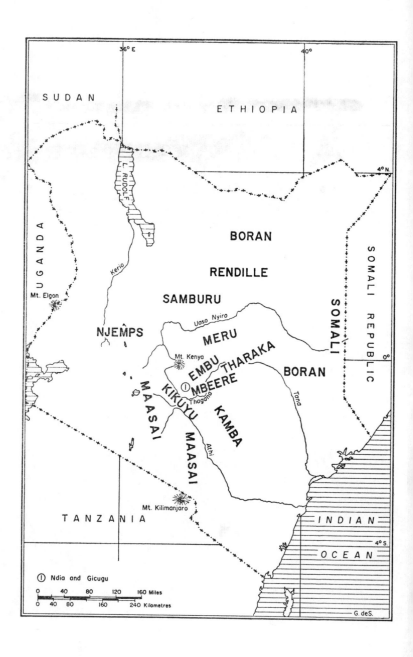

SUDAN

ETHIOPIA

36° E

40°

4° N.

UGANDA

L. RUDOLF

Kerio

Mt. Elgon

BORAN

RENDILLE

SAMBURU

Uaso Nyiro

NJEMPS

MERU

Mt. Kenya

EMBU

THARAKA

MBEERE

BORAN

KIKUYU

Thagana

SOMALI

SOMALI REPUBLIC

0°

MAASAI

KAMBA

Tana

MAASAI

Athi

TANZANIA

Mt. Kilimanjaro

INDIAN

4° S.

OCEAN

G. deS.

① Ndia and Gicugu

0   40   80   120   160 Miles

0   40   80   160   240 Kilometres

GODFREY MURIUKI

A HISTORY OF THE KIKUYU
1500-1900

1974
OXFORD UNIVERSITY PRESS
NAIROBI LONDON NEW YORK

Oxford University Press, Ely House, London W.1

GLASGOW NEW YORK TORONTO MELBOURNE WELLINGTON
CAPE TOWN IBADAN NAIROBI DAR ES SALAAM LUSAKA ADDIS ABABA
DELHI BOMBAY CALCUTTA MADRAS KARACHI LAHORE DACCA
KUALA LUMPUR SINGAPORE HONG KONG TOKYO

Oxford University Press, P.O. Box 72532, Nairobi

TO WARUGURU AND NJERI

Contents

Page

PREFACE   vii

INTRODUCTION   1

CHAPTER 1 The physical setting   25
        2 Migration of the Mount Kenya peoples   37
        3 Migration and settlement of the Kikuyu   62
        4 The Kikuyu and their neighbours   83
        5 The social and political structure   110
        6 Prelude to British rule   136
        7 Conclusion   167

BIBLIOGRAPHY   180

INDEX   186

MAPS   1 Kikuyu plateau: physical features   27
        2 Kikuyu plateau: ecological zones   31
        3 Migration of the Mount Kenya peoples   50
        4 The dispersal of the Kikuyu   59
        5 Kikuyu plateau: land alienation   172

Preface

This book is the first systematic attempt so far undertaken to collect and analyse the historical traditions of the Kikuyu. It demonstrates that among the Kikuyu, genealogies of the *mbari*, or kinship groups, are a more fruitful source of historical evidence than the popular myths of origin, which are practically worthless.

A close study of the former indicates that the Kikuyu are an amalgam of diverse elements drawn from a wide area. An analysis of the Kikuyu society, based on kinship groups and the *mariika* (age sets) system, also shows that it was profoundly influenced by the mode of the initial immigration and the subsequent pattern of settlement. The *mariika* system provided manpower for public duties and was a vital vehicle for education and social control. By the end of the nineteenth century, this society was characterized by two factors: it was highly competitive and egalitarian.

Relations between the Kikuyu and their neighbours are also examined. It is shown that there were no basic differences in the social relationships between the Kikuyu themselves, the Kikuyu and the Maasai or the Kikuyu and their Bantu cousins around Mount Kenya. The bad reputation of the Kikuyu, in particular, is revealed to have originated from the Kamba and the coastal traders and this had disastrous results to the subsequent contact between the Kikuyu and all newcomers.

Finally, the initial establishment of British rule, largely by force, is examined. Western civilization was imposed on the conquered with far-reaching repercussions to their way of life.

This book grew out of a Ph.D. thesis which was presented to the University of London in 1969. Its completion was greatly assisted by the generous co-operation of many people and institutions. I was financially supported by the Rockefeller Foundation throughout the period of research. I am full of gratitude to the

Foundation for its most generous grant, which enabled me to conduct my research both in Kenya and in Britain.

My deep thanks go to Professor Roland Oliver of the School of Oriental and African Studies, University of London, for his kindness, constructive criticism, patient supervision and untiring counsel.

Several librarians and officials made available the material that I required, especially the staff of the Kenya National Archives, the Public Record Office, the Church Missionary Society Library in London and Rhodes House, Oxford.

I am also grateful to Mr T. G. Benson, then of the School of Oriental and African Studies, London, for drawing my attention to the existence of the Barlow Papers; to Dr Alan H. Jacobs, 'Orangai' (the tall one) of the University of Nairobi, who made his research notes on the Maasai freely available; to the late Col. R. Meinertzhagen for permitting me to use his private papers; and to the Ainsworth family for giving me access to John Ainsworth's private papers.

In the early stages of my fieldwork, I was assisted with interviewing by students and pupils of several institutions. I wish to thank the former principal and students of Kagumo Teacher Training College, and the headmasters and pupils of Ruthagati, Kabiru-ini, Kirimara, Kiaritha-ini, Kanjuri, Gikumbo and Gatondo Secondary Schools in Mathira, Nyeri. I was also assisted by administrative officials in Nyeri, Murang'a and Kiambu districts, for which help I am grateful indeed. In particular I wish to thank the chiefs and their assistants in these districts.

I am most obliged to all my informants; it is a pleasure to record my appreciation of their co-operative and voluntary service, and to recall generous hospitality even in the most humble homes. Many thanks are due also to my colleagues at the University of Nairobi, who read the manuscript and made valuable criticisms and suggestions.

Finally, I am grateful to my wife, Njeri, who was not only a constant source of encouragement but also fully shared in the preparation of this book. She assisted with the interviewing of the informants, transcribed the interviews from tapes, typed several drafts and drew the maps. I can never thank her enough for her unsparing help.

INTRODUCTION

In the last two decades the African continent south of the Sahara has witnessed radical changes. And while focus on these changes has largely been centred on the process of decolonization, a much less-publicized but integral part of this revolution has been the historian's reappraisal of the study and teaching of African history. African history is no longer regarded to be an appendage of European history, nor is its subject matter the colonial exploits of the missionaries, explorers, traders and administrators. African history has come of age and has rightly established itself as a respectable academic discipline in Africa and in other parts of the world, particularly Europe and North America.[1] This reversal of fortunes has been largely accelerated by the emergence of the hitherto dependent territories into independent states. Aware of the importance and the role of history in uniting and maintaining a nation, these new states have been loudest in the call for a re-interpretation of their history. Unity and stability are of vital importance to them since many of them are composed of heterogeneous, and artificial, units that are often strained by endemic forces; a phenomenon commonly called tribalism. But this need for a new approach to African history has not been solely, or even mainly, confined to the political practitioners. On the contrary, the coming of age of African history is due to the efforts of a new generation of Africanists which has been at the forefront of the new interpretation of, and approach to, African history.

These scholars have particularly emphasized the brevity of the colonial period with which the bulk of the extant studies have

---

1. R. Oliver, *African History for the Outside World*, an inaugural lecture delivered on 13 May 1964; R. Oliver (ed.), *The Middle Age of African History*, London, 1967, pp. 92-7.

tended to be concerned. Also, the subject matter of colonial history has been shown to be limited in scope and the general characteristic of these studies is that they have been conditioned by the climate of the colonial era. Consequently, they have emphasized the activities of the foreigners to the virtual exclusion of the African peoples, and the picture that emerges is far from complete. They have tended to portray the foreigners as a catalyst in a sea of hitherto docile and dormant recipient communities. Yet, whenever a closer study has been undertaken, this conclusion has been shown to be unten-able.[2] Furthermore, the colonial era cannot be understood properly, or analysed, without taking into account the preceding period. This has led the students of African history to the conclusion that the continent's history must necessarily be a history of, and for, Africa. That is, a history which, while inevitably including much about outside influences from Europe and Asia, will also attempt to give them their proper weight. These outside influences are hence only one, albeit an important one, of the many factors that have influenced the course of African history. Seen in this light, the history of Africa ceases to begin with the incursions of the Arabs and the Europeans into Africa, as formerly portrayed in the history curricula of colleges and schools and, to some extent, in current textbooks. It becomes the study of the African people in the past and present. Accordingly, it conforms to the historical tradition of the theme of history being the study of man and his actions,[3] or as Professor Oliver has so aptly put it, '... history is the history of Man, and not just of European man, or even of so-called civilized man'.[4]

Faced with a scarcity of written sources, or even their non-existence, historians have primarily relied on oral traditions for the reconstruction of African history. But this has presented its own problems. As Vansina has shown, oral traditions do not exist in a vacuum; they have a purpose and function to fulfil in any society and are therefore conditioned by the political and social structure.[5] But if this creates difficulties, these are neither peculiar

2. For example, Mutesa, the Kabaka of Buganda, did not invite missionaries because of his desire for Christianity *qua* Christianity but as a political weapon. J. M. Gray, 'Mutesa of Buganda', *Uganda Journal*, vol. 1, 1934, pp. 22-49.
3. M. Block, *The Historian's Craft*, Manchester, 1954, pp. 10-11, 25-6.
4. Oliver, inaugural lecture, op. cit., p. 17.
5. J. Vansina, *Oral Traditions: A Study in Historical Methodology*, London, 1965, chapter 4 and pp. 170-3. This is a general historical problem as P. Weiss has argued—'Since our idea of the reasonable is in good part

to Africa, nor are oral traditions necessarily more unreliable than the written sources.[6] No historian can be entirely divorced from the society in which he lives and to that extent this will influence his judgement and values. Moreover, the problem of African historiography is not an isolated entity; it is part of the world-wide problem of the nature of history, and history, it has been argued, can only arrive at probabilities but never at certainties.[7]

In the study of oral traditions, it has been implied that centralized societies are better able to preserve their oral traditions than the acephalous ones.[8] This view seems to underrate the oral traditions of the latter societies and perhaps this is not surprising for, individual researchers have in the past concentrated their efforts on the centralized societies due partly to the difficulties involved in collecting oral traditions of the acephalous societies. Until recently little work has been done on acephalous societies but this pattern is rapidly changing. In Kenya alone, the studies carried out lately by Jacobs, Were and Ogot indicate that our ignorance of the uncentralized societies has been partly due to neglect.[9] This study will show that far from there being a poverty of oral traditions among such societies, their social and political structure only calls for a different approach in the retrieval of their traditions. Whereas traditions in the centralized societies were often controlled and rigidly regulated by a narrow circle of courtiers, those in the uncentralized societies were spread among much wider groups

a function of social experience, all histories have a tribal side, reflecting the assumptions and evaluations shared by the members of a society.' See P. Weiss, *History: Lived and Written*, Illinois, 1962, p. 11.
6. For a discussion of the African historiography, see 1st, 2nd and 3rd Conferences on History and Archaeology held at the School of Oriental and African Studies, University of London, edited by R. A. Hamilton (1955) and D. H. Jones (1959), and in the *Journal of African History*, vol. 3, 1962 respectively; J. Vansina, R. Mauny and L. V. Thomas (eds.), *The Historian in Tropical Africa, Studies Presented and Discussed at the Fourth International African Seminar at the University of Dakar, Senegal, 1961*, London, 1964; M. Posnansky, *Prelude to East African History, Papers Read at the First East African Vacation School in Pre-European History and Archaeology, December, 1962*, London, 1966.
7. 'The historian never arrives at certainty; he rarely ends with more than a not altogether sifted totality of plausible, hypothetical, guessed-at and imagined formulations of what had been.'—P. Weiss, op. cit., p. 45.
8. J. Vansina, op. cit., p. 173, and R. Oliver in Vansina, Mauny and Thomas (eds.), op. cit., p. 309.
9. A. H. Jacobs, 'The Traditional Political Organization of the Pastoral Masai', unpublished Ph.D. thesis, Oxford, 1965; G. S. Were, *A History of the Abaluyia of Western Kenya, c. 1500-1930*, Nairobi, 1967; B. A. Ogot, *History of the Southern Luo, Migration and Settlement*, Nairobi, 1967.

such as the heads of families and lineages, or experts in judicial, political and religious processes of the tribe. This difference appears to be marginal rather than fundamental; in the former case the custodians of oral traditions are known and easily identifiable, while in the latter this is not the case. Here the researcher has to cast a more widespread net, because every lineage head or expert may have something of importance to contribute.

Besides, it should be borne in mind that there are advantages and disadvantages to the study of both the official and private traditions.[10] Centralized societies such as Rwanda and Buganda, maintained (official) traditions which conveyed information of public importance. Because of their functional importance, such traditions were so rigidly controlled by social or political groups in authority that in some societies, traditions which contradicted the official version were explicitly suppressed. Also, facts which did not help in maintaining the *status quo* were either omitted or falsified. There is no doubt, however, that official traditions were more carefully transmitted, special attention being paid to accuracy. It is also true that official traditions seem to go much further into the past than private traditions, although a serious drawback is that by their nature they are less trustworthy as historical sources, official history being more subject to distortions than private history. In contrast, private traditions do not need official ratifications or control. These are transmitted at random and consequently are open to change according to the whims or inclination of the individual. There is no need, though, for the individual to distort events of the past since private traditions only defend private interests, and the fulfilment of social function is of secondary interest.

Although my study of the Kikuyu did not start until October 1966, my interest in the African history goes back to my undergraduate days at Makerere University College, Uganda, where I read history between 1961 and 1964, under the revised external syllabus of the University of London.[11] My appreciation of the role of oral traditions in the study of African history, however, arose from the participation in a vacation school organized by the British Institute of History and Archaeology in East Africa held in December, 1962.[12] It was then that I realized how little I knew about the pre-colonial

10. Vansina, op. cit., pp. 84-6.
11. For details, see Oliver, inaugural lecture, op. cit., pp. 4-6.
12. Posnansky, op. cit.

history of East Africa, or indeed of the Kikuyu. Luckily, I was soon afterwards assisted by the History Department of Makerere College to spend April and May of 1963 in Nyeri district familiarizing myself with oral evidence relating to the establishment of the British administration in that part of Kikuyuland. My initiation had thus begun.

The months of October 1966 to June 1967 were spent at the School of Oriental and African Studies, University of London, making a general survey of the background material available in Britain. These documentary sources were later supplemented (in July and August 1967) by further sources at the Kenya National Archives, Nairobi. The more important primary sources are the works of Routledge, Hobley and Leakey, while general ethnographical surveys are to be found in the works of Cagnolo and Kenyatta.[13] Most of the existing material is ably summarized by Middleton and Kershaw in their contribution to the Ethnographical Survey of Africa.[14] Other primary sources dealing with specialized aspects of Kikuyu society are the articles contributed by K. R. Dundas (1908-9), McGregor (1909) and Tate (1904, 1910-11).[15] Another important source is the report on *Native Land Tenure in Kikuyu Province*, dealing specifically with land and the related subjects. Besides, Barlow and Lambert have also made major contributions to our understanding of the Kikuyu society. Barlow was perhaps the most thorough and painstaking student of the Kikuyu there has yet been, and it is on his original linguistic work that Benson's standard *Kikuyu-English Dictionary* is based.[16] His private papers are also an extremely important source and contain his research

13. W. S. and K. Routledge, *With a Prehistoric People, the Kikuyu of British East Africa*, London, 1910; C. W. Hobley, *Bantu Beliefs and Magic, with Particular Reference to the Kikuyu and Kamba Tribes of Kenya Colony*, London, 1922; C. Cagnolo, *The Akikuyu, Their Customs, Traditions and Folklore*, Nyeri, 1933; L. S. B. Leakey, 'The Southern Kikuyu Studies', unpublished MS, 1938 (hereafter Leakey, MS); J. Kenyatta, *Facing Mount Kenya*, London, 1938.

14. J. Middleton and G. Kershaw, *The Kikuyu and Kamba of Kenya*, London, 1965.

15. H. R. Tate; 'The Native Law of the Southern Gikuyu of British East Africa', *Journal of African Society*, vol. 9, 1910, pp. 233-54 and vol. 10, 1911, pp. 285-97, and Kenya National Archives (hereafter KNA), ref. PC/1/4/1; K. R. Dundas, 'Notes on the Origin and History of the Kikuyu and Dorobo Tribes', *Man*, vol. 8, 76, 1908, pp. 136-9 and vol. 8, 101, 1908, pp. 180-2; A. W. McGregor, 'Kikuyu and Its People', *Church Missionary Review*, 1909, pp. 30-6.

16. T. G. Benson (ed.), *Kikuyu-English Dictionary*, Oxford, 1964.

notes dealing with all aspects of Kikuyu society, including their oral traditions. Lambert, on the other hand, summarized the existing traditional history of the Mount Kenya peoples and attempted to reconstruct a history of their migration.[17] But his work could be criticized on two grounds. As indicated in chapter 2, he assumed that all the Mount Kenya peoples came from Shungwaya, whereas only Meru traditions suggest this. Secondly, although he recognized the importance of the *mariika* system in constructing a chronology and the essential principles governing their formation, yet he failed to use this evidence to its conclusion, which would have permitted him to extend the chronology back to the sixteenth century, without having to resort to the doubtful 'average rate of occupation' or the 'co-efficient of expansion'.[18]

Another unique and indispensable primary source is *The Kenya Land Commission, Evidence and Memoranda*.[19] This is the product of the Royal Commission dispatched, under Sir Morris Carter in 1932, by the British government to inquire into the land problem, an incessant cause of political friction in Kenya. It is particularly valuable as a record of the situation in Kikuyuland in the second half of the nineteenth century, and of the initial contacts between the Kikuyu and the Europeans. It also gives graphic surveys of the manner in which the Kikuyu adjusted themselves under the new regime in this century. But a word of caution is necessary about this and the other sources. From 1920 onwards, land had become a controversial issue between the government, the Kikuyu and the white community. To the extent that land and Kikuyu traditions of origin and migration are interrelated, it is important to distinguish between the material collected before and after 1920. Much of the later work, whether contributed by the Kikuyu or the Europeans, was politically inspired. The written contributions by Dundas, Routledge, McGregor, Barlow and Tate are therefore more valuable and reliable in their treatment of the Kikuyu traditions. Similarly, one should be wary of much of the evidence contributed by the

---

17. H. E. Lambert, 'The Social and Political Institutions of the Tribes of the Kikuyu Land Unit of Kenya' (hereafter Lambert, MS).
18. H. E. Lambert, *The Systems of Land Tenure in the Kikuyu Land Unit*, Communications from the School of African Studies, University of Cape Town, 1950, (hereafter 'Lambert, 1950'), p. 35.
19. HMSO, *Kenya Land Commission, Evidence and Memoranda*, 3 vols. and *Report*, London, 1934 (hereafter *KLC*). Particularly useful is the original evidence which contains more details. This is housed in the Lands Department, Nairobi.

professional politicians, such as the officials of the various Kikuyu political parties.

Several recent studies have a bearing on my field of study. The study of the Maasai carried out by Jacobs influenced my researches in one respect.[20] His findings on the relationship between the Maasai tribes and their sedentary and agricultural neighbours proved to be valuable where they affect Kikuyu/Maasai relations. In his study of the establishment of British rule in Kenya, Mungeam briefly discusses how this was carried out among the Kikuyu.[21] And Rosberg and Nottingham, in their survey of nationalism in Kenya, examine the manner in which the Kikuyu readjusted themselves to British rule in the first quarter of this century.[22] They also attempt to answer the question why the Kikuyu were among the first people to display political consciousness in Kenya and, in particular, why this led to the Mau Mau uprising. Finally, in his two studies, Sorrenson discusses the land issue, particularly land consolidation, and the genesis of white settlement as well as the Kikuyu land grievances arising therefrom.[23]

Though the Kikuyu proved to be fairly richly-covered by written sources, it became clear, nevertheless, that no systematic survey of their traditions had been carried out. Nor had any analysis of their expansion and settlement been undertaken in any depth. Consequently the field work, undertaken between September 1967 and July 1968, was the most important part of my research. The strategy for the collection of the oral data was influenced by several factors. The pattern of migration and settlement, discussed in chapter 3, was one of the important considerations. From my reading of written sources, it was evident that the Kikuyu had originally spread into Gaki and Kabete from the vicinity of the Metumi/Gaki border. This expansion was undertaken ridge by ridge by small bands of kinship groups. But bifurcation and hiving off of the clans and sub-clans had occurred, in the course of time, leading to individual clans being widespread all over Kikuyuland. To be able to trace this expansion and hiving off, it became necessary to

20. Jacobs, op. cit.
21. G. H. Mungeam, *British Rule in Kenya 1895-1912: The Establishment of Administration in the East Africa Protectorate*, Oxford, 1966.
22. C. S. Rosberg and J. Nottingham, *The Myth of 'Mau Mau': Nationalism in Kenya*, Stanford, 1966.
23. M. P. K. Sorrenson, *Origins of European Settlement in Kenya*, Nairobi, 1968 and *Land Reform in the Kikuyu Country*, Nairobi, 1967.

conduct interviews ridge by ridge, following for convenience the administrative units. I commenced the research from the frontiers and worked inwards—that is, from the most recently settled areas to the centre of dispersion.

Another important factor was the manner in which the oral traditions were transmitted in Kikuyu society, which as already noted is uncentralized and segmentary. Kikuyu traditions are neither controlled nor regulated by any one section of the community, they are largely free, informal and widely diffused.[24] The more popular traditions which occur throughout Kikuyuland are often too vague and unhelpful. Clan or lineage genealogies, therefore, are of greater significance and the heads of the clans and lineages are perhaps the best sources by virtue of their status as custodians of family affairs. But their role has become obsolete in this century and, with the rapid increase in population, new *mbari*, or sub-clans, have been formed and have dispersed all over Kenya. By 1962 it was estimated that 30 per cent of the Kikuyu lived outside their own districts.[25] This figure has become even higher since independence because many of them have taken up land in the Kenya highlands, formerly settled by white farmers. For example, although Nyeri, Murang'a and Kiambu were recently enlarged, the 1969 population census showed that 34 per cent of the total Kikuyu population lived outside their homeland.[26] This dispersion throughout Kenya made it impracticable to collect traditions clan by clan. It was more convenient to collect their traditions family by family, or *mbari* by *mbari*. But whatever approach was adopted, it had to satisfy two criteria—to tap the best available sources, while at the same time covering as wide a cross-section of the population as was possible. At this point, it is appropriate to say a few words about the educational system of the Kikuyu.

From an early age, a Kikuyu child was informally taught some of the tribal traditions. Tales, riddles and proverbs formed an important source of amusement for the young as they sat round the fire-place waiting for the evening meal to cook. Gradually, the children

24. Vansina, op. cit., pp. 121-9.
25. Kenya Government, Statistical Division of the Ministry of Economic Planning and Development, *Statistical Abstract*, Nairobi, 1967, p. 36.
26. Kenya Government, Ministry of Finance and Economic Planning, *Kenya Population Census 1969*, Nairobi, 1970, vol. 1., p. 69-76. There were, for example, 341, 480 Kikuyu living in the Rift Valley Province alone.

would in turn learn to relate this newly gained experience to their friends, brothers and sisters. This tradition has been part of primary school life in the Kikuyu country for a considerable time. A period is set aside each week during which pupils narrate their favourite folk tales to their classmates, or test each other's memory with riddles. It is considered a real shame for a pupil to be unable to do this. When the children grow a little older, they enter the second stage of this informal education. Boys are taught by men, especially their fathers or grandfathers, the necessary manly skills—fighting, herding and clearing the bush for cultivation. They learn basic things about their *mbari*, for example the family genealogy, the boundaries of their land, their debtors or creditors, and so on. The girls, in their turn, learn from the womenfolk the essential knowledge and skills befitting their role in society. Being well-acquainted with traditional education was essential, for a departure from the accepted norms and deportment was considered a serious offence, because it brought shame to the family. And since individual merit and achievement were regarded to be the criteria for leadership, no individual would have wished to remain ignorant of the forces which held the society together. This was an important incentive to learning.

By far the most important stage of education was reached when boys and girls were initiated in order to become adult members of the community. The neophytes underwent formal instruction on tribal lore at the hands of experts, called *atonyi*, who advised their pupils on all aspects of the initiation rites. During this period, the neophytes lived in temporary huts built in the home of the sponsor where the ceremonies took place. Instruction at this stage was most opportune because initiation marked an individual's transition from childhood to adulthood. This will be discussed further in chapter 5. After this girls continued to learn informally by assuming more responsibilities in the homestead and by being taught more about their role as girls and mothers, under the discerning eye of their more experienced womenfolk. The *anake* (circumcised boys) served as warriors before graduating to become elders of the tribe. But it was only after an apprenticeship period as junior elders that they would qualify to become senior elders, and would thus be permitted to hear cases or officiate as priests in the many rites and ceremonies that marked Kikuyu life. It was this group which formed the real depository of Kikuyu traditions, whose chief duty was to ensure the welfare of the community by co-ordinating the various facets of tribal activity, a duty that demanded extensive knowledge of tribal lore. This group formed the core of my informants as far as was practicable. But as the Kikuyu say, *kirira ti ukuru*—knowledge is not the prerogative of the old. There were younger men who, because of their duties, had acquired extensive knowledge of their society, in their roles as headmen, chiefs, teachers, court assessors, interpreters or clerks. In fact the above axiom proved all too true, in that the harsh conditions in the large villages built during the Mau Mau war had taken a heavy toll on the elder group and I had to depend rather heavily on the younger men.

Having isolated the class of people which was likely to provide useful informants, the problem of choosing the actual informants still remained. This was carried out in two ways. In some parts of Kabete (Kiambu) and Gaki (Nyeri), I already had contacts who introduced me to their own families or any other people whom they thought could be useful, or those who were regarded as experts by the local people. I considered this to be by far the best method. First, in most cases the inhabitants of every village or ridge knew who were the experts in their midst, some of whom were even known beyond their own locality. Secondly and more important, the advantage of this method was that an atmosphere of confidence between the potential informant and me was generated. I considered this to be of prime importance. Wherever possible I took my contact with me during the actual interviewing, so that he could introduce me properly and allay any mistrust. Mutual confidence was most important, because the colonial period had left behind an attitude of mistrust and suspicion towards anyone attempting to probe into personal or family affairs such as I was attempting to do. It was impossible, though, to confine myself to this approach, particularly in those areas where I was a stranger. In such situations I had to seek the help of the administrative officials, and here the problems of some officials being reluctant to help, or conveniently forgetting appointments made previously, had to be faced. I was aware, too, that in the past District Commissioners had collected traditions in a *baraza* (open air meeting), something that I had no wish to repeat. Indeed, there had been a surfeit of such *barazas* during the many committees and commissions of inquiry that had visited Kikuyuland. I was also apprehensive that where the government might have problems of its own, my work could be seriously hampered if I became too closely identified with it. For these reasons, I was anxious to eschew official assistance wherever I could, although administrative officials can quickly and easily provide important informants, and chiefs in particular know the areas and people under their jurisdiction very well. They will usually know who are the experts and from whom they themselves might have sought advice in the course of their duties. I found that a popular chief was an asset, an unpopular one a major liability. Most of the chiefs left as soon as they had introduced me to the potential informants, except for a few whose enthusiasm and keenness were enough for them to endure the drudgery of a lengthy interview.

I had several advantages from the outset, for, being a Kikuyu and having been brought up in my maternal grandfather's home, a traditionally orientated family, I had imbibed much of the traditional lore. I also had done some teaching, which gave me valuable contacts throughout the Kikuyuland. But the most important factor was the changed political climate. I was to remember this fact many times during the course of my research. In the colonial period land was one of the major political issues that agitated the Kikuyu. The Crown Land Act of 1915, the Maxwell Committee of 1929 and the Carter Commission of 1932-3 had brought about changes which seriously seemed to undermine the Kikuyu rights to land. One of the arguments put forward was that the Kikuyu, being as much immigrants as the Europeans, had no special claim to the land. It was also maintained that the Kikuyu, having originally acquired their rights to land by conquest, had surrendered this in turn to their European conquerors. Furthermore, it was argued that the Athi had no right to sell, give or surrender land. Thus Kikuyu tribal history became very much intertwined with their rights to land, hence it was a taboo for any Kikuyu to discuss the past frankly where this seemed even remotely to contradict, or in any way undermine, their claim to the ownership of land prior to the dawn of the colonial era. This mood was radically altered by the attainment of independence in December 1963. People were now ready to discuss their past truthfully and without misgivings. This was particularly noticeable in the relevant information on expansion and the various methods used in the acquisition of land, discussed in chapter 3.

There were two methods open to me—to hold either group or individual interviews. The former involved a number of informants who were assembled together, and who were asked to express their opinion about a particular issue. Discusssion would follow, and agreement would be reached finally. This method was only found to be useful when eliciting a particular type of information, such as a list of age groups or trading commodities, where group effort would supplement individual contributions. The method, however, had some major drawbacks. A forceful and respected personality can dominate the whole proceedings to the exclusion of all the others; he can play a far greater role in choosing a particular variant of a tradition than his knowledge warrants, especially where vested interests are at stake. But a more serious drawback is that in a group interview the participants have a dual function: they are the source of the data as well as its analysts. There is the danger here that they might decide to tell only what they think one should know. I found it more politic to record all the variants of any one tradition and afterwards I had to decide for myself what to accept. The ideal method was to hold individual interviews conducted in the informant's environment; the home atmosphere generally gave the latter a feeling of self-confidence which was vital to a successful interview. The researcher became the informant's guest and, so long as mutual confidence had been established first, the informant did not feel inhibited, as so often happens in a group interview. There was no need, too, to exaggerate his importance or even hide his ignorance, as he would have been tempted to do in the presence of his peers.

But there are no firm rules and, despite my preference for individual interviews, I sometimes had to accept group sessions, especially when I relied on the assistance of chiefs in seeking potential informants, and it was not unusual to find that he had collected a dozen or so people at his headquarters. Whenever this happened, I either reduced the group to a manageable size or concentrated on family genealogies alone. In the latter case, I noted the more knowledgeable informants and visited them individually and at their homes later on. If two or more informants chanced to belong to the same *mbari*, I recorded all the versions of their genealogy, particularly points of divergence. My work was often made easier by the informants themselves, by their suggestion of who knew most about a particular issue in their locality.

My fieldwork started in Nyeri (Gaki) district in September 1967. Nyeri was chosen first because this being my home district I had more contacts there than anywhere else and I began by drawing up a questionnaire, on the basis of which I hoped to be able to discover the most useful informants. These were handled for me by the pupils of two secondary schools but the experiment proved a failure and was thereafter abandoned. While the pupils and teachers were enthusiastic, it became obvious that for the pupils to be capable of producing worthwhile material, an initial period of training would need to be followed up by very close and constant supervision. Effective supervision could not be exercised over such a large number of assistants. However, the deciding factor was the nature of Kikuyu traditions. They are not of the type that is amenable to a questionnaire, being largely narrative in form. I therefore prepared a guide which consisted of a list of topics, and the relevant questions that I wished to be covered. This time I was luckier to have the assistance of students from the Kagumo Teacher Training College during their vacation. After an initial briefing session, a programme was drawn up to ensure adequate supervision. They were visited once a week during which a practical session was held; an informant of their choice was interviewed by me to demonstrate the proper way of conducting an interview as well as framing questions. I then went over the scripts of their interviews, after which they were required to seek further information on points that were unclear or particularly valuable.

This group was a distinct improvement on the first one, but even here the temptation of quick and haphazard work, in order to enhance emoluments, became apparent, as when one of the students claimed to have conducted twenty-nine interviews of different informants in four days! The results did not seem to justify the plan wholly, and ultimately I grew wary of assistants and decided to do the rest of the work on my own. Luckily, from February 1968 my wife was of great help, she transcribed the interviews from tapes, thus leaving me free to concentrate on interviewing.

Most of the interviews were recorded on tapes. It was made clear to my informants that our discussion would be taped (unless there was any objection on their part), in order to avoid any suspicions. The tape recorder was widely accepted and only a negligible number objected to it, and they only did so when discussing what they thought were sensitive points which reflected unfavourably on the character and integrity of individuals or *mbari*.

The problem of whether informants should be paid was being

widely discussed in Kenya at the time of my fieldwork and even gave rise to an article in the local press. This practice is objectionable on two counts; it will make it increasingly difficult for *bona fide* students of limited means to undertake any meaningful research of this type. A greater danger is that once payment of informants becomes fashionable, it will not take long before spurious information is invented for sale. Certainly I had no wish to add to this problem; it was my practice not to do anything that would give the impression that I was interested in buying information and interviewing proceeded as soon as I had been introduced to a prospective informant. At the end of it and as a token of gratitude, I then offered the informant a pound of sugar or tea, or a roll of snuff which I had bought beforehand. Only two of my informants demanded payment, otherwise everyone was enthusiastically co-operative about the project, and I was given every assistance.

Chronology is a basic requirement in any attempt to place historical events in perspective. Historical time has been called 'the very plasma in which events are immersed, and the field within which they become intelligible'.[27] Yet this is one of the main difficulties confronting a historian in Africa who utilizes oral traditions as a source of evidence. The problem arises because African societies did not measure time exactly. Consequently oral traditions or sources only give a vague picture of the absolute chronology of the events that they relate. In an attempt to overcome this problem, scholars have resorted to the use of lists of kings or rulers, generations and age differentiation systems, in order to establish a reasonable chronological framework. This study makes use of the last two—generations and age systems—in trying to establish a reliable chronology of the traditional history of the Kikuyu.

The Kikuyu did not have a seven-day week, and the day was divided into portions corresponding to the position of the sun in the sky. For reckoning time durations longer than a day, the Kikuyu depended mainly on the lunar month, as were their activities, which were planned to correlate with the various phases of the moon's cycle. Each of the phases bore a particular name, and these names reflected the predominant weather characteristics in each period. The year was divided into two major and two minor seasons (see chapter 1) according to the weather and the agricultural activities. Broadly the *gathano* and *themithu* seasons were

27. Bloch, op. cit., pp. 27-8.

amalgamated with *kimera kia njahi* and *kimera kia mwere* respectively. Each of these seasons consequently lasted for approximately six months and formed the Kikuyu year, *mwaka* or *kimera*. It is important to bear this in mind when considering the age system. In discussing their past, the Kikuyu very often indicate the time factor by such phrases as, 'at the time of Iregi', 'when the Manguca were warriors', or 'the Mungai did it'. This is an indication that not only are they very historically minded but also that their *mariika*, or age sets, act as milestones of chronology. This features has led many previous writers to note the potential importance of the *mariika* for establishing a reliable chronological framework, and several lists of them have been collected in various parts of the country. However, some of these lists are very muddled and inaccurate. It is therefore necessary to be cautious of the various facets of age differentiation, as well as the various shades of meaning of the word *riika*. I am not concerned here with *riika* in the sense of age grade, which is a status role commonly ascribed to individuals at a certain age and in many societies. My concern is with *riika* in the sense of age sets or age groups which are coeval, corporate groups whose members are recruited through specific criteria. This word is not at all precise, as shown in chapter 5, and this may have been the source of confusion. Depending upon the context, it may refer to generation (moiety), or to three slightly different kinds of initiation sets, comprising either all the neophytes who underwent circumcision in any one year, or an army contingent embracing several initiation sets, or an exclusively female initiation set.[28]

No special problem is posed by the generation sets since these are fairly uniform throughout the Kikuyu country. Again, the exclusively female initiations present no problem, since this event was annual. It is the male initiation sets which pose serious difficulties in the attempt to trace their proper sequence. This is particularly so since the bulk of the existing literature gives little clue as to their mode of formation. My own modest research on the subject indicates that there were two systems of army and initiation set formations. As shown in chapter 5, there were two systems of formation; one was operative in Kabete (Kiambu) and most parts of Metumi (Murang'a), with the exception of areas bordering on Gaki (Nyeri); the second one was operating in Gaki and the adjacent parts of Metumi.

28. See figure 1, p. 16

RULING GENER-ATIONS	GAKI (*Nyeri*)		METUMI (*Murang'a*) KABETE (*Kiambu*)	
	ARMY SETS	INITIATION SETS	ARMY SETS	INITIATION SETS
1898 ? MWANGI	Ndumia or Ngunjiri (Right hand)	1898 Nuthi (start of an army set)	Kienjeku	1898 Kienjeku (start of an army set)
	1889-97 Muhingo		**1894-7** Muhingo	1897 Ndutu/ Nuthi* 1896 Kagica* 1895 Kibiri/ Nduriri* 1894 Ruharo*
1862-97±5 MAINA			**1885-93** Mutung'u or Mburu	1893 Mutung'u 1892 Nyongo 1891 Gicere 1890 Ngigì 1889 Ngando/ Muing'oto 1888 Uhere 1887 Mburu 1886 Ngaruiya 1885 Kiniti
	1884-8 Ndirangu or Ndung'u (Left hand)	1888 Thugu or Nyuguto 1886 Wamwega 1884 Muricu		
	1875-83 Muhingo		**1881-4 Muhingo**	
			1872-80 Njenga or Mbira Itimu	1880 Boro 1879 Wanyoike 1878 Ngunga/ Mwirigi 1877 Ruhang'a 1876 Ngugí 1875 Kiambuthi 1874 Kiriira 1873 Mang'uriu 1872 Muiruri
	1870-74 Ndiritu (Right hand)			
			1868-71 Muhingo	
	1861-9 Muhingo		**1859-67** Mbugua	1867 Mbugua 1866 Gucu Nduike 1865 Nguo ya Nyina 1864 Wangigì 1863 1862 ? 1861 ? 1860 ? 1859 ?
1827-61±10 IREGI	**1856-60 Manguca**			
	1847-55 Muhingo		**1855-8 Muhingo**	

Figure 1: The Mariika formation

* Girls' initiation sets only.

The former system—the Metumi system—was based on a *muhingo* (closed period), which lasted for nine *imera* (seasons) or *miaka* ('years')—four and a half calendar years—during which no initiation of boys took place at all.[29] But it should be noted that initiation took place on the tenth *kimera* (season) which in effect meant that it took place after five calendar years, since as a rule initiation took place only during the *themithu* after the *mwere* (millet) harvest. This was followed by annual initiations for the next nine calendar years before the next *muhingo* was imposed. These nine initiation sets formed one army contingent or regiment set. It is only to be expected that the system in Metumi and Kabete should coincide, Kabete having been so recently occupied that there had not been time for the development of a different pattern. And it was generally agreed by my informants that the first initiation set to be circumcised in Kabete was the Mungai. Furthermore, the oldest elders who crossed the southern Cania river into Kiambu are said to have been of the Ndemi generation. A comparison of all the lists of sets that were collected confirms this, despite the fact that these sets have not been in operation to any effective degree in this century.

Lambert, who alone has discussed the regiment sets in the whole of Gaki, implies that there were wide divergences in the various localities. Indeed, he concludes that the system in Tetu, Aguthi, Mathira and the areas close to Metumi followed different systems. This conclusion is not borne out by the evidence I collected. Moreover, Lambert overlooks one important factor, that Gaki was an area that had very close ties with the Maasai and one where their influence would be most marked. This is made evident by the division of sets into the right-hand (*tatane*; Maasai, *tatene*) and the left-hand (*gitienye*; Maasai, *kedyanye*), and also by the distinction made between the first set to be initiated after a *muhingo*, called *muricu*, which was considered to be senior to all the others and whose name remained the official one for the whole regiment set. These two features are similar in all parts of Gaki without exception, and it is relevant to point out that this was borrowed from the Maasai. A third feature that was common to all of them is that their *muhingo* was imposed for nine calendar years, and finally, a careful study of the various lists collected clearly indicates that their names were remarkably similar if not identical. Taking all these factors into consideration, it seems that the Gaki pattern was

29. Two *imera* or Kikuyu *miaka* are equivalent to one calendar year.

widespread in the whole of the district or county, and not as localized as Lambert suggests.

One problem still remains in connection with the Gaki system. How long did it take to form a regiment or army contingent? My information on this is conflicting and muddled. But I am inclined to think that, since this was essentially based on the Maasai system, it took fourteen calendar years or thereabouts to form a regiment, nine of which were *muhingo* years. Therefore it must have taken five calendar years to complete a regiment set. In some areas there was initiation in each of those years while in others initiation sets were spaced over a year or two depending upon the locality. Hence, after the *muhingo*, two, three or more sets were formed. This appears to be the only plausible explanation of the differences in the number of sets that formed a regiment. Furthermore, it is this feature that would seem to account for the apparent divergences noticed, but not accounted for, by Lambert. The need for a standing army meant that in some parts, notably in Mathira and Tetu, a minor *muhingo* was imposed after the *muricu*—the first initiates after a major *muhingo*—had been initiated. It should be noted, too, that in these two areas there was close co-operation and migration to and fro, as Wang'ombe's movements demonstrate.[30] Finally, the evident divergence shown by the lists from the Metumi/Gaki border should be attributed to the fact that for *mariika* purposes this was a no man's land. Above all, and despite all the apparent discrepancies, the *muhingo* was observed at the same time over a wide area; the *ituika* process also took place, at the same time, nearly all over Kikuyuland. Moreover, an examination of figure 1 shows that the closed period, or *muhingo*, as well as the open period for the formation of army regiments, overlap considerably under both the Metumi and Gaki systems. These two features not only help us in arriving at approximate periods, but are important consider-ations when assessing the importance of the age sets in establishing a reliable chronology.

Two important features of the *mariika* emerge. First, they were central to an individual's life, and secondly they were also regular, or periodic, depending on the sex. And because of their importance it was most unusual, if not impossible, for an individual not to know how they operated or fail to recite the names of past sets.

---

30. G. Muriuki, 'Kikuyu Historical Texts', 1969, unpublished, pp. 226, 235 and 308, (hereafter 'KHT').

And although the regiment sets were formed irregularly, they can still be measured with reference to the female initiation sets as far back in time as the latter can be remembered. For the majority of people, however, it is the regiment sets that mattered most and were best remembered, even though it is no longer possible to discover exactly how they were formed.

There is a mass of oral evidence that enables us to calculate with reasonable certainty the dates corresponding to the various sets that have been enumerated by the informants. Take Kabete, for example. We are told that the Europeans camped at Kiawariua, Lugard's Dagoretti, when Njenga and Ngigi were warriors and that the latter were neophytes at that time. We are also told that Mutung'u (smallpox) were initiated at a period when the Kaputiei and Loita were fighting each other, when the Maasai took refuge among the Kikuyu after a cattle epidemic, and that in the same year Waiyaki was arrested and deported. We are informed, too, that Mutung'u were *ihii* (uncircumcised boys) when Kiawariua was ransacked and also during a Maasai raid at Mbari ya Gicamu's. Uhere, an older set, is also said to have been preparing for initiation when Nyanja and Ruara passed through Kikuyuland. And turning to the written sources, there is extensive corroborating evidence: Waiyaki was arrested in August 1892,[31] the Maasai took refuge among the Kikuyu in large numbers around 1892-3, and, after being maltreated by the Kikuyu, they sought Hall's help and built their *manyatta* (kraals) at Fort Smith towards the end of 1893;[32] Kiawariua was established by Lugard in October 1890;[33] von Höhnel and Teleki passed through Kabete in September 1887;[34] Hall noted the presence of smallpox around Fort Smith in October 1892 and its spread further north in Konyu (the southern part of Mathira),

31. M. Perham, *The Diaries of Lord Lugard*, London, 1959, vol. 3, p. 408.
32. The Maasai took refuge after the Morijo war, see Jacobs, op. cit., pp. 100-3; J. Ainsworth to IBEAC, 15 February 1894 in Foreign Office (Africa series)—hereafter FO—correspondence ref. FO2/73; Hall to Col. Hall, 24 November 1894; Hall's diaries for 20, 21, 29 September and 8 November 1893; Hall to IBEAC, January 1894 in FO2/73. Hall's Papers are in Rhodes House, Oxford.
33. Perham, op. cit., vol. 1, pp. 309-11, 317-48; J. W. Gregory; *The Great Rift Valley*, London, 1896, p. 91; Boedecker in *KLC*, vol. 1, op. cit., p. 703.
34. The Kikuyu thought that Qualla (Dualla) and Kijanja, both caravan leaders to von Höhnel and Teleki, were the important people since it was with them that they negotiated for toll. Hence their visit has always been referred to as that of Ruara and Nyanja. See L. von Höhnel, *The Discovery of Lakes Rudolf and Stefanie*, London, 1894, vol. 1, pp. 286-361.

Gaki was noted by Gregory in 1893.[35] Finally, the Gicamu raid occurred in May 1892.[36] Taking all this evidence into account, together with the practice of having initiation after the millet harvest, it seems certain that the Uhere set was initiated in 1888, Ngigi in 1890 and Mutung'u in 1893. Further evidence shows that the Mutung'u marked the completion of a regiment set which was followed by a *muhingo*. This *muhingo* was lifted by the initiation of the Kienjeku initiation set in 1898.

Lambert, Leakey, Beech, Knight and Tate have given varying dates for their various lists of the *mariika*.[37] No adequate explanation is offered, however, for the gaps in their lists, for instance the different dates given for the Ngigi and Mutung'u sets. If we are right in accepting that the Mutung'u should have marked the end of one regiment set, then the first initiation to inaugurate this new regiment should have been taken place in 1885. I strongly feel that the Kabete *mariika* are suspect between 1890 and 1902, because in this period that region experienced traumatic changes which threw their social structure into a turmoil. The constant raids by the servants of the Imperial British East Africa Company, followed by disease and famine which devastated the area, meant that there was neither time nor initiative to bother with what were complicated rituals that demanded time and wealth. Further north in Metumi, no such disruptions took place, as is clearly shown by their *mariika*, which are more complete.[38] To conclude, the regiment set completed by Mutung'u in 1893 should not have been called Njenga; it should have been called either Mburu or Mutung'u, Njenga being an earlier regiment set. But the Mburu/Mutung'u regiment set was never completed, and in the eyes of the Kikuyu, theirs was the age of disaster and shame becauses the tribe had been defeated by the British and decimated by disease and famine. For all these reasons, there was no glory to be associated with the set and it was not unusual, therefore, that they chose, albeit unconsciously, to be

35. Hall, diary for October 1892; Gregory, op. cit., p. 195. Note the fear expressed by the Mathira at the northern border that Gregory might bring in the disease if allowed to pass through. See Gregory, op. cit., p. 158.
36. Purkiss to Portal, 31 January 1893 in FO2/60.
37. H. E. Lambert, *Kikuyu Social and Political Institutions*, London, 1965 (hereafter 'Lambert, 1965'), chap. 2; Leakey, MS, chap. 18; Beech in KNA/PC/ CP/1/4/2, pp. 31-2; Knight in *KLC*, vol. 1, pp. 900-2 ;Tate in the *Journal of African Society*, vol. 10, op.cit., pp. 286-9.
38. 'Barlow Papers', The Library, University of Nairobi, file on *Mariika*; Cagnolo, op. cit., pp. 198-202; Champion in KNA/KBU/3/12.

RULING GENERATIONS	REGIMENT (ARMY) SETS	
	METUMI (*Murang'a*) KABETE (*Kiambu*)	GAKI (*Nyeri*)
Maina **1862–97±5**	1885–93 Mutung'u 1872–80 Njenga	1884–8 Ndung'u/ Ndirangu 1870–74 Ndiritu/Ngunjiri 1856–60 Manguca
Iregi **1827–61±10**	1859–67 Mbugua 1846–54 Mungai 1833–41 Gitau	1842–6 King'ori
Ndemi **1792–1826±15**	1820–8 Kang'ethe 1807–15 Wainaina 1794–1802 Njoroge	1828–32 Ndirangu 1814–18 Ndigirigi 1800–4 Ndiang'ui
Mathathi **1757–91±20**	1781–9 Ng'ang'a 1769–77 Kinyanjui 1756–64 Njuguna	1786–90 Thiuri 1772–6 Ngithitu 1758–62 Matu 1744–8 Tatua
Ciira **1722–56±25**	1743–51 Kinuthia 1730–38 Karanja	1730–34 Thuita
Cuma **1687–1721±30**	1717–25 Kimani 1704–12 Kamau 1691–9 Kiamuhia	
Manduti **1652–86±35**	1678–86 Cege 1665–73 ? Kiarii 1651–9 ? Mbironde	
? Agu **1617–51±40**		
? Tene **1582–1616±45**		
? Mamba **1547–81±50**		
? Manjiri **1512–46±55**		

Figure 2: The Mariika

associated with the Njenga, the regiment that had the honour and reputation of having been a terror to the Maasai. Hence they are called Njenga, derived from *cenga* (cut), or Mbira Itimu, meaning spear spinners, a picturesque image of spinning spears as the regiment marched to battle. This conclusion accords with the lists collected in Metumi. A tentative arrangement based on this conclusion is shown in figure 2. When pressed to enumerate the regiments beyond the Thuita, most informants in Gaki mentioned the ruling generations or claimed that they did not know of any others.

I have regarded Kianjagi and Ruhonge, which appear in the Limuru and Kikuyu/Kiambaa lists, to be local names of some of the sets already listed elsewhere in the make-up of the Mutung'u regiment. From the Mbugua regiment set onwards, it is impossible to find out the right order of the constituent initiation sets, and even Njenga itself presents some problems among its earlier sets. Indeed, as one called Wainaina told Barlow in 1932, from Gucu Nduike (see figure 1) the lists became less precise. This comment is supported by the lists collected by Champion and Cagnolo, which very clearly indicate the *muhingo* between the Mutung'u and Kienjeku, and also between Mburu and Boro. Further back than that it is impossible to pick out the girls' sets. Lastly, only a few informants mentioned regiments earlier than Kamau, and here my lists agree with extant sources.

It was possible to draw up a tentative list for Gaki (see figure 2) using similar techniques. Once again, lists collected earlier have been compared and contrasted with those obtained recently. This proved to be a more complicated area because of the local variations, but when compared with the all-embracing generation sets, the result does not appear to be too divergent. For example, Ndung'u, which was sometimes called Manguca, was, according to informants outside the area, the same as Mutung'u (mistakenly called Njenga) in Kabete.

Several initiation sets made up a regiment and several regiments a generation. According to most informants, Mwangi took over from Maina during the *muhingo* and before the Kienjeku and the Nuthi (see figure 1), in Metumi and Gaki respectively, were initiated. That would fall between 1889 and 1898 and, according to Kenyatta, this event took place between 1890 and 1898.[39] There are

39. Kenyatta, op. cit., p. 190.

references, too, to the *ituika* having occurred towards the end of the nineteenth century. *Ituika* was a protracted affair said to have taken years to complete, and for this reason it is not surprising to hear that it may have indeed been in the process for such a long period. This account will assume that preparations for it were taking place between 1890 and 1898. This does not seem unreasonable for, according to Barlow, the Irungu generation was in the process of taking over the running of the country from the Mwangi between 1925 and 1932.[40] Lambert thinks the Irungu should have taken over in 1924/5, Beecher saw preparations for it in 1931/2 and an administrative officer noted it in 1929.[41] It is apparent, therefore, that the Irungu generation was trying to effect the transfer of power from 1924 to 1932, a period of nine years. If the Mwangi eventually took over in 1898 and should have relinquished office in 1932, they would have been in office for thirty-four years. This is in general agreement with the views of most informants, who say that each generation ruled for a period of thirty to forty years. If we take thirty-five years as the average period of office, the result seems to tally with the Kikuyu traditions, as shown in figure 2. The sequence of the sets has been determined by the elimination of those names—such as Karirau and Gumba—which refer to specific incidents and which in all probability are names of either regiments or initiation sets. Terms such as the Tene (long ago) and Agu (ancestors) are admittedly vague and could refer to any of the earlier generation sets. But on the other hand, the period from the era of creation, Manjiri, to the appearance of internal dissension among the ancestors, Manduti, could hardly have covered only two generations, as some of the lists that enumerate the generation sets imply. Furthermore, nearly all those who collected lists of generations at the turn of the century were told that there had been no less than ten to twelve generations previous to the Mwangi generation; others were told that there were many more although no one could enumerate all of them with any confidence.[42] Indeed, the existing evidence is contradictory and tenuous, and we cannot deduce with any

40. Benson, op. cit., p. 467.
41. Cagnolo, op. cit., pp. 86, 120-1; Lambert, ms, op. cit., p. 361; KNA/PC/CP/1/1/2, op. cit., p. 47; and L. J. Beecher, *A Kikuyu-English Dictionary*, 1935, Kahuhia, Fort Hall, p. 68.
42. McGregor (pp. 32-3) enumerates eleven; Beecher (p. 68) twelve; K. R. Dundas (*Man*, 1908, vol. 8, pp. 181-2) ten; Tate (*Journal of African Society*, vol. 10, p. 290), eleven.

certainty the number of generations which preceded the Manduti. For example, McGregor, the first author to enumerate the generation sets, was told that since the creation of the world there had been 'ten ages or dispensations'. Yet he enumerates eleven generation sets in his lists up to the Mwangi, and calls the Iregi the seventh age.[43] However, he assures us that none of the Iregi was alive in 1909. To offset the lack of evidence of generations, which obviously exists, before the Manduti, we shall retain the Tene and Agu, despite their vagueness, for lack of better descriptive terms.

The Ndemi and Mathathi are sometimes interchanged by individual informants. Here the Mathathi will precede the Ndemi following the lists collected early this century. The fact that the Mathathi commemorate the period of the initial decorating of bodies with red ochre, a feature that seems to have been borrowed from the Maasai, suggests that this occurred earlier than the period of the rapid expansion commemorated by the Ndemi. The remainder of the generation sets have been regarded as a summary of Kikuyu traditional history: consequently since the Manjiri refers to the period of creation, this should come before the Ciira, for example, which represents the period when the Kikuyu greatly increased in numbers. But evidence becomes more definite and reliable only after the Manduti generation.

43. McGregor, op. cit., p. 32.

Chapter 1

THE PHYSICAL SETTING*

THE Kikuyu,[1] who numbered just over two million at the 1969 population census, make up the largest group of the north-eastern Bantu and inhabit the Central Province of Kenya.[2] At the end of the nineteenth century, they probably numbered slightly over 500,000 souls.[3] Prior to the Independence Constitution of 1963, when their area was considerably increased, they occupied only about 320,000 hectares.[4] Their homeland is divided into three administrative districts—to the north is Nyeri (or Gaki), to the south is Kiambu (or Kabete) and in the middle is Murang'a (or Metumi), which is traditionally considered to be the tribe's ancestral and spiritual home.[5] But these political divisions were, however,

* For the physical environment of Kikuyuland, see HMSO, *A Handbook of Kenya Colony and Protectorate*, London, 1920, pp. 43-51; B. Dickson, 'The Eastern Borderland of Kikuyu' in the *Geographical Journal*, vol. 21, 1903, pp. 36-9; R. Crawshay, 'Kikuyu: Notes on the Country, People, Fauna and Flora' in the *Geographical Journal*, vol. 20, 1902, pp. 24-49; S. J. K. Baker, 'The East African Environment' in R. Oliver and G. Mathew (eds.), *History of East Africa*, Oxford, vol. 1, 1963, pp. 1-22; H. J. Mackinder, 'A Journey to the Summit of Mount Kenya' in the *Geographical Journal*, London, vol. 15, 1900, pp. 453-86; HMSO, *Report of the East Africa Royal Commission, 1953-5*, London, 1961, pp. 8-9; and Kenya Government, *National Atlas of Kenya*, Nairobi, 1970.

1. This study excludes the Ndia and the Gicugu although they regard themselves and are regarded by their neighbours as Kikuyu. The proper spelling should be *Mugikuyu* (sing.), *Agikuyu* (pl.) for the people, *Gikuyu* for their country and *Gigikuyu* for their language. But to avoid confusion and in view of its wide currency in modern usage I shall stick to 'Kikuyu', the anglicized form, for all three.
2. *Kenya Population Census, 1969*, listed 2,201,632 Kikuyu on pp. 69 and 73. This figure excludes 216,988 inhabitants of Kirinyaga district. Compare with Kamba 1,197,712 Meru 554,256, Embu 117,969, Tharaka 51,883 and Mbeere 49,247.
3. Routledge, op. cit., pp. 7 and 80; Boyes, op. cit., p. 296.
4. For example Nyeri has been enlarged from 86,100 hectares to 325,600 hectares, Murang'a from 150,200 hectares to 243,700 hectares and Kiambu from 83,000 hectares to 242,000 hectares. See *Statistical Abstract*, 1967, p. 2.
5. Gaki is a small ridge in Aguthi, Nyeri; Metumi is the ridge between Irati and Maragua rivers; and Kabete is the region to the north-west of Nairobi between Uthiru and Kibiciku and up to Wangigi market.

rather vague and indeterminate at the turn of the century and indeed only coalesced during the colonial period.

Kikuyuland is a dissected plateau of approximately 160 kilometres in length from north to south and 50 kilometres in width from east to west. Its altitude ranges from about 1,000 metres to over 2,500 metres above sea level, and has many natural landmarks. To the north it is dominated by Kirinyaga (Mount Kenya), a three-peaked massif of an extinct volcano, rising to 5,600 metres; to the west its border follows the Kikuyu escarpment of the Rift Valley which merges to its north with the Nyandarua (Aberdares) Range which rises to over 4,300 metres; and to the east and south lies Kianjahi (Ol Donyo Sabuk) and Kiambiruiru (Ngong hills) respectively. The whole plateau, moreover, tilts to the south-east from the mountain and foothills into the Mbeere and Kaputie plains. The northern boundary of the plateau is clearly marked by Nyeri hill and a low line of hills bridging the Nanyuki-Nyeri corridor to Nyandarua and Kirinyaga. This plateau is characterized by two features—deep, narrow gorges which have been furrowed by the numerous parallel streams flowing into the Thagana and Athi rivers, and parallel ridges running easterly. A cross-section of the country from north to south therefore depicts a series of parallel ridges and valleys a few of which are broad but most of which are very narrow.[6] These features of the Kikuyu plateau have influenced the pattern of settlement and the political as well as social organization of the Kikuyu to a considerable degree, as we shall see in chapters 3 and 5. This terrain also proved to be as disheartening as it was cumbersome and exacting to the early foreign travellers who traversed the Kikuyu country.[7]

The Kikuyu escarpment and the Nyandarua Range are drained by south-eastward flowing streams. All the tributaries north of the Ndarugu river (see map 1) join the Thagana river, while those to its south join the Athi river. Kirinyaga, with its permanent snow cap, is the source of many tributaries which are fed by the glaciers and flow south-westwards to join and form the mighty Thagana river before it curves eastwards on its journey to the coast. Among some of the major tributaries are the north Cania, the Gura, the Maragua, the north and south Mathioya, the Thika, the south Cania,

6.   Crawshay, op. cit., p. 27; Dickson, op. cit., pp. 36-7; *Handbook*, pp. 44 and 98.
7.   Note, for example, von Höhnel's experience in *The Discovery of Lakes Rudolf and Stefanie*, vol. 1, pp. 301, 315-16, 322 and 328.

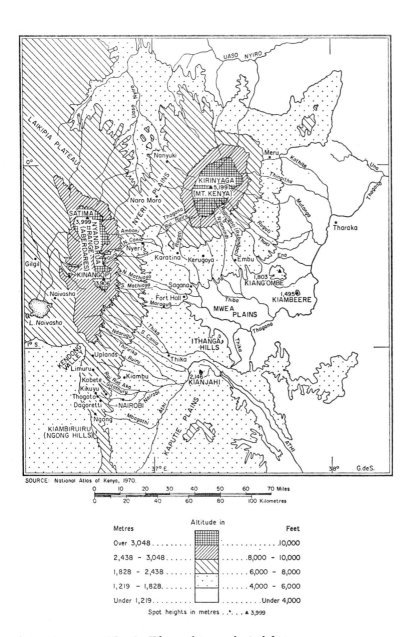

Altitude in		
Metres		Feet
Over 3,048	▦	10,000
2,438 – 3,048	▨	. . . . . .8,000 – 10,000
1,828 – 2,438	◫	. . . . . . .6,000 – 8,000
1,219 – 1,828	⬚	. . . . . . .4,000 – 6,000
Under 1,219	☐	. . . . .Under 4,000

Spot heights in metres . .ˑ . . . ▲ 3,999

Map 1—Kikuyu plateau: physical features.

the Ndarugu, the Ruiru and the Rui rua Aka (the Women's River, or as it is commonly mis-spelt, Ruaraka).[8]

This topography has resulted, to a great extent, from the geological structure of the plateau.[9] It is covered by an irregular gneiss basement on which a sheet of tertiary lava flow has been superimposed. The volcanic activity has also given rise to volcanic piles such as the Nyandarua and Kirinyaga. The plateau slopes from the north-west to south-east because of the subsidence of the country to the south, while the Laikipia plateau is thought to have remained intact. Over the years, this structure has been exposed to the agents of denudation resulting in waterfalls where exposed gneiss crosses the streams. Examples are the Gura Falls on the Gura river, Cania Falls on the south Cania river, Fourteen Falls on the Athi river and the famous Seven Forks Falls on the Thagana river, the site of the extensive Kindaruma hydroelectric project. Heavy rainfall, especially, has enabled the streams to furrow deep and winding valleys as they flow over the gneiss and granitic rocks of varying hardness. Consequently, the Kikuyu plateau is a trenched and denuded plateau of ridge and valley.

To the north of the low line of hills marking the beginning of the Nyeri-Nanyuki corridor lies the Nyeri plain, which is hemmed in by the Nyandarua and the Kirinyaga massifs. The plain itself is marked by shallow valleys separated by intervening grassy plains anything up to eight kilometres wide, while its slopes are dissected by deep, steep-sided valleys. At the turn of the century, this formed a natural home for the Purko and the remnants of the Laikipiak Maasai, who were only separated from their neighbours, the Kikuyu, by a thin fringe of primeval forest to the south—a useful defensive barrier in case of need. Far from being the 'traditional enemies' of popular literature, the Maasai and the Kikuyu had extensive trade relations, had intermarried and even on occasion, had made military alliances against their common neighbours. A more significant consideration, however, is that a sizeable section of the Kikuyu is of the same stock as the semi-pastoral Maasai, especially those Maasai tribes which formerly inhabited Laikipia. The much publicized Maasai/Kikuyu wars were no more serious or numerous than those between the Kikuyu themselves, and even then they

8. It is so-called because a Dorobo woman used to guard one of the fords and demanded toll from travellers.
9. Baker, op. cit., pp. 1-3; *Handbook*, pp. 93-100 and *National Atlas o Kenya*.

were a much later development, dating from the nineteenth century. On the contrary there have been very close ties between the two peoples which, in turn, have led to cultural fusion, a process which has left a deep imprint on the Kikuyu, as we shall see in chapter 3. The Maasai were also the neighbours of the Kikuyu to the west, where they were separated from each other by the forested Nyandarua range running from north to south for about 140 kilometres. The former also occupied the vast, broad and undulating Kaputie plains beyond the Kiambiruiru and here, too, they were separated from the Kikuyu only by a forest fringe.[10]

There were other neighbours besides the Maasai. The country lying to the east of Kikuyuland is inhabited by their cousins—the Meru to the north-east; the Ndia, Gicugu, Mbeere and Embu to the east; and to the south-east, the Kamba with whom the Kikuyu are especially closely related.[11] It is also from these areas that the ancestors of the Kikuyu originated, as shown in chapter 2.

Other significant neighbours of the Kikuyu were the Athi (Dorobo) who were living in the forests in Kikuyuland at the turn of the century. Their importance cannot be over-emphasized, because of the part they played in land acquisition, the ivory trade and the origin and migration of the Kikuyu. It will be argued, in chapter 3, that not only are the Athi the ancestors of some of the Iloikop (semi-pastoral Maasai) but also of a good many Kikuyu sub-clans. And it was this common ancestry, between the Iloikop and the Kikuyu, especially in Nyeri, that may have made possible the extraordinarily good relations between specific Maasai and Kikuyu families.

In Kenya, as indeed in the rest of East Africa, rainfall is to a very considerable degree determined by relief. Hence the Kikuyu country, with its high altitude, has a higher rainfall than the lowlands of Kenya and this may average from 1,000mm in the lowlands to over 1,750mm in the highlands per annum. This orographic rainfall decreases gradually towards the lower altitude until in Nanyuki, to the north of the area, it is only 500mm to 750mm annually. In the Mwea plains, to the east, rainfall is under 750mm and rapidly decreases to below 500mm in Tharaka. But its

10. J. Thomson, *Through Masailand*, London, 1885, pp. 310-14, 319-20; von Höhnel, op. cit., p. 302; Routledge, op. cit., p. 7; Mackinder, op. cit., p. 463; *Handbook*, pp. 44, 46, 47; Gregory, op. cit., p. 157.
11. Middleton and Kershaw, op. cit.; 'Lambert, 1950', chap. 1; 'Lambert, 1965', chap. 1.

reliability is even more decisive; while this is generally good in Kikuyuland, it is very poor elsewhere. For example, east of Embu town the probability of getting less than 500mm of rain per annum is 10 to 20 per cent and reaches 30 per cent in Tharaka. In such areas, therefore, the threat of drought becomes very pronounced, which in turn enhances the possibility of frequent famines. The prevalence of droughts and famine in an ecologically marginal region might have significantly contributed to the migration of the Kikuyu group.

The Kikuyu plateau and its environs is divided into three eco-logical units. To the east lies the arid, woody or shrubby grassland zone which is less than 1,500 metres above sea level. This ecological unit is characterized by low, unreliable rainfall of between 500mm and 750mm per annum. It is the home of wild animals such as the wildebeeste, hartebeest, bushbuck, warthog, bush pig, gazelle, impala, buffalo, giraffe, lion, leopard and hyena. Some of these animals—particularly the bushbuck, the warthog and the bush pig—are host to tsetse fly, particularly *Glossina pallidipes*. The area is not suitable for arable agriculture and is acutely susceptible to frequent, if not semi-permanent, famines.

The second ecological unit is a narrow zone to the east of an imaginary line drawn from Ngong to Murang'a, Kerugoya, Embu and Meru towns, and running from the north-east to the south-west. Eastwards it gradually merges with the scrubby grassland ecological unit. Generally referred to as the scattered woodland, the zone lies between 1,000 metres to 2,000 metres above sea level and has an average rainfall of between 750mm to 1,500mm. Although the fauna is similar to that in the first zone, the scattered woodland unit is of higher agricultural potential and supports a sparse population.

A large area of the Central and parts of the Eastern Province, however, fall into the forest region ecological zone which can be further sub-divided into two units. First, there is the so-called Kikuyu and star grass zone, characterized by high rainfall (1,375mm to 2,250mm per annum) and high altitude (1,800 metres to over 2,100 metres above sea level). Its abundant foliage supports such animals as the buffalo, the rhino and the elephant, while bush babies, colobus monkeys and other smaller animals teem in the glades. This zone is also heavily populated by man due to its potential for intensive agriculture. Three major cash crops—

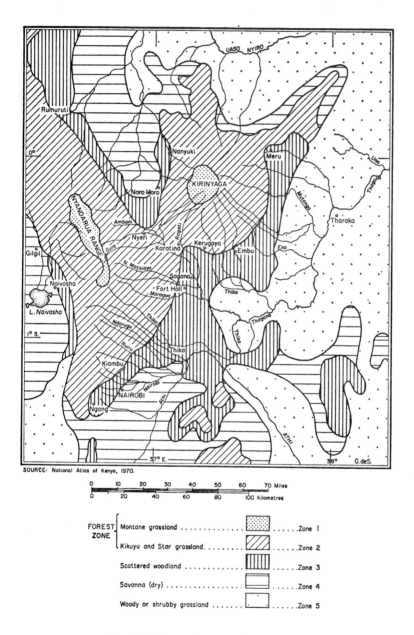

SOURCE: National Atlas of Kenya, 1970.

```
0      10     20    30    40    50    60    70 Miles
0      20    40    60    80    100 Kilometres
```

FOREST ⎰ Montane grassland . . . . ░░░░ . . . . . Zone 1
ZONE ⎱ Kikuyu and Star grassland . . . . ▨▨▨ . . . . . Zone 2

Scattered woodland . . . . ▥▥▥ . . . . . . Zone 3

Savanna (dry) . . . . ▭ . . . . . . Zone 4

Woody or shrubby grassland . . . . ▭ . . . . . . Zone 5

Map 2—Kikuyu plateau: ecological zones.

pyrethrum, coffee and tea—are grown in this region. The second sub-division is the montane grassland zone, a moorland, petering out to the barren land at high altitude on the peaks of Mount Kirinyaga and the Nyandarua range. It is a zone of limited potential and its acidic soil, very high rainfall and cold conditions can only support bracken and other montane flora such as tussock grasses and giant groundsel.

Like the rest of the country, there are two rainy seasons because of the effects of the south-east and north-east trade winds blowing from the Indian Ocean towards the inter-tropical convergence zone at the equator. The long rains fall between March and May, and the short rains between mid-October and December. Due to this incidence of rain the Kikuyu divide the year into two seasons corresponding to the rainy seasons; *kimera kia njahi* (*Dolichos lablab* season) from March to about July and *kimera kia mwere* (millet season) from October to December. Sandwiched between these two are the cold, drizzly months of July to September, called *gathano*, and the bright, sunny and fair-weather months of January, February and March called *themithu*. Each of the lunar months was named according to the weather prevalent at the time.[12]

Another important factor in settlement pattern is the incidence of malaria and the tsetse fly. Eastwards of an imaginary line drawn between Nairobi, Murang'a, Embu and Meru towns, there is a high incidence of malaria. This malarial belt runs from Meru to the north-east to Tsavo to the south-east.[13] In addition, the region is also infested with human and animal trypanosomiasis vectors, especially a corridor running north to south and between Embu and Tharaka. In the Embu-Meru area to the east of Mount Kenya, the major tsetse-fly species are *Glossina pallidipes* and *Glossina longipennis*. There are also small pockets which harbour *Glossina brevipalpis*.[14] *Glossina pallidipes* is a human and animal disease-carrying species which thrives in the open grass and thickets over a wide area, while *Glossina longipennis* and *Glossina brevipalpis* are animal-infecting flies. But Kikuyuland, in contrast, has a low incidence of malaria and none of the human or animal

12.   Baker, op. cit., pp. 9-14; Gregory, op. cit., p. 26; *Handbook*, pp. 124-30, 148-55; K. R. Dundas, 'Kikuyu Calendar', *Man*, vol. 9, 19, 1909, pp. 37-8; Benson, op. cit., pp. 6, 492; Cagnolo, op. cit., pp. 7, 194-6.
13.   *National Atlas of Kenya*, p. 47.
14.   ibid. p. 45.

trypanosomiasis, mainly due to the high altitude and other climatic factors. It is conceivable, therefore, that Kikuyu pioneers might have migrated in order to escape the scourge of malaria and trypanosomiasis in particular. This would not be an isolated, or even unique, case. Lambrecht has shown that tsetse flies have had considerable impact on the economy and population movements in such diverse regions as South Africa, Zaïre and the interlacustrine region of East Africa.[15]

Besides an unusually adequate rainfall, Kikuyuland is also endowed with moderate temperatures. Its deep red soil, derived from the volcanic tuffs, was rich in humus from the cleared primeval forest and hence made the land very productive. It was therefore an ideal habitat for the agricultural, hardworking Kikuyu who for a long time made it the granary of their neighbours as well as for the European and Swahili caravans which passed by or through their country, especially in the nineteenth century. The main traditional food crops were bananas, sweet potatoes, yams, arum lily, various types of *mwere* (finger or bulrush millet) and *muhia* (sorghum), *njahi* (*Dolichos lablab*) and *njugu* (cowpeas). Maize, which now constitutes the staple food, was introduced only probably towards the end of the eighteenth or early nineteenth century.[16] It is no exaggeration to say that Kabete, for example, became to the caravans what Cape Town had been to the passing ships in the seventeenth century. The Kikuyu produced food far in excess of their needs in order to be able to trade with their neighbours.[17] Trade, therefore, was an important activity both internally and externally, external trade was, however, more important, especially with the Maasai and the Dorobo.

Although the Kikuyu were chiefly agriculturalists, they also kept an appreciable number of livestock, chiefly sheep and goats

15. F. L. Lambrecht, 'Aspects of Evolution and Ecology of Tsetse Flies and Trypanosomiasis in Prehistoric African Environment', *Journal of African History*, vol. 5, London, 1964, pp. 1-24.
16. Routledge, op. cit., p. 42.
17. Mackinder, op. cit., pp. 457, 460-2; von Höhnel, op. cit., pp. 302, 315, 332, 335; Gregory, op. cit., p. 192; Bishop A. R. Tucker, an extract from *The Times* of 24 January 1892 in FO 2/57; Sir Gerald Portal to Lord Rosebery, 24 May 1893 in FO 2/57; F.D. Lugard, *The Rise of our East African Empire*, vol. 1, Edinburgh, 1893, pp. 323, 328, 418-19; M. Perham (ed.), op. cit., vol. 1, pp. 285, 314, 316; Thomson, op. cit., pp. 307, 309; J. R. L. MacDonald, *Soldiering and Surveying in British East Africa, 1891-4*, London, 1897, pp. 109, 111, 115; A. Arkell-Hardwick, *An Ivory Trader in North Kenia*, London, 1903, pp. 50-4, 345.

(*mburi*), and cattle. The latter were few and perhaps because of their scarcity, they were the prerogative of the wealthy in the community. Sheep and goats were on the other hand much more common and they played an important role in the life of the ordinary Kikuyu. They were slaughtered during various ceremonies and sacrifices, they were paid as dowry, and their skins provided bedding as well as clothing. The Kikuyu, therefore, had a mixed economy, and besides the pastoral/agricultural pursuits, some families specialized in iron-work, tannery, bee-keeping and barter exchange, especially with their neighbours.[18]

The ridge and valley topography, which is such a charateristic feature of Kikuyuland, considerably influenced the nature of the original settlement, the acquisition of land and subsequent land tenure. Similarly, the original settlement patterns affected the interplay of forces within the social and political organizations that evolved eventually. The immigration into, and the settlement of, the Kikuyu plateau was a slow process, which was spearheaded either by individual pioneers or small family groups which staked claims to particular ridges. Consequently land was occupied ridge by ridge by the pioneers, who were later joined by their kinsmen, or alternatively attracted diverse elements into their sphere. The chief bases of claim to land were either the first clearance of the virgin forest (*kuuna*), or the initial hunting rights. This, however, did not apply to most parts of Kabete, where most of the inhabitants claim to have bought their land from the Athi.

Being primarily an agricultural people, the Kikuyu have been deeply attached to their land, which has been regarded by them as having more than an economic value. Largely because of the mode of migration and the topography there developed neither the tribal nor the individual ownership of land as we shall see in chapter 3.[19] Land was owned by the *mbari*[20] and its administration

18. Middleton and Kershaw, op. cit., pp. 17-22; Cagnolo, op. cit., pp. 31-41; Routledge, op. cit., pp. 38-48, 66-102, 105-7; Kenyatta, op. cit., pp. 53-92.

19. For a discussion of the Kikuyu land tenure, see M. P. K. Sorrenson, *Land Reform in the Kikuyu Country*, chap. 1; Kenyatta, op. cit., chap. 11; Middleton and Kershaw, op. cit., pp. 48-52; 'Lambert 1950', op. cit., chap. 4-8; Routledge, op. cit., pp. 3-7; evidence by various informants to be found in 'Barlow Papers'; M. H. Beech, 'Kikuyu System of Land Tenure', *Journal of African Society*, vol. 17, 65, 1917, pp. 46-59 and no. 66, 1918, pp. 136-44; *Kenya: Native Land Tenure in Kikuyu Province*, op. cit.; J. Fisher, *The Anatomy of Kikuyu Domesticity and Husbandry*, London, 1964, pp. 177-226; L. S. B. Leakey, 'Land Tenure in the Native Reserves', *East African Standard* of 8 and 15 September, 1939 and

was entrusted to a *muramati* (guardian or custodian) who was the nominal head of the *mbari*. *Mbari* ownership of land was further reinforced by the people's religious beliefs, especially reverence for ancestors, which fostered a deep attachment to ancestral lands. The *mbari* land tenure was a safeguard against exploitation by any one member of the clan, however strong or influential he might have been. Moreover, in a society in which communal solidarity was essential for survival, the welfare of the less fortunate members was ensured by the rest of the community. Anyone without land, for example, became a *muhoi* (tenant-at-will) on someone else's land, with the assurance that save for misconduct his tenancy would be secure. Indeed the *ahoi* (tenants-at-will) were always welcome, mainly near the frontiers, where manpower was in great demand for performing various tasks. It was the *ahoi* phenomenon, among other factors, that led to the dispersal of the ten clans all over the country at the turn of the nineteenth century. This has been instrumental in obscuring the original pattern of settlement in many cases, and in spite of the *mbari* ownership of the land. But there was little conflict between the *mbari* and their *ahoi*, for apart from the delicate balance between the seemingly competing interests of the *ahoi* and the *mbari*, both operated under the stringent demands of a customary code that safeguarded their respective interests. With the coming of the white man and the introduction of a cash economy, however, this balance of interests was upset, and subsequently the *ahoi* were adversely affected. They posed grave social and administrative problems in the first decades of the twentieth century as an uprooted peasantry and now mainly constitute the landless sector of the Kikuyu community.

Finally, the ridge, besides being the basis of *mbari* land, was an important link in the political and social chain that cut across the kinship ties. The elementary family, *nyumba*, consisting of a man, his wife or wives and their children, was the core of the Kikuyu society. Several *nyumba* traced their origin to a common male ancestor several generations back and formed a *mbari*, which may have numbered anything from a few hundred to several thousands. The various *mbari* traced their ancestry to the original ten *mihiriga*

A. R. Barlow, 'Kikuyu Land Tenure and Inheritance', *Journal of East Africa and Uganda Natural History*, no. 45-6, 1932, pp. 56-66.

20. A lineage or a sub-clan, depending on numbers, tracing its origin to a common male ancestor a number of generations back. See 'KHT'.

(clans). As well as the *nyumba* being the primary unit in the social framework, it was also the immediately operative political unit. Each *nyumba* formed a *mucii* (pl. *micii*), the homestead, and the various homesteads were grouped together into an *itura* (pl. *matura*), a collection of dispersed homesteads. The *itura* was the focus of the social and political interaction in everyday life, and was in many ways a closely-knit community. The *matura* were, in turn, linked together to form a bigger administrative unit, the *mwaki*,[21] which in turn would be part of a *rugongo* (pl. *ngo'ngo*), a ridge. The ridge was by far the largest administrative unit under normal circumstances but in times of crisis, mutual need or country-wide ceremonies, an *ad hoc* alliance of several ridges might emerge and act in concert. This grouping was designated a *bururi*, an indeterminate term which could have meant anything from the whole of the Kikuyu country to a mere handful of ridges. A particular *mbari* or even clan might have been predominant in one administrative unit, such as an *itura* or ridge, but this was not always the case since the various clans and *mbari* were widely dispersed.[22]

21. The unit occupied by those who assisted each other with hot embers to light fires. *Mwaki* (sing.) means fire; plural *miaki*.

22. Middleton and Kershaw, op. cit., pp. 23-32; Kenyatta, op. cit., pp. 1-2, 5-6, Cagnolo, op. cit., pp. 20-2; Fisher, op. cit., pp. 5-20.

Chapter 2

MIGRATION OF
THE MOUNT KENYA PEOPLES

THE country now inhabited by the Kikuyu people was originally covered by a vast primeval forest, which was sparsely inhabited by the Gumba and Athi hunters and berry gatherers. It attracted the Kikuyu because of its adequate rainfall, cool temperatures and fertile soil, unlike the region skirting it towards the eastern border. After its occupation, it was with a deep sense of gratitude that the Kikuyu came to feel that God had given them 'a very pleasant country indeed, that does not lack food, or water, or land'.[1] This statement is a succinct summary of the basic factors that have influenced their migration and settlement through the generations.

Kikuyu pioneers in the area are said to have been preceded by the Maitho/Maitha a Ciana, the Gumba, the Athi and the Dorobo.[2] Opinion varies, however, as to whether these four were distinct groups, or a related people. Beech, Stoneham and Boyes record that the original inhabitants were the Maitha/Maitho a Ciana, 'enemies or eyes of small children', a dwarf-like people who were displaced by the Gumba and the Athi/Dorobo.[3] Hobley, on the other hand, says that the Maitho/Maitha a Ciana were displaced by the Athi, who were the true Dorobo and descendants of an ancestor called 'Digiri'.[4] And commenting on their own ancestry,

1. R. Macpherson, *Muthomere wa Gikuyu: Ng'ano*, Nairobi, 1944, p. 5.
2. M. W. Beech, 'Pre-Bantu Occupants of East Africa', *Man*, vol. 15, 1915, pp. 40-1; H. F. Stoneham, 'Notes on the Dorobo and Other Tribes', *KLC*, vol. 2, op. cit., pp. 2061-2; K. R. Dundas, 'Notes on the Origin and History of the Kikuyu and Dorobo Tribes', *Man*, vol. 8, 1908, pp. 136-9.
3. Beech, op. cit., p. 40; Stoneham, op. cit., p. 2061 and Boyes, op. cit., p. 298.
4. C. W. Hobley, 'Notes on the Dorobo People and Other Tribes: Gathered from Chief Karuri and Others', *Man*, vol. 6, 1906, pp. 119-20. See also his notes on the Dorobo in *Man*, vol. 3, 1903, pp. 33-4 and vol. 5, 1905, pp. 39-44 and in KNA/PC/CP/1/1/1/.

the Dorobo told K. R. Dundas that 'they, the Masai and the Kikuyu, are the descendants of a common ancestral tribe called Endigiri, and that their ancestors came from beyond Mount Kenya'.[5] In a footnote, Dundas explained that the Endigiri or Muisi were known to the Kikuyu as Maitha a Ciana, a name that was 'said by some to have been applied originally to all the Dorobo or Asi'.[6] It is evident, however, that the term Maitho/Maitha a Ciana was only fashionable particularly in Metumi and some parts of Gaki. Routledge and McGregor, both of whom worked in those parts, identify Maitho/Maitha a Ciana as the same people as the Gumba.[7] In this respect, it is significant to note that the Cuka, the Mwimbi the Muthambi, the Igoji, the Imenti, the Embu and the Tharaka do not seem to have any recollection of such a people as the Maitho/ Maitha a Ciana, whereas they clearly recall the Gumba. Moreover in the recently collected data very few people could recall the former, and those who did thought that they were the same people as the Gumba.[8] In view of this, it would seem that although the term Maitha/Maitho a Ciana might have originally meant the ancestors of the Gumba, later on it specifically referred to the Gumba or, in very rare cases, to the Athi in general, depending upon the context.

Lambert was also doubtful of the identification of the Athi with the Dorobo.[9] The apparent ambiguity implied both by the extant literature and the oral data has arisen out of two factors. The Kikuyu word *athi* (hunters, sing. *mwathi*), was used to mean either an individual who practised hunting as a way of life, irrespective of ethnic grouping, or more specifically, a tribe whose economic activities were largely centred upon hunting and gathering. And apart from the inherent ambiguity in meaning of the word *athi*, its obscurity was further deepened by the reluctance of the Kikuyu to discuss any issue which seemed likely to undermine their rights to land. The political controversy centring on the alienation of land to white settlers generated an atmosphere of mistrust that precluded any honest discussion of oral traditions which embraced the sensitive issue of land. This reluctance was more pronounced whenever the Kikuyu were approached by people who appeared unsympathetic to their interests. On the other hand, material

5.   K. R. Dundas, *Man*, vol. 8, p. 139.
6.   ibid., p. 139.
7.   Routledge, op. cit., pp. 3-5; McGregor, op. cit., p. 31.
8.   'KHT', pp. 75 and 104.
9.   'Lambert, 1950,' chap. 4.

collected prior to the emergence of organized political consciousness among the Kikuyu, that is, prior to 1920, as well as the data I have collected recently, demonstrate without doubt that 'Athi' and 'Dorobo' are alternative names for the same ethnic group. The former was commonly used in Gaki and Metumi, and the latter in Kabete. In Gaki and Metumi, though, 'Athi' has come to mean the early Kikuyu pioneers to some people, just as in Kabete it simply means the Dorobo hunters, who are reputed to have sold them land. Still, these two attitudes towards the Athi/Dorobo are not necessarily contradictory, since some of the Kikuyu *mbari* trace their ancestry to Athi ancestors. From the above discussion, there seems to be little doubt that the Kikuyu were preceded by two distinct, but perhaps related, groups of people; and in all probability these were the Gumba and the Athi/Dorobo. This conclusion accords with Routledge, the first scholar to have seriously investigated the cultural traditions of the Kikuyu.[10]

Little is known of these people, nor do the informants clearly distinguish between them. The Gumba or the Maitho/Maitha a Ciana, who were the first group to come into contact with Kikuyu pioneers, are said to have been a race of hunting dwarfs, rather like the pygmies, who lived in roofed-over, dug out caves or tunnels. Estimates of their height ranges from two to four and a half feet, but they are said to have been stocky, clever and rather retiring. Besides hunting with bows and arrows, and gathering, they are also known for their bee-keeping and their skill in iron-working and pottery. The innumerable depressions that exist all over the Kikuyu country are regarded to be the sites of former Gumba homes.

The contact between these hunters and the Kikuyu pioneers is important for two reasons. The Kikuyu claimed, according to Northcote, that they were taught the art of iron-working and smelting by the Gumba.[11] If this is so, theirs was an important contribution, since the Kikuyu were enabled to clear the forest for cultivation by using iron tools. It also appears that it was from them that the Kikuyu borrowed the rituals of circumcision, clitoridectomy and some features of the age system. This view would tend to rule out the possibility of the Kikuyu having borrowed their *mariika* (age differentiation) system from either the Maasai or the Galla. The *mariika* system was in operation long before the

10. Routledge, op. cit., p. 3.
11. Beech, *Man*, vol. 15, pp. 40-1.

Maasai and Kikuyu communities came into contact and when they
did, it was only Gaki which was heavily influenced by the Maasai
pattern of the age system. As to the Galla, Haberland has shown
that not only is their importance in the cultural history of eastern
Africa overrated but, as he concludes, 'it is not possible to maintain
that the Galla were responsible for the diffusion of the age-grade
(*gada*) system ... The formation and dissemination of the gada-
system probably lie as far back as the disintegration of the eastern
Hamitic language group into several distinct languages'.[12]

The second group that the Kikuyu pioneers came into contact
with were the Athi. Like the Gumba, they were also hunters and
gatherers who neither cultivated nor possessed livestock. They
obtained the latter from their neighbours in case of need. The Athi
played a very significant role in the life of their Kikuyu neighbours;
they were important trading partners, selling animal products
such as ivory, hides and skins, as well as acting as middlemen
between the Kikuyu, the Maasai and the coastal traders. They also
sold land to the Kikuyu, especially in Kabete, in exchange for
livestock which, apparently, they sought avidly. This interdependence between the two communities persisted right up to the nineteenth century, and this is evident from the number of caravans that
sought these neighbours' aid when attempting to procure food
from the Kikuyu. Mianzini, for example, was an important victual-
ling site because the Athi, who had settled in the Kinale forest,
acted as trading intermediaries between the caravans and the
source of food in the heart of Kikuyuland.[13] Further north there
was also a colony of the Athi, living in the Nyeri plains and in the
Mount Kenya forest. Here, too, they had trading contacts with
their Kikuyu neighbours as well as the Swahili and Arab traders.
Ndoro, like Mianzini, seems to have been an important resting and
trading centre.[14]

Extant sources—as indeed the Kikuyu oral traditions—do not give
a clear picture of the differences, or relationship if any, between
the Gumba and the Athi. There are, however, striking similarities
in habitat, material culture and their economic and social organization. The only significant difference between the two communities,

12. E. Haberland, *Galla Sud-Athiopiens*, Stuttgart, 1963, English summary,
     p. 771.
13. G. A. Fisher, *Das Masai-Land*, Hamburg, 1885, pp. 47-8, 81, 99.
14. Boyes, op. cit., pp. 165, 189-90; Fischer, op. cit., p. 98; von Höhnel,
     op. cit., pp. 351, 364, 366; Gregory, op. cit., pp. 157-61.

as far as the traditions go, was their respective stature; the Gumba are said to have been dwarf-like, in contrast to the Athi who are described as resembling their Bantu and Plains or Highlands Nilotic neighbours. However, according to some Kikuyu opinion, the two groups lived side by side and even intermarried;[15] yet other Kikuyu traditions describe the two predecessor communities as separate and distinct groups. Whatever the true position may have been initially, there is no doubt that the Athi have assimilated a considerable section of the Gumba, some of whom are known to have sought refuge in the forests following Kikuyu encroachment on their hunting grounds. Dorobo traditions, as recorded by K. R. Dundas, are not so ambivalent; they claim that the Dorobo were divided into the Gumba, who hunted in the plains, and the Okiek (the Athi of the Kikuyu) who lived in the forests. And as noted above, they asserted that they, the Maasai and the Kikuyu, were the descendants of a common ancestral tribe, the 'Endigiri', who had migrated from beyond Mount Kenya.[16] It should be noted, in this regard, that according to Meru traditions a group of the Il Tikirri (plains Nilotic speakers) was still living to the north-eastern fringe of the Tigania plains in the first half of the eighteenth century.[17] Secondly, some Kikuyu pioneers are said to have emigrated from the region of Tigania as discussed below.

Whereas we can determine what became of the Athi when they came into contact with the Kikuyu, the fate of the Gumba is shrouded in mystery and myth. The traditions of the Mwimbi, Cuka, Embu and Kikuyu aver that the Gumba fled *en masse* after being frightened by the appearance of helmeted hornbills (*magogo*, sing. *igogo*). One day, the story goes, the helmeted hornbills settled on a tree and started cawing. The Gumba thought that the *magogo* were shouting 'Over there! Over there!',[18] thereby directing an army of warriors to attack them. Thoroughly disconcerted, the Gumba migrated, and either disappeared into the ground, or moved westwards, or northwards, the details varying with each informant. This, however, is a rationalization, or an

15. Routledge, op. cit., p. 5.
16. K. R. Dundas, *Man*, 1908, pp. 138-9.
17. See J. Fadiman, 'Early History of Meru', *Aspects of Pre-Colonial History of Kenya* edited by B. A. Ogot (forthcoming).
18. The Kikuyu light-heartedly take the birds as saying '*O hau! O hau!*' when cawing.

oversimplification, of a more complex process. And although this tradition is devoid of details, it points to some important factors.

The apparent flight of the Gumba is suggestive of a worsening of relations between them and the Kikuyu, a process which might have taken a considerable period of time. A number of factors may have influenced the situation, the chief of which would be the intrusion of the proto-Kikuyu elements into a predominantly Gumba domain. The clearance of bushland for agricultural purposes was in itself a direct threat to the Gumba way of life and, more especially, of their livelihood. It is conceivable, therefore, that faced with this danger they were not slow to retaliate. This, in turn, would have set in motion a chain reaction of retaliatory and counter-retaliatory measures which could only be stopped by one group deciding to migrate in order to avoid annihilation. In any case there would have been a lot of scope for misunderstanding, if not quarrels, once the two groups were living in proximity to each other. The Gumba were not weaklings, and armed with their bows and arrows, they could have defended themselves effectively against the intruders. But it is much more likely that the intrusion of human habitation, and the destruction of the bushland, forced some of the wild animals to retreat to the primeval forests higher up the plateau or to scatter over the vast plains. The retreat of the wild animals, the main source of livelihood for the Gumba, made it necessary for them to follow the animals either into the high mountain forests or south-wards across the plains. This argument rules out the idea of a Kikuyu conquest, which is not supported by the available data. The Kikuyu 'obtained the country by a system of peaceful penetration, effected by individuals, or small bands of individuals united only by family ties'.[19] This does not rule out the occasional conflict, some of which will be referred to in later chapters. Such conflict was not, of course, confined to the Gumba and the Kikuyu alone; intra-clan and inter-*mbari* fights were all too common among the Kikuyu themselves. It is also important to remember that, given the acknowledged ability of the Gumba as a fighter, and especially his prowess in using bows and arrows in a terrain he knew well, it is unlikely that the intruders would have made much headway in the face of a determined opposition. On the contrary, it is much more likely that both groups realized that it was of mutual benefit to live amicably; the Kikuyu needed the hides and skins that were available from

19. Routledge, op. cit., p. 3.

the Gumba as much as the Gumba needed some of the agricultural products of the Kikuyu. The available evidence tends to support the view that they reached a *modus vivendi*, but in the interim there was settlement amongst, and intermarriage between, the two peoples, the descendants of such marriages becoming full members of their respective Kikuyu clans while at the same time retaining some of the aspects of a hunting and gathering economy. It is very probable that it was this group of semi-Kikuyu, semi-Gumba which made up the bulk of the pioneers who initially settled in the secondary nuclear area of dispersal, that is, in Gaki and Metumi. There is enough evidence supporting such a view. First, several eponymous *mbari* founders—such as Kanja of Kirimukuyu (Mathira), Magana of Mahiga (Uthaya), Kambaire of Karima (Uthaya), Ithemukima of Kahuhia (Kiharu) and Thuthuni of Kihoya (Kangima)—are said to have been hunters.[20] Moreover, it was generally agreed by my informants that most of the earliest pioneers were either hunters or pastoralists.[21] Secondly, other informants claimed that the Kikuyu themselves are descendants of the Gumba.[22]

This process of absorption was to continue when the Kikuyu came into contact with the Athi. While some of the latter migrated into the forests of Nyandarua and Kirinyaga or settled among the Maasai, others adopted the Kikuyu way of life, by undergoing a ceremony of mutual adoption which made them full members of the Kikuyu community. The only reminder of this process is perhaps preserved in the Kikuyu attitude to wild game—it was taboo for some sections of the community to touch it.

> The Achera, the Ambui, the Ethaga, and the Anjiru, may eat wild game. In two other clans, the Angari and Aizerandu, some may eat wild game and some may not. This difference is accounted for by tradition, that in each there were originally two brothers, one of whom went and killed game and the other did not, and their respective descendants adhere to the precedent thus laid.[23]

Thus complete assimilation has almost taken place; today the only remnant of the Athi as an ethnic group is to be found among their descendants around Kambaa, in the Limuru division of Kabete, where they were settled by the colonial government after

20. 'KHT', pp. 3, 4 and 8, 42-56, 57-60, 89-90 and 100-2.
21. ibid., pp. 8, 67, 71, 73-4, 75, 77, 80-1, 83, 91 and 98.
22. ibid., pp. 52, 63, 71 and 119.
23. Routledge, op. cit., pp. 21-2.

being ejected from Kinale forest in the 1930s. But even here it is fairly difficult to trace them and it can be safely argued that this chance encounter between these groups had profound consequences on both.

It is also necessary to bear in mind that the Gumba, as said above, hunted mainly in the open grassland rather than in the forests. Secondly, the Kikuyu pioneers migrated from as far afield as Tigania, Igembe, Tharaka, Cuka, Embu and Mbeere. Yet, in each of these areas the new immigrants encountered the Gumba and as recently as the second half of the eighteenth century, for example, the Gumba were living in considerable numbers in the Mwimbi region, where they were a real threat to the Mwimbi people.[24] The Embu also claim that they were nearly defeated by the Gumba towards the end of the eighteenth century.[25] In light of the above, it seems much more likely that the proto-Kikuyu initially encountered the Gumba in eastern Meru and that contact continued till their arrival in the highlands.

The traditions of these people do not give adequate information of where, and when, the initial encounter took place. And for this reason any attempt to provide the answers must remain speculative until we have confirmatory data. However, a close examination of the generation and military sets might provide useful clues. By the middle of the seventeenth century, several basic features of the social and political structure of the Kikuyu had emerged. The organization of the ruling generations goes back to the early decades of the sixteenth century, while the military sets date from the middle of the seventeenth century. And none of the informants claimed that these lists were exhaustive, on the contrary, they alleged that there might have been others which they had forgotten. And if the initiation ceremony was borrowed from the Gumba, as has been suggested above, then the encounter between the Gumba and the proto-Kikuyu must have taken place several generations before the middle of the seventeenth century. Significantly, the clan system had evolved by mid-seventeenth century, and matriarchy had been superseded by a patrilineal and a patrilocal social and political organization; such a transformation can hardly

24. Fadiman, op. cit.
25. For the information on the Embu, Cuka and Tharaka, I am indebted to Mr. H. S. K. Mwaniki, Research Fellow of the Institute of African Studies, University of Nairobi, who has been conducting research in the area.

be expected to have been completed overnight. The middle of the seventeenth century, however, has been taken as a basis for discussion simply because from then onwards, evidence becomes reasonably reliable, with specific episodes being associated with each of the generations. There is, too, a close parallel between the system of age differentiation among the Ndia and the Kikuyu, as opposed to that of the Meru. Finally, the traditions of the Kikuyu state unequivocably that their clans had already evolved by the time they crossed the Thagana river into Metumi and Gaki. It can be assumed that all these social upheavals took place before the Kikuyu arrival in their present homeland.

The gradual expansion by the vanguard of the Kikuyu pioneers pushed the forest fringe further and further back until they reached their final area of dispersal around the Metumi/Gaki border. The relations between the Gumba and the incoming Kikuyu pioneers worsened and a fight ensued at Giitwa and Karirau.[26] The deterioration of relations between the two groups, together with the effects of the receding forest fringe, eventually drove the remnants of the Gumba deeper into the extensive forests of the Kikuyu plateau where they joined the Athi. And as the Kikuyu increased in number their clearing of the forests gained momentum, and in the words of Routledge, 'the Akikuyu pushed on and on. Their progress was like that of the locusts—the ranks at the rear, finding food supply exhausted, taking wing over the backs of the main body to drop to ground in the forefront. And as locusts clear a sturdy crop, so have the Akikuyu cleared the forest'.[27] This intrusion by newcomers, who made additional and different demands on the natural resources, forced the Gumba and the Athi, too, either to adapt themselves to the new environment or to seek a new habitation.

As well as fleeing from the approaching Kikuyu others formed a symbiotic relationship with the cultivators, but despite mutual economic convenience, contact was kept to a minimum by a sizeable number on each side.

Nevertheless, this stage of rapid expansion did not occur until the last decades of the nineteenth century. After the Giitwa and Karirau episodes, little is heard of the Gumba apart from the battle at Gathagana, at the confluence of the Gura and Thagana rivers, where the last group, which had allegedly prevented expansion

26. 'KHT', pp. 85, 88. 94-5 and 109-10.
27. Routledge, op. cit., p. 6.

into Mathira, was defeated. It is also said that this forced the Kikuyu to destroy the natural bridge which had hitherto been there, in order to contain the Gumba, who used it to cross into Mukurue-ini division.[28] Oral traditions are not firm about the time this confrontation occurred. But it seems to have taken place during the Iregi generation, that is, in mid-nineteenth century. Most probably this coincided with the Barabiu invasion, and it might have involved some of the remnants of the Gumba and Athi who were then living in the Mount Kenya forest. This implies that the Gumba were only present in any appreciable numbers in the country towards the east of Metumi, their numbers tailing off in the eastern borders of the Kikuyu plateau. This view agrees with Dorobo traditions, that the Gumba hunted in the plains and the Athi (Okiek) in the forests. Certainly the Gumba are almost unheard of in Kabete and by the time the Kikuyu elements reached their final centre of dispersal in the plateau, the Gumba had virtually ceased to exist as an ethnic group.

Three things might have happened to the Gumba; they might have been absorbed by either the Athi or the Kikuyu pioneers, they might have settled amongst the latter group after abandoning their way of life, or they might have been expelled, taking refuge in the plains to the north and the south-east of the Kikuyu plateau.[29] And even though oral traditions state artlessly that the Gumba scattered and 'disappeared' to the four corners of the globe, it is quite clear this is a cover for a possible massacre, which occurred about mid-nineteenth century. There are other parallels elsewhere in East Africa. For example, most traditions in Uganda claim that the Bacwezi simply 'disappeared', but they were in fact defeated by later immigrants such as the Babito.[30]

There are two main myths which attempt to explain the origin of the Kikuyu. One of them relates that a man who had four sons called them at his death-bed to apportion his possessions. He had four articles—a herding staff, a quiver of arrows and a bow, a stabbing spear and a digging stick. Depending upon the choices

28. 'History *irĩa ũiguanĩirũo nĩ athuri arĩa akũrakũrũ—1.8.42*' in 'Barlow Papers' (Unsorted Miscellaneous File). Others give different, but related, reasons for the destruction of the bridge. See 'KHT', pp. 2 and 21.

29. 'KHT' pp. 74-5.

30. J. B. Webster, 'Migration and Settlement of the Northern Interlacustrine Region', typescript, Department of History, Makerere University, Uganda, n.d., pp. 4-12.

they made, the four sons became the ancestors of the pastoral Maasai, the Kamba, the Athi and the agricultural Kikuyu respectively. Very few people recall who this man was and only Tate records that the man was a Mumbeere living east of Mbeere.[31] But the most popular myth is that which associates the Kikuyu with the Mukurue wa Gathanga. God appeared to Gikuyu, we are told, and allotted to him all the land to the south-west of Mount Kenya.[32] Gikuyu and his wife Mumbi (the Adam and Eve of the Kikuyu) made their home at Mukurue wa Gathanga, and while there they had nine daughters. The latter became the ancestors of the 'full nine' clans.[33]

These myths are clearly unhelpful and only two points are worth noting. First, there is the implication that the Kikuyu might have migrated from beyond Mbeere and that they might be related to their neighbours. Secondly, the possibility that the area around Mukurue wa Gathanga was a significant one in the evolution of the Kikuyu. Otherwise, the study of *mbari* genealogies is far more rewarding. Indeed, while the Mukurue region retains some significance, it can no longer be regarded as the cradle, for there is evidence to show that some of the *mbari* came from as far afield as Meru, Mbeere, Cuka and Ndia. Igembe, Tharaka, Ithanga and Thagicu are places that are also frequently mentioned.

While it is difficult to name any one specific cause of the initial sparking off of the proto-Kikuyu migration, several factors may have been of great importance. Ecologically, the Igembe and the Tharaka probably experienced, as they still do, a very poor climate, they had few resources and were susceptible to famine whenever the rains failed, as we have seen in chapter 1. The area also has a high incidence of malaria, as well as human and animal trypanosomiasis. In contrast, the area to its west was not only a potentially attractive

31. H. R. Tate, 'The Native Law of the Southern Gikuyu of British East Africa', *Journal of African Society*, vol. 35, 1910, pp. 233-54; Routledge, op. cit., pp. 283-4.
32. Kenyatta, op. cit., pp. 3-6; 'KHT', pp. 7, 65, 138. No satisfactory explanation was given why the ancestors were called Mumbi and Gikuyu. The only plausible information offered was that a man met a woman who was making pots (*kumba*), and that this woman discovered that the man was sheltering under a wild fig tree, *mukuyu*. On marrying they called each other by nicknames, a usual Kikuyu custom, associated with the circumstances of their initial meeting. Thus the man called the woman Mumbi (potter), while the woman called him Gikuyu (of the fig tree).
33. 'Full nine' means ten; it was courting disaster to count people or livestock. There are ten clans, the Aicakamuyu being the descendants of an unmarried mother from one of the other nine.

agricultural land but it was also sparsely populated by nomadic hunters. It seems reasonable to assume that this area, now known as Mbeere and Cuka, was a welcome refuge to those immigrants suffering from the ravages of famine or even diseases. But people sometimes adapt themselves to their environment even when conditions are harsh. There might have been other factors therefore compelling the proto-Kikuyu to migrate. A sudden increase in the population, for instance, would have depleted the already meagre resources and, secondly, a foreign invasion would have sparked off migration. In this case, the Galla impingement might have acted as a catalyst to migration and it is significant that in Meru traditions one of the factors which led to migration was their ill-treatment by the Nguntune, a light-skinned race.[34] And some of the Tharaka in particular claim to have found the Galla living in their present land at the time of occupation.[35] From the sixteenth century onwards, the Galla, in search of new areas for settlement, migrated in all directions from the overcrowded southern part of the Ethiopian highlands. By the middle of the sixteenth century some of them had advanced as far south as the mouth of the Juba river on the east coast of Africa.[36] It should be noted, too, that according to Kikuyu traditions, the early part of their history was marked by internal tension as well as raiding. The Manduti and Cuma generations (from the middle of the seventeenth century to the first half of the eighteenth) are best remembered for their raiding and fighting. Tradition also describes the Mathathi and Ndemi generations as the era of expansion by, and influx of, most of the Kikuyu pioneers.[37] This coincides with two major phenomena—the arrival of the ancestors of the Meru into their present homeland in the first half of the eighteenth century, and the worsening of the relations between the Gumba, on one hand, and their neighbours the ancestors of the Meru and Embu on the other.[38] All the above factors might have combined to give impetus to Kikuyu migration. As well as these major causes of migration, secondary issues helped the phenomenon, and indeed an examination of *mbari* genealogies

34. 'Lambert, 1950', chap. 2 and E. R. Shackleton, 'The Njuwe', *Man*, vol. 30, 1930 pp. 201-2.
35. A. M. Champion, 'The Atharaka', *Journal of the Royal Anthropological Institute*, vol. 42, 1912, pp. 69-70.
36. Haberland, op. cit., pp. 772-3.
37. 'KHT'. See section on migration and settlement, particularly in Gaki and Metumi.
38. Fadiman, op. cit.; Mwaniki, personal communication.

reveals that each *mbari* had its own particular and peculiar reasons for deciding to migrate. Various reasons were cited, among which were internal family or *mbari* quarrels, criminals fleeing from justice, adventurous individuals setting out for a new environment, fear of witchcraft, natural disasters such as famine or disease, and a search for better new homes in cases of persistent misfortunes in the previous ones.[39] Tradition, for example, recalls several serious famines which have afflicted the Kikuyu and their neighbours virtually throughout their history. These are: the Famine of Sweeping the Courtyard at the time of Agu (probably between 1637 and 1645); the Famine of Small Bones at the time of the Karanja warriors (1730-8); the Famine of Kimorori at the time of the Njihia initiation set (1863); the Famine of Necklaces at the time of Muhaguya initiation set (1884) and the Famine of 'Europe' in 1901.[40]

The emigration of the proto-Kikuyu from Meru and Tharaka, or a detailed study of their migration via Mbeere and Ndia, lies beyond the scope of this book. This should not, however, preclude some general observations about these other groups. The Kikuyu proper and the Cuka have no traditions of ever having migrated from the coast, let alone Shungwaya. The Embu and Kamba, according to the researches recently carried out among them, do not have traditions that recall their emigration from the coast either.[41] It is the Meru congeries alone that claim to have come from a place to the east called 'Mbwa'. According to the Embu, the Mbeere and the Kikuyu, their ancestors originated either from the east or north-east of the present Mbeere country. In the event and on the basis of the available evidence, it is quite clear that the ancestors of the Tharaka, Cuka, Mbeere, Embu, Ndia, Gicugu and of the Kikuyu migrated from Tigania and Igembe in Meru. This migration was well under way by the middle of the fifteenth century. There does not seem to be any historical evidence, therefore, for the

39. The Kikuyu believed that if one was dogged by misfortune, migration to a new area might alter the course of events. See 'KHT', pp. 1-192, particularly pages 125, 138-41, 144, 150-1, 153-4, 185-6 and 192.
40. The names of the famines are based on Cagnolo (pp. 199-202), while the dates are based on my own chronology. There have been other famines in this century such as the ones in 1917 (called the Famine of Thika), 1943 (the Famine of Mianga [cassava]) and 1948 (the Famine of Muthua [white termites]).
41. S. C. Saberwal, 'Historical Notes on the Embu of Central Kenya'; J. Forbes Munro, 'Migrations of the Bantu-Speaking Peoples of the Eastern Kenya Highlands: A Reappraisal', *Journal of African History*, vol. 8, 1967, pp. 29-38 and 25-8 respectively.

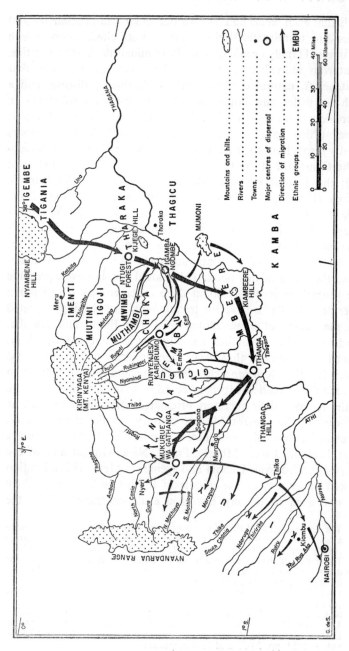

Map 3—*Migration of the Mount Kenya Peoples.*

conclusion popularized by Lambert and thereafter accepted by scholars, that the branch of the north-eastern Bantu inhabiting the Mount Kenya region came from Shungwaya. The probable historical relationship between these groups can be worked out if we take into consideration the traditions of migration as narrated by the various ethnic groups.

The most common myth among the Embu is that of Mwene Ndega and his wife, Nthara. The couple, so the story goes, had a son, Kembu, and daughter, Werimba. Kembu made Werimba pregnant and consequently the two ran away towards the Kieni area. The other children of Mwene Ndega misbehaved in a similar manner and fled likewise, thereby spreading to populate Embuland.

According to Cuka traditions, however, the Cuka, Embu and Tharaka are very closely related. They are said to be descendants of three sisters who migrated from Tigania or Igembe or both places. On leaving Tigania and Igembe, they are said to have settled around the Ntugi forest. The mother of the Tharaka, Cia-Mbandi, was left there and she gave offspring to the Tharaka, while CiaNthiga (the Eve of the Embu) and CiaNgoi (the Eve of the Cuka) pressed ahead and settled at Igambang'ombe. CiaNthiga and CiaNgoi apparently quarrelled at this stage and the former crossed the Tharia and Thuci rivers into modern Embuland, while the latter went up the ridge to settle at Magumoni.

Finally, the Mbeere say that a fight was provoked by a serious quarrel between the sons of two brothers or, step-brothers. After this episode one of the brothers decided to migrate. He eventually became the ancestor of the Mbeere. Indeed, the Mbeere regard the Embu as 'children of our daughters', while the Embu in turn regard the Mbeere as 'children of an Embu daughter'. Subsequently, the Mbeere migrated following the Thagana river and halted near the Kiambeere hill. Some of the migrants settled there, others crossed the Thagana river into modern Kambaland, while the rest migrated westwards until they reached the Ithanga hills, at the confluence of the Thika and Thagana rivers. From Ithanga it is said that people dispersed to Mwea, Mbeere hills, and some even to Embuland. The final group hived off, migrating towards Murang'a.

Apart from these traditions, and those of the Kikuyu proper, two other major pieces of evidence are worth considering. In a pioneer article on the historical linguistics of the Mount Kenya peoples, Bennett argues that Thagicu is a group of dialects, or very closely related languages, that are spoken to the east and south of Mount Kenya.[42] It includes the Kikuyu, Kamba, Embu, Mbeere, the Meru (Cuka, Muthambi, Mwimbi, Igoji, Imenti and Tigania) congeries and the Tharaka. Segeju and Sonjo, though spoken near Tanga in Tanzania, also belong to the Thagicu language group. He sub-divides the Thagicu group into two—the northern and the southern Thagicu.[43] The Northern Thagicu includes the Tharaka and the Meru cluster, while the sourthern Thagicu covers the rest of the dialects. On the basis of highly technical linguistic data, Bennett advances the hypothesis that, 'The name "Thagicu" is, in various forms and various ways, associated with all the major subdivisions of the group, and *there is some reason to believe that it was in fact the name of the tribe* from which they are all derived.'[44]

Another linguist, Ehret, appears to support this view.[45] Evidence on the Thagicu is rather scanty. But they are mentioned by several people. Dundas reports that the actual Kikuyu were said to have come from 'two tribes called the Shagishu [Thagicu] and Ngembe [Igembe]'.[46] McGregor also reports that the inhabitants of Kikuyu 'country began their immigration from the northwest of the mountain from Chagicho [Thagicu] and made their first settlement at Mazeras [Mathira] on the southern slopes'.[47] There is no doubt that previously, the Thagicu were better known and even more widespread than they are today. At the moment, they are to be found east of Mbeere and in Tharaka country. Besides, the present Mavuria location of Mbeere is traditionally called Thagicu. Most of the early European travellers, for instance, record having heard or come across them to the east of Kikuyuland.[48]

The second evidence comes from archaeology. In the course of my field research work, I stumbled across an iron-age site at Gatung'ang'a, a small village in the Mathira division of Nyeri district. The site was subsequently excavated in May and June 1971

42. Patrick R. Bennett, 'Dahl's Law and Thagicu', *African Language Studies*, vol. 8, University of London, 1967, pp. 127-59.
43. ibid., pp. 141-2 and map on p. 130.
44. ibid., footnote 1, p. 128. Italics mine.
45. C. Ehret, *Southern Nilotic History: Linguistic Approaches to the Study of the Past*, Illinois, 1971, p. 43.
46. K. R. Dundas, *Man*, vol. 8, 1908, p. 137.
47. McGregor, op. cit., p. 31.
48. Note, for example, Arkell-Hardwick who shows that 'Dhaicho' was in an area south of Nyambene hills but north of the Thagana river. See map facing p. 368 in Arkell-Hardwick, op. cit., and Fisher, op. cit., p. 98.

and the finds were analysed and radio-carbon dated.[49] The finds included potsherds, iron slag, pieces of hammerstones, tuyères and some iron-slag heaps. A close study of the 230 decorated sherds, found at the site, indicated that Gatung'ang'a pottery was similar to the Kwale ware.[50] It included such specific Kwale traits as bowls with up-turned, bevelled rims and necked pots with fluting below the neck. The most prominent decorative motif is the rocked zig-zag line. This characteristic links it with pottery found at such diverse sites as Gatare Forest Station (Nyandarua Range), Karen in Nairobi, Kathpat Estate in Kiambaa (Kiambu district), Kyambondo and Kyanga in Machakos district and Ngungani in Chyulu hills. Other decorative motifs link the Gatung'ang'a site pottery to that found at Don Dol and Kantana in Laikipia district, in the Kilomba and Kisima rock-shelters in Machakos and Narok districts respectively, and at Njiiri's School in Murang'a district.

Further archaeological analysis of the material revealed that it was possible to divide it into two groups—phase A, which is older, and phase B. Apart from Kwale-type pottery, phase A had an obsidian industry showing blade technique, and there was some evidence of probable iron working and animal domestication. Kwale-type pottery was missing in phase B but there was ample evidence of intensive iron working and domesticated animals, particularly the cow, sheep and goat. The archaeological evidence and C 14 dating indicated that at Gatung'ang'a there was continuous occupation from about the twelfth to the fourteenth century.[51] Siiriänen concludes that the population that made the pottery—found at Gatung'ang'a, Usangi hospital, Pare hills and sites

49. Ari Siiriänen, 'The Age Site at Gatung'ang'a, Central Kenya: Contributions to the Gumba Problem', Azania, vol. vi, 1971, pp. 199-232.
50. R. Soper, 'Kwale: an Early Iron Age Site in South-Eastern Kenya,' Azania, vol. ii, 1967, pp. 1-17.
51. Siiriänen, op. cit.. The Geology Department of the University of Helsinki gave the following C14 dates:

HEL—222 layer 2   810 ± 130 B.P. = A.D. 1140
HEL—223 layer 2a   820 ± 130 B.P. = A.D. 1130
HEL—224 layer 3   850 ± 150 B.P. = A.D. 1100
HEL—225 layer 3   690 ± 100 B.P. = A.D. 1290
HEL—226 layer 3   600 ± 80 B.P. = A.D. 1350

Layer 2: dark grey layer, containing abundant iron slag and pieces of charcoal; c5 to 25cm.
Layer 2a: similar to 2; lighter in colour; c2 to 50cm.
Layer 3: red loamy soil, the upper part of which (c20 cm) contained pieces of iron slag.
Layer 2 and 2a are Phase B and Layer 3 is Phase A which is older, but probably there has been a disturbance of the soil leading to contamination between layers.

mentioned above—was probably ethnically the same as that responsible for the Kwale ware. He concludes, 'the excavations at Gatung'ang'a seem to show that there already existed in the eastern highlands of Central Kenya a Bantu-speaking population before the arrival of the Kikuyu in the sixteenth century'.[52]

The linguistic and archaeological evidence presented here calls for a re-examination of the oral traditions. The oral data collected from the secondary nuclear area of dispersal mentions several initial *mbari* founders, whose origin is rather obscure. There are, for example, Kanja in Kirimukuyu (Mathira), Magana and Kamoko in Mahiga (Uthaya), Kambaire in Mukurue-ini and Karima, Ithemukima in Kahuhia and Thuthuni in Kihoya (Kangima).[53] Magana is perhaps the most interesting pioneer. Originally he came from Mathira before he entered Aguthi, where he did not stay for long either. His hunting activities eventually took him to Mahiga where he is said to have met Kamoko, a pastoralist.[54] Finally, Magana probably married Nduguti or Nyanjugu, a descendant of Kambaire.[55] It is noteworthy that Kanja and Magana came from Mathira, the region where, according to McGregor, the Thagicu made their first settlement.[56]

Secondly, the initial pioneers are portrayed as having been largely a group of hunters, together with a few pastoralists. This is confirmed by the fact that claim to land has been based primarily on the initial hunting rights and grazing, or ultimately on the clearing of the virgin land. This supports the evidence, or indication, of there having been no agriculture at the site at Gatung'ang'a. It appears reasonable to assume from the oral, linguistic and archaeological evidence gathered so far, that the main body of the Kikuyu group was preceded by early iron-age, Bantu-speaking, occupants who depended largely on hunting for their livelihood, though there were some pastoralists. Most probably these were the Thagicu, who spread from Meru to Kambaland and from Tharaka to the Kikuyu plateau.

Finally, it was the Thagicu who heavily intermingled with the previous populations such as the Gumba and the Il Tikirri, leading to a cross-fertilization of ideas and institutions at a formative stage

52.   Siiriänen op. cit., pp. 223-4.
53.   'KHT', op. cit., pp. 3-4 and 8, 42-56, 57-60, 89-90 and 100-2.
54.   ibid., pp. 42-56.
55.   ibid., pp. 55-9.
56.   McGregor, op. cit., p. 31

and before the arrival of the present occupants. This, then, formed the first stage in the colonization of the highlands by the Mount Kenya peoples.

The second stage probably began in the middle of the fifteenth century, or perhaps earlier. An analysis of the traditions of the Kikuyu and their cousins clearly shows that some of the ancestors of the Embu, Tharaka, Cuka, Mbeere and the Kikuyu migrated from the present-day Igembe and Tigania area. But no clear reasons are advanced for this population movement. However, apart from the reasons cited above, we are further told of a 'a brother making a sister pregnant and the two thereby becoming social outcasts'; it is claimed that 'there was oppression and hence people ran away'; or 'two brothers quarrelled and one of them migrated'. Such explanations are in accord with Kikuyu traditions, which definitely state that the early period of the Kikuyu history was an era of internal tension and raids. The Cuma era was characterized, as has been mentioned before, by raiding, while its predecessor, the Manduti, is said to have been the era of 'evil doers', 'worthless people', and 'sinful people'.[57] It seems clearly evident, therefore, that a serious social sin was committed at the time of the Manduti, and in the eyes of the Mount Kenya peoples, nothing can be more serious than incest, such as a brother making his sister pregnant.

During the course of their migration, the pioneers appear to have avoided the hilly regions of Imenti, Mwimbi and Muthambi as well as the low-lying Thagana river valley. Trekking south-wards, they halted around the Ntugi forest or Matiiri, between the Thingithu and Mutonga rivers.[58] A section of the trekkers who settled at Matiiri, and thereby joined the Thagicu and their descendants, are the Tharaka. Further migration brought the rest of the pioneers to the confluence of the Mutonga, Maara and Ruguti rivers. Here, too, one section broke off moving up the ridges towards Mount Kenya. These eventually became the Cuka. The rest of the migrants trekked south-westwards until they once more halted at Igambang'ombe, just north of the confluence of the Thuci and Tharia rivers. This became an important centre of dispersal. One section crossed the Thuci to form the present-day Embu, while a second group advanced up the ridges, towards Mount

57. Tate, *Journal of African Society*, vol. 10, 1911, p. 290; Routledge, op. cit., p. 9; K. R. Dundas, *Man*, vol. 8, 1908, p. 181.
58. See map 3, p. 50.

Kenya, and settled at Magumoni, thus uniting again with the group that had earlier broken off the main body of pioneers at the confluence of the Mutonga, Maara and Ruguti rivers. These two groups are the ancestors of the Cuka.

The group that crossed the Thuci river into Embu advanced to Karurumo and finally reached Mwene Ndega's sacred grove, near present-day Runyenje's market. The region around Mwene Ndega's grove was the first settlement in Embu, and immigration into the area was spearheaded by the Igamuturi and Kina clans. A study of the Igamuturi genealogy indicates that some of their earliest ancestors were born there towards the end of the fifteenth century or very early in the sixteenth century. It was from this region that people dispersed to settle in Gikuuri, Maranga, Kevote, Nvuvoori, Kieni and Nginda. This group finally evolved into the Embu.

Meanwhile, from Igambang'ombe the other group of pioneers moved southwards, along the Thagana river valley, until they reached Kiambeere hill, where they made a settlement. *En route*, one group branched off to settle in the region of the Mumoni hills and up to modern Kindaruma. A few people also remained behind at the Kiambeere hill. Today these are the Mbeere people. However, this was not the end of the journey, for yet another group continued trekking and finally settled around Ithanga, at the confluence of the Thagana and Thika rivers. This took place perhaps late in the sixteenth century. The available evidence describes Ithanga as a major centre of dispersal for the Embu, Mbeere, Ndia, Gicugu and the Kikuyu pioneers. For example, one group dispersed to settle in Mwea or Mbeti, thus joining the rest of the Mbeere pioneers. This particular group later on subdivided, some of them finally colonizing the lower and drier parts of Embu country. The second major group advanced towards the present-day Embuland and settled in Mavuria, Nthawa, Ivurori and Kamwimbi. The third group trekked westwards towards Kirinyaga, Nyeri and Murang'a, and thus reached the proverbial 'Mukurue wa Gathanga'. In this study we are primarily concerned with the latter group—that is, those who finally settled in Nyeri, Murang'a and later on in Kiambu, to become the Kikuyu proper.

The latter are an amalgam of several groups of people, which may or may not be related. First, a tiny minority of my informants believed that the Kikuyu were descendants of the Baci or Ethiopians; or descendants of a Rendille man who came from Meru and settled at Gathanga; or that the Turkana and Baci are relatives of the Kikuyu.[59] Still others thought that the Kikuyu were descendants of the Gumba.[60] However, the majority of my informants, particularly those from the secondary nuclear area of dispersal, claimed that their ancestors came from either Meru, Igembe, Cuka, Mbeere and especially from Ithanga.[61] It is evident, however, that one section of the Kikuyu proper migrated from Igembe and Tigania. The early administrators, for example, were told by the Kikuyu that they had migrated from Igembe.[62] Dundas also reports that the actual Kikuyu were said to have come from 'two tribes called the Shagishu and Ngembe'.[63] It was this Igembe group that migrated southwards to the Tharaka country, thereby becoming the ancestors of the Kikuyu cousins, such as the Tharaka, Cuka, Mbeere and the Embu. Equally it was these people who are likely to have had contact with the Il Tikirri, Nilotic speakers living in the Tigania plains.

In the course of their migration southwards, the Igembe group appears to have encountered a large concentration of the Thagicu along the Thagana river valley and close to Ithanga. This encounter undoubtedly, led to cultural fusion between the two groups, particularly around the important centre of dispersal at Ithanga. But while some of the Thagicu eventually became the ancestors of the Tharaka, Mbeere and Kamba in particular, others can be easily identified as the ancestors of the Kikuyu. Some *mbari*, for example, forcefully assert that their ancestors migrated from Kambaland or Mbeere and specifically mention Thagicu.[64] Routledge was also told that the Kikuyu came 'from the tribe of the Akamba' at the time of the Mathathi, that is, in the second half of the eighteenth centnry.[65] Dundas is even more specific. According to the information he collected, the Agaciku and Aceera clans originated from the Kamba people.[66] It is being suggested tentatively that these Kamba elements that are referred to were most probably the Thagicu, or their descendants, who were living along the

59. 'KHT', op. cit., pp. 33, 38, 41, 94, 115 and 130.
60. ibid., pp. 41, 52, 63, 71 and 119.
61. ibid. See section on migration and settlement, particularly pp. 8, 18, 20, 27, 30, 68-80, 82-5, 91-105, 106-26, 130, 146, 165 and 171.
62. See KNA/PC/CP/1/1/1.
63. K. R. Dundas, *Man*, vol. 8, 1908, p. 137.
64. 'KHT', pp. 1, 17, 30, 31, 138.
65. Routledge, op. cit., pp. 9 and 12.
66. K. R. Dundas, *Man*, vol. 8, p. 137.

Thagana river valley on the northern border of Kitui and Machakos.
Besides the Thagicu, the Igembe group impinged upon the Gumba,
an eastern Cushitic-speaking family group. The Gumba are recalled
by nearly all the Mount Kenya peoples; for example the Embu,
Kikuyu, Muthambi, Mwimbi, Igoji and the Imenti have traditions
about them. Thus the Igembe and Thagicu groups are likely to
have mingled with the Gumba in the Tharaka and Mbeere regions.
The former groups gradually displaced or assimilated the Gumba,
thereby establishing a new ethnic group. This process presumably
occurred during their gradual migration through Mbeere country
and especially during their sojourn in Ithanga. One is therefore
inclined to think that Mukurue wa Gathanga, the Garden of Eden
of the Kikuyu traditions, is likely to have been located at Ithanga,
rather than at Gakuyu near Gathuki-ini in Murang'a. Certainly
the physical environment connoted by the word, a place of sand,
does not fit the present site around Gakuyu. And since the period
of evolution of the Kikuyu to become a distinct group had passed
by the time they reached the area around Mukurue wa Gathanga,
having by then acquired all the basic characteristics of their culture,
this presupposes a lengthy period of consolidation *en route*. The
fact that they share some features with the Ndia, such as the military
sets, in contrast to their other cousins, tends to support this argument.[67] Ithanga is also said to have been the source of iron ore
(*muthanga*), which was smelted to produce pig iron used in the
making of vital implements, especially for forest clearing, for which
axes and *minyago* (pointed digging sticks) were the common
instruments, although for the giant trees they would light a fire at
the foot of the tree and continuously scrape the charred portion,
meantime heaping more dry leaves and small branches to keep the
fire going. No giant of the forest could withstand such an onslaught.

For these reasons, Ithanga and Mbeere regions were the most
important centres of consolidation, more important even than the
famous Mukurue wa Gathanga. It was probably in the former places
that the various proto-Kikuyu elements evolved into the Kikuyu
proper. This—in spite of the fact that some earlier informants, for
example the Kikuyu of Mathira who told Barlow that they originated
from Mukurue wa Ithanga—sounds a more likely theory of Kikuyu
migration.[68]

67. 'Lambert, 1965', chapters 3 and 5.
68. See Unsorted Miscellaneous File in 'Barlow Papers'; also 'KHT', pp. 1-31.

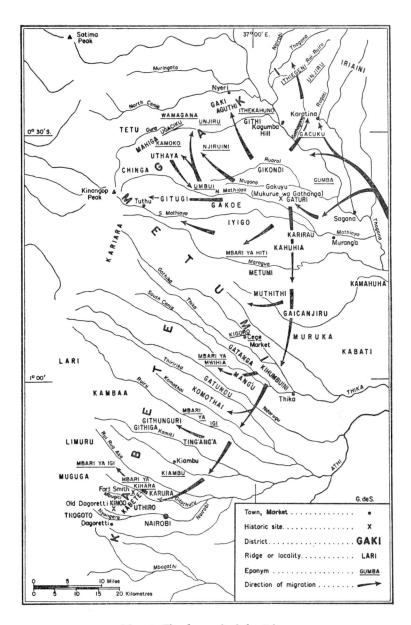

Map 4—The dispersal of the Kikuyu.

From the region of Ithanga the Kikuyu pioneers trekked in small groups towards the west leaving some of their kinsmen *en route* who today form the Gicugu and the Ndia. Orde-Browne thought that the Cuka were the descendants of the original inhabitants of their present homeland.[69] However, and as shown above, current research shows that their ancestors hived off from the main body of migrants before the former reached the Mbeere region. Thus by the time the Kikuyu pioneers immigrated into Ndia they had absorbed nearly all the ethnic groups that have contributed to their physical characteristics, except the Gumba and Athi whom they continued to absorb and the Maasai whom they came across at a much later stage. An administrative officer in Embu recognized the complexity of assimilation and migration that had occurred in this area when he remarked that 'some say [they came] from the plains round the Lonya Sabuk, others from the east of the Tana, while still others state they came from the north'.[70]

The last main group of pioneers to invade the highlands were ancestors of the Meru cluster. Oral traditions recently collected reveal that, save for the Cuka, the ancestors of the Meru were a small agricultural community living at 'Mbwa' on the Kenya coast.[71] These ancestors also had domestic animals such as sheep, goats, short-horned cattle and small dogs. Fadiman thinks that these pre-Meru were living on the Manda island probably as late as A.D. 1700. Consequent upon persecution by a people called Nguo Ntune, probably the Arabs, they trekked southwards until they came across the Thagana river, near the sea. Following the southern bank of the river, they reached what traditions refer to as a desert. Further migration through the desert-like zone and lightly wooded grassland brought them to the present Tharaka and Mbeere areas. It should be noted that all the members of the Meru congeries, then known as 'Ngaa', recall having journeyed through Mbeere on their way towards Mount Kenya. In the first half of the eighteenth century, they reached the confluence of the Mutonga and Ena rivers, and then they crossed northwards into Tharakaland where they impinged upon the Thagicu resulting in considerable intermarriage. At a place called Igaironi or Kagairo, near the eastern side of Ntugi hill, the

69. G. St. J. Orde-Browne, *The Vanishing Tribes of Kenya*, London, 1925, pp. 17-27, 63-4; and 'Mount Kenya and Its Peoples: Some Notes on the Chuka Tribe', *Journal of African Society*, vol. 15, 1916, pp. 225-31.
70. See KNA/PC/CP/6/4/1.
71. The following section is based on Fadiman, op. cit.

'Ngaa' subdivided into the various clusters that now form the Meru people. The Mukunga moiety advanced northwards towards Tigania, while the Murutu cluster expanded westwards into the present Mwimbi area, leaving behind a section in Tharaka which became absorbed by the latter. Eventually the Murutu further subdivided into the ancestors of the present Muthambi, Igoji and perhaps the south Imenti. Likewise, the Mukunga splintered into the forefathers of the present Igembe, Tigania and north Imenti. But the Miutini are likely to be descendants of a varied group, which most likely consisted, originally, of splinter groups from Imenti, Igoji, Mwimbi and Muthambi.

By 1750 small groups of proto-Meru had begun to invade the foothills of Mount Kenya and the Nyambene forests. This vanguard of pioneers probably consisted of hunters, who demarcated their hunting grounds by marking on trees or erecting stones as boundary marks. However, the drift of migration was up the ridges and towards Mount Kenya.

Chapter 3

MIGRATION AND SETTLEMENT OF THE KIKUYU

DURING the Cuma generation, at the turn of the seventeenth century, immigration into northern Metumi and southern Gaki was well underway. It seems to have been accelerated by, among other things, internal dissension, which in turn led to raiding on a large scale. It is suggested that this tension arose between the farmers and the nomads.[1] But for an industrious agricultural community, the dry and sandy areas of Gaturi and lower Githi, which border on Ndia, offer no attraction. The area is also most inaccessible from the east, being ringed by a series of deep, tortuous gorges which are formidable even today, despite modern technology. Any pioneer is more likely to move further west to Gathuki-ini and Njiru, or to south Mathira and Mukurue-ini divisions. And despite land shortage among the Kikuyu, certain sections of Gaturi and lower Githi have remained very sparsely populated, or completely empty of people, up to the present day.

On reaching the forested highlands, a further period of consolidation ensued, during which the Kikuyu evolved as a distinct group before fanning out towards Gaki and Kabete. This consolidation involved two important aspects. Hitherto, the proto-Kikuyu had migrated largely as hunters, or pastoralists, through a wooded grassland ecological zone that was not particularly suited to agriculture. Now they were entering areas of high agricultural potential.[2] Thus, the evolution of a way of life to suit the ecology was desirable, if not essential. Secondly, the emergence of the Kikuyu as a distinct group from their cousins signified the successful re-grouping of many elements of diverse origin around a new focus. It is from this perspective that the myth of Mumbi,

1. Hall's report to IBEAC of 13 March 1894 in FO2/73.
2. See map 2, p. 31.

Gikuyu and Mukurue wa Gathanga should be considered. Two functions seem to have been served by the claim that the origin of all the Kikuyu people was at the Mukurue wa Gathanga and that God was responsible for settling Gikuyu and his wife Mumbi there originally. It acted as a focus, or symbol, of unity, thereby welding together the various disparate elements into one people. Thus the idea of one monolithic people—called the Kikuyu—emerged, obscuring, but not entirely wiping out, the diversity inherent in the heterogeneous origins of their forefathers. This phenomenon is neither unique nor peculiar to the Kikuyu people. The Baluhya, Meru and Kalenjin congeries have buried their differences in this century in order to meet new and external challenges. Secondly, and equally important, this has legitimized Kikuyu claims to the ownership of land, since their present homeland was bestowed upon their mythical ancestors by Providence.

It appears that the routes of migration in those days were along the river valleys and, when it became necessary, the migrants crossed the rivers by natural bridges (*morumathi*, sing. *urumathi*). Several of these are mentioned, such as the ones at Gathagana and Kianjege on the Thagana river, and the one over the Komothai river in Kabete. From Ndia the pioneers migrated to the area around Sagana Station; some might have crossed into Gaturi but most of them appear to have veered northwards into southern Mathira before crossing into Mukurue-ini via the natural bridges at Kianjege and Gathagana.[3] Those who remained in Mathira, however, encountered strong opposition at first from a sizeable section of the Gumba and the Athi, but finally it was the Barabiu who forced them to cross into Mukurue-ini division during the Iregi generation, in the first half of the nineteenth century. Thus the initial Kikuyu settlers in Mathira were forced to seek safety amongst the rest of the Kikuyu. Consequently, it was the region between the Gura river, to the north, and the North Mathioya river, to the south, that became the secondary nuclear area where the Kikuyu pioneers finally evolved into Kikuyu proper: a distinct group from their closest cousins, the Gicugu and the Ndia. This epoch was characterized by the intermittent harassment of the Kikuyu settlers by the remnants of the Gumba and the Athi; but the most notable aspect was the continued assimilation of these groups, their

3. McGregor records that on migration from Thagicu the Kikuyu settled in Mathira to begin with. See McGregor, op. cit., p. 31.

quarrels notwithstanding. Indeed, these early occupants of the Mount Kenya region have left a deep imprint on the Kikuyu and their cousins.

The numerous physical types seen amongst them bear testimony that the Kikuyu represent a fusion of many different ethnic elements. The aboriginal hunting gathering peoples have also enriched the Kikuyu language. As Ehret has noted, 'Among the Bantu-speaking Thagicu group of peoples, a few Southern Nilotic loanwords go back to proto-Thagicu, as their attestation in both Kikuyu and Kamba indicates, while other such words apparently occur in one descendant language, Kikuyu, and are therefore more recently borrowed'.[4] The loanwords include the names of wild animals, trees, three generation sets (the Cuma, Maina and Mwangi) and ceremonial dances for circumcision.[5] There is no doubt that some of the words and cultural traits were borrowed, at various stages of contact, from the plains Nilotic speakers such as the Il Tikirri, the Dorobo, the Athi and the Maasai. However, it should be noted that many of them were acquired from the eastern Cushitic-speaking peoples in the first instance.[6] It is probable, therefore, that the Thagicu, or proto-Thagicu, might have acquired some of these eastern Cushitic cultural characteristics directly from the eastern Cushitic-speaking elements. The most important of these traits are circumcision and clitoridectomy as the major initiation rites, as well as the Cushitic prohibition against eating fish and, presumably, the idea of a cycling age-set system. It is likely, though by no means certain, that these features might have been borrowed from the Gumba.

According to the traditions, the Ciira generation was characterized by an increase in population around the secondary nuclear area. It is not surprising, therefore, that it was in this period, during the first half of the eighteenth century, that appreciable numbers began to fan out westwards towards the Nyandarua massif, southwards towards Kabete and northwards into Uthaya and Aguthi. North-eastwards, expansion along this frontier was a slow one, and the situation did not change until the time of the Ndemi and Mathathi, when a spate of expansion into Mathira gained momentum. This influx of settlers continued unabated until the Iregi

4. Ehret, op. cit., p. 43.
5. ibid., appendix D6, pp. 139-40.
6. ibid., chap. 4.

generation, in the first half of the nineteenth century, when a major setback occurred. Some time in the nineteenth century the Barabiu, the Galla and the Somali launched a major attack in the Kenya highlands. Some of the Kikuyu in Mathira and Tetu were driven back into Mukurue-ini and the southernmost parts of Mathira division.[7] Others took refuge as far east as Kiini in Ndia, as happened to Njiri Kibii of Magutu during the time of the Ndigirigi warriors, or in the first three decades of the nineteenth century.[8] While in Mukurue-ini division, the Mathira and Tetu people experienced considerable hardships. Their livestock was attacked and decimated by diseases and the Mukurue-ini people did not welcome them at all. They ill-treated them and during the initiation ceremonies, taunted them as cowards. It is also suggested that some of the Gumba and Athi remnants might have joined the Barabiu to attack the Kikuyu.

Faced with this reversal of fortunes, the refugees from Tetu and Mathira rallied together and determinedly attacked the Gumba at Gathagana in the Thagana valley. The confrontation was so serious that the Kikuyu were forced to destroy the natural bridge at Gathagana in an attempt to contain the Barabiu, who had used it to cross into Mukurue-ini division. The most popular story is that Munjuku, a medicine-man, used suet to create a crack in the natural bridge and at the same time he is said to have given the hornbills 'medicine' to scare away the Gumba, who fled northwards towards the plains. This resembles other popular accounts about the disappearance of the Gumba. The reality was quite different, and the Kikuyu must have mobilized all their forces against a formidable protagonist in what must have been a once-for-all campaign. In fact the Barabiu were only defeated by the allied forces of the Maasai, the Athi and the Kikuyu. Thus, the generation named Iregi, or revolters, commemorates the defeat of the Barabiu rather than the overthrow of the despotic rule of 'King' Kikuyu.[9]

This frightening experience at the hands of the Gumba and their allies forced the Kikuyu to adopt new defensive tactics. On the frontiers, it became essential to have outposts manned by warriors. Two or more were chosen from each village and their duties involved patrolling the borders for raiders. A contingent

7. McGregor, op. cit., p. 32; K. R. Dundas, *Man*, vol. 8, p. 138; 'Barlow Papers' (History *iria iiguaniiruo ni athuri aria akurakuru* 1.8.42).
8. 'KHT,' pp. 26 and 28.
9. Kenyatta, op. cit., p. 186.

manned the guard posts for a continuous period of three to four months, during which they were maintained by public food contributions. Secondly, in the interior of the country, warriors lived in special huts (*gaaru*), where they could easily be rallied together for counter-attack in case of need. Thirdly, a war cry (*mbu*) was adopted as a sign of alarm at the approach of an enemy, or to call attention to any other disturbance. From then on, warriors in Nyeri district were able to defend themselves and their homeland against their enemies effectively.[10] Most of these tactics were borrowed from the Maasai; indeed, the Nyeri people readily admit that they were taught them by a warrior who had lived among the Maasai.

The rate of expansion in Mathira, and indeed in Tetu and the south-western outskirts of Kabete, was in the nineteenth century conditioned mainly by the relations existing between the Kikuyu and the Maasai. Both groups appear to have reached some mutual understanding which resulted in widespread intermarriage between them. Close co-operation hastened the rate of absorption of the Maasai through intermarriage, especially when they took refuge in the Kikuyu country because of famine, disease, or internal conflict in their areas. In particular the Purko and Laikipiak wars of about 1875 forced many Maasai to seek shelter with the Kikuyu *mbari*, among whom, they allege, they already had many relatives. This was a significant feature of Maasai/Kikuyu relations, that although they were quite often at war with each other, there were always friendly relations between specific families on both sides, the majority of whom had kin-connections[11]. And although no statistics are available, the impression given by the informants is that perhaps half or more of the population in Mathira and Tetu is of Maasai origin, or has Maasai blood. Indeed, there are large *mbari* in these areas which are predominantly Maasai and which still retain contact with their Maasai kinsmen up to the present day.

However, congenial relations with the Maasai were intermittent. They became very strained at times, if not actually ruptured, and the Kikuyu were sometimes forced to retreat into the lower reaches of southern Mathira and Tetu, while others emigrated altogether. This did not, however, deter expansion, and on the eastern frontier of Mathira, which was relatively peaceful, the Kikuyu had reached

10.   'Barlow Papers' (History *iria iiguaniiruo ni athuri.*)
11.   Personal communication with Jacobs.

the outskirts of Iria-ini and Magutu locations by the beginning of the nineteenth century. And the Konyu and the Kirimukuyu, who bore the brunt of the Maasai raids, had reached Karura and Ruthagati by the same time. Gathu-ini and Wamurogi salt-licks were battle grounds in this period, where the Kikuyu took their livestock for watering. But there is clear evidence that it was not until after the 1880s that they effectively occupied the area north of the Rui (river) Ruiru, and this understandably coincides with the great cattle epidemic and the Purko and Laikipiak wars. The observations of the early travellers, who journeyed through this area, help us to determine the location of the frontier to a precise degree; Gregory, for example, found that there was extensive cultivation around the Gathu-ini salt-lick when he travelled through the northern frontier in 1893. And Boyes and Mackinder found that towards Magutu the Kikuyu had effectively occupied the area up to and around the Kiamuceru hill by 1898 and 1899.[12] Further to the north, occupation did not take place across the Thagana river until the colonial period and especially after the eviction of the Maasai from the Nyeri plains to make way for the European settlement schemes. This is corroborated by oral evidence.[13]

At the close of the nineteenth century, the Mathira had almost evolved into a sub-tribe, a process which dated back to the first half of the eighteenth century. Their extensive assimilation of Ndia elements, and the widespread absorption of the Maasai and the Athi, led them to acquire singular characteristics, such as their distinctive dialect, which set them apart from the rest of their kinsmen, even within Gaki district itself.[14] Their emergence as a sub-tribe was only arrested by the arrival of the British, without whose intervention they would have very likely evolved into a sub-tribe such as the Ndia and the Gicugu. The only difference in this case would have been that such a group would have become a sub-tribe more akin to and closely associated with the Maasai. And their neighbouring Maasai would not have been like the other Maasai either; the Laikipiak Maasai, for example, were distinct from the other pastoral tribes precisely because they had absorbed large numbers of the

12. Gregory, op. cit., pp. 157-61, 189-92; Boyes, op. cit., pp. 167-78, 180-99; Mackinder, op. cit., pp. 462-4.
13. See evidence by the government officials, settlers and the Kikuyu in *KLC*, vol. 1, pp. 82-110, 510-48; 'KHT', pp. 2, 11, 12-13.
14. K. R. Dundas records that the Iria-ini, in particular, represent a fusion of various tribes such as the Laikipiak and the Dalalekutuk Maasai. See his article in *Man*, vol. 8, 1908, pp. 136-7.

original Athi or Gumba, who gave up hunting and gathering to become pastoral or semi-pastoral.[15] It is this feature more than anything else which they shared with their Mathira neighbours, who had also absorbed some of the Athi or Gumba. It is even conceivable that their congenial and friendly relations may have sprung from their sharing a common Gumba or Athi origin. However, this is a topic that requires further investigation.

Immigration northwards into Uthaya was spearheaded by the Aithiegeni clan which had initially settled around Gikondi. According to tradition, the pioneer settler at Gikondi was a certain Kambaire Munjuri, who later immigrated to Karima together with his four sons—Ngai, Gitene, Kirumwa and Maigua. This was perhaps at the time of the Cuma generation, that is, about the end of the seventeenth century and the beginning of the eighteenth. Further north, Kamoko, who is alleged to have been a herdsman, is said to have been joined by a Mumbui hunter, Magana, a man who is reputed to have ranged far and wide—from Mathira to Wamagana (named after him)—before settling with Kamoko at Mahiga in the first half of the eighteenth century.[16] Other pioneers spread across the Gura river into Aguthi from Tambaya, but expansion further north was considerably slower, only reaching the vicinity of the North Cania river towards the end of the nineteenth century.[17] This slow rate of expansion is explained by the Maasai threat, and is similar to the situation in Mathira. But here, as in Mathira, extensive intermarriage between the two peoples took place, with the same consequences. In effect, by the nineteenth century, the two groups were conducting joint raids not only against their own people, but as far away as Ndia and Cuka.

Between the Cuma and the Ciira generations, that is, from the late seventeenth to mid-eighteenth century, there was unimpeded expansion westwards towards Nyandarua. This expansion was along the ridges, particularly between the north Mathioya and Boyo rivers. Here the Kikuyu met with little opposition, except by a few Athi who were routed at the confluence of the Boyo and southern Mathioya rivers—at Karirau. But despite the absence of serious opposition they did not reach the foot hills of Nyandarua until the middle of the nineteenth century. By then they were approaching the montane

15. Jacobs, personal communication.
16. 'KHT', pp. 42-56.
17. Routledge found them clearing the forest around the banks of the North Cania river in 1902. See Routledge, op. cit., pp. 7-8.

grassland zone with its acidic soil, high rainfall and cold conditions. It was perhaps this discouraging weather that forced them to migrate southwards across the ridges and along the Kikuyu and star grass zone, which is of high agricultural potential. Many of the people who now live in Kabete spread there from Iyigo and the Gathuki-ini region, together with those who were forced to retreat from some parts of Gaki by Maasai, or Athi, threats. The advance southwards went ahead steadily, until the Kikuyu reached Muruka and Gatanga where Maasai opposition began to worry them. But this southward migration did not take place until the Mathathi generation in the second half of the eighteenth century and was preceded, in the Cuma generation (late seventeenth to the mid-eighteenth century), by migration into Kahuhia and Weithaga, which overspilt into Muthithi in the second half of the eighteenth century. And evidently it was the warriors initiated when the Mathathi generation was in power who provided the bulk of the pioneers who crossed the South Cania river into Kabete. Thus the peak of expansion across the South Cania river occurred in the first half of the nineteenth century, but it should be remembered that actual occupation was preceded by a period of exploration and the initial immigration is likely to have begun late in the eighteenth century, if not earlier. Many of the informants allege that the first batch of warriors to be initiated in Kabete was the Mungai, about the middle of the nineteenth century, and that it was only the Mbugua (initiated in the first two decades of the second half of the century), amongst whom the majority were initiated in Kabete.[18] By that time the frontier had advanced as far south as the Rui rua Aka, the Women's River.[19]

The southward expansion by the Kikuyu apparently led to a concentration of the Athi in Kabete, just as their expansion north-wards had led to the same phenomenon taking place around Kirinyaga. It is even feasible that this might have led to their consoli-dation once more. It was not politic, therefore, for the vanguard of the Kabete pioneers to have antagonized them, let alone to have tried to drive them forcibly away. The Maasai were also on the Kaputie plains and an alliance by the two groups would have presented the Kabete with formidable obstacles, especially because pioneering was still undertaken by individuals or small groups.

18. 'KHT', pp. 141, 147, 151, 160, 181.
19. This is incorrectly spelt Ruaraka in all the published maps and books.

For all these reasons, it was important that the Kabete should come to terms with the Athi, if their expansion was to be effective. It is to be expected that in these fringe areas of occupation, and in contrast to the situation further north (in Gaki and Metumi), some families had to buy land, and this seems to be the case in most parts of Kabete, with the exception, perhaps, of certain localities of Gatundu division.[20] Contrary to the view expressed by Lambert and others, the Athi were not eliminated, nor were they cheated of their land by guile and chicanery.[21] They were too strong and well-armed to be so easily driven off, but a more significant factor is that the Kikuyu way of life and that of the Athi were complementary. In particular, the symbiotic relationship between the Kikuyu and the Athi was conducive to mutual understanding and co-operation wherever this was practicable. This process is made evident by the existence of some *mbari*—such as Mbari ya Muniu of Githunguri—which are of essentially Athi ancestry, while a still greater number have Athi blood. The Athi who sold their land also retained friendly relations with the buyers; these transactions were preceded by an elaborate code of procedure which has made land negotiations be likened to marriage proceedings. It was imperative in all these negotiations that land was only sold after close and firm ties had been established between the two parties. Thus the Kikuyu acquired land by a 'process which consisted . . . partly of alliance and partnership and partly of adoption and absorption, and partly of payment'. Certainly it was not by a process 'largely of force and chicanery'[22]

The oath of mutual adoption was an even more serious affair, not to be lightly taken. Both parties swore a solemn oath to be like brothers in all matters, not to shed each other's blood or cause each other harm in any way. Both parties also undertook to help one another in times of need. Consequent on having undergone the ceremony, the Athi were full members of whatever *mbari* adopted them, and were henceforth protected from any molestation by outsiders or within the *mbari*. A good example of this mutual dependence is Kihara, who protected some Athi whom he had adopted when they were molested.[23] Athi and Kikuyu relations were

20.   'KHT', pp. 134-6.
21.   *KLC*, *Report*, p. 93.
22.   ibid.
23.   See especially evidence by Muiruri Muinami and Wanjugu Marimbi in *KLC* (original evidence), vol. 7, or its summary in *KLC*, vol. 1, pp. 284-5.

so complex as to defy generalization.[24] Each individual Kikuyu
or Mwathi developed special relations with his benefactor. However,
sharp practice by unscrupulous individuals on both sides existed;
some Kikuyu, such as Gatonye Munene and Waiyaki Hinga,
are alleged to have maltreated their Athi, and equally some Athi
are alleged to have sold the same piece of land to different individuals
at the same time.[25] Such instances should not be seen as isolated
cases, for powerful *mbari* along the frontiers finally became a
menace to everybody, whether they were Athi or Kikuyu. These
seem to have attracted a clientele of warriors and to have behaved
in a manner reminiscent of the private armies of medieval Europe.
The Mbari ya Munyori (or Thumbi), for example, is alleged to have
dispersed the Mbari ya Mbuu from their land around Kiambu
(named after their ancestor Mbuu) despite the fact that both are
closely related Ambui *mbari*. The Mbari ya Mbuu subsequently
migrated to Thimbigua. Wang'endo is also said to have driven
away the Mbari ya Muya from their land.[26] Indeed, it was generally
agreed that only large and strong *mbari* could effectively acquire
land at the frontier.[27]

Immigration southwards had been conducted along the traditional
lines of small family groups spearheaded by individuals but after
Rui rua Aka, and as the frontier advanced southwestwards, greater
defence was necessary the nearer the immigrants approached the
Maasai border. It became impossible thereafter for singlehanded
pioneers to blaze the trail; this role was assumed by the *mbari*, which
had many warrior sons or else attracted a clientele of fighting followers. On the other hand, a group of brave warriors invited a motley
of interested parties to join them, who helped in either defending the
newly-acquired land, or in purchasing it where this was applicable.
It was this phenomenon that strained the traditional social organization, these *mbari* or individuals usurped the traditional balance
of power by taking the law into their hands, such as often

24. 'KHT', pp. 133-4, 136, 137, 141-3, 144-5, 148, 151, 154-5, 158-62, 163,
    164, 166-8, 172, 173, 175-80, 182-4, 187-9 and 190-2. Even Kihara, who
    was reputed to have treated his Athi well, was alleged to have chased
    some of them away later. See 'KHT', pp. 154-5.
25. Evidence by A. Muthuri, Waiganjo and Lewis Kaberere in *KLC* (original
    evidence), vol. 7, or its summary in *KLC*, vol. 1, pp. 223-9, 265-8; 'KHT'
    pp. 160-2, 170, 178, 183, 188-9 and 190-2.
26. 'KHT', pp. 153-4, 176 and 178.
27. ibid., pp. 179-80.

flouting the code of behaviour by refusing to pay blood money.[28]

In about a century the Kikuyu had effectively inhabited the area between the south Cania and Nairobi rivers. This was a fairly rapid expansion and may be related, to a great extent, to an increase in population. The decline of Maasai power, though not of crucial importance, was also a contributory factor. Immigration into Kabete spanned the period between the life of the Kinyanjui and the Mungai warriors, who were initiated in the second half of the eighteenth and the middle of the nineteenth century respectively. Many of the informants assert that very few of the Kamau, Kimani or Karanja generations of warriors emigrated from Metumi. Many of them are said to have died of old age around Muruka and Gatanga, unable to cross the South Cania river. Similarly it was agreed by my informants that either none of the Iregi elders—who were the ruling generation from about the second to sixth decade of the nineteenth century—immigrated into Kabete or that only a few of them managed to do so.[29] The first batch of warriors to have encountered and fought with the Maasai are said to have been the Gitau and Wainaina warriors, who were initiated in the first half of the nineteenth century. This encounter took place in the vicinity of Thika. So there had been a steady advancing of the frontier, and by the middle of the nineteenth century the Kikuyu had reached the locality of the Karura river from where they were thrusting towards the Maasai border. The Maasai were in fact not very far away, as they occupied the area around Nairobi, and the stretch of land between Ngeca and Kiambaa at the time the Ngigi warriors, initiated in 1890, were children. During the 1880s the Kikuyu were settling in the area between the Karura and Nairobi rivers, and also towards Muguga. The penetration of Karura ridge was spearheaded by Iguku, of Mbari ya Gathagu, and Ndungata, of Mbari ya Muya.[30] However, several people led the advance towards the Nairobi river and Muguga; Gatonye Munene made his *kihingo*, a fortified cluster of homesteads (pl. *ihingo*), in the 1880s at Muguga and Waiyaki Hinga moved to Mbugici (near Fort Smith)

28. Tate records that the Aceera, Anjiru, Agaciku, Aithiegeni and Ambui were the most powerful and were constantly engaged in fighting each other over property. They also refused to pay blood money. See Tate, op. cit., p. 237. See also 'KHT', p. 158.

29. 'KHT', pp. 133-4, 137, 141, 146, 162, and 166.

30. ibid., p. 157.

from Karura between 1884 and 1890.[31] Other prominent pioneers who had *ihingo* at the frontier were Mucene Cege at Uthiru, Muthondu Nduru and Gatama at Kirungii (now Westlands), Mbari ya Wahothi close to Kikuyu Station and Kiratu at Limuru.[32] None of the pioneers, however, had gone beyond the Nairobi river by the time Lugard established his fort at Kiawariua (Dagoretti) in 1890. There were no signs of cultivation around the area and Thogoto was at that time a thick forest. Westwards, the pioneers had just approached Limuru; the Lari salt-lick was in fact a battle-ground, it being necessary for cattle to be guarded by warriors when they went for watering. All the same, immigration continued unabated and with the increase in population the Kikuyu began to expand westwards into Nyandarua, having hitherto only occupied a stretch of land parallel to the Kaputie plains.

Traditional Kikuyu land tenure has aroused considerable interest and controversy all through the colonial period. It has even been claimed that their political consciousness stems from the problem of land alienated for white settlement. The main question has been whether or not the so-called '*githaka* system' existed and, secondly, what it meant if it did, and thirdly whether it was uniform throughout Kikuyuland. But before deciding whether or not the system existed, a discussion of the original pattern of migration and the subsequent system of land acquisition might be useful.

The system of land tenure that emerged was governed mainly by the initial process of the acquisition. The procedure of individual pioneers striking out on their own led them to exploit the natural resources along the ridges and towards the Nyandarua in most parts. However, expansion in Mathira was northwards and towards Kirinyaga (Mount Kenya), but with the same results. The burden of the data indicates that in the early stages at least, the vanguard of the pioneers seem to have been a fringe community of hunters who trapped wild animals, collected wild honey or hung beehives on trees in the forests. They were followed by pastoralists and agriculturalists at a later stage. And although the original pattern of settlement has now largely been obliterated by various factors, a study of the place

31. von Höhnel found Waiyaki at Mukui (Karura) in 1887 and he had migrated to Mbugici when von Höhnel returned from his trip to Lakes Rudolf and Stefanie. See von Höhnel, op. cit., pp. 298-315. Lugard found him at Mbugici in 1890 and by 1894 had claimed the area between Mbugici and Thogoto. See also 'KHT', pp. 163 and 190.

32. 'KHT', pp. 165-92.

names reveals that they represent, especially in Metumi and Gaki, the names of the original settlers. Some of the well-known eponymous ancestors are Magana (Wamagana), Kambaire, Kigoro, Gitiha and Mbuu (Kiambu). Furthermore, in some areas—such as Njiku, Unjiru and Ithiegeni—the eponyms represent the original clan settlements after their initial immigration.[33] Some of these clan settlements are regarded to be the spiritual homes of the clan, where clan reunions used to be held. The settlements were invariably acquired on a ridge basis, each clan settling in its own ridge. It is clear, therefore, that the nature of the terrain, in conjunction with the nature of immigration, were of vital importance in influencing the pattern of land tenure that emerged. Land acquisition was on the basis of first come first served, and the initial activities carried out in exploiting the natural resources in time came to be accepted as the basis for land ownership. And when the agriculturalists appeared on the scene and cleared the virgin forest, that, too, came to be accepted as a criterion for claim to land ownership. Anyone who acquired land by any of these methods claimed to have acquired it by *kuuna* (cutting down virgin forest land), or *mutego* (trapping). There were also other ways in which individuals, family or *mbari*, could have acquired land, as for instance through marriage. It was customary for in-laws to offer one another land. Equally, friends could present each other with gifts of land. Besides, land could be transferred, or forcibly taken, by another *mbari* as blood money in lieu of livestock, particularly where a *mbari* was unable or unwilling to meet the necessary fine.[34] In such cases, however, the land could be redeemed if the required compensation was paid in full. A poor man often attached himself to a rich man's daughter and after marriage continued to cultivate portions of land alloted to the girl when young. Finally, and at a later stage, land could be acquired by buying from the Athi or the other Kikuyu.

Apart from later developments, land initially belonged to an individual or a small group of closely related people. But with the increase in population, this circle grew wider through the generations to include the descendants of the original pioneers. The essential thing is that such a group had a strong community interest born of the need to defend themselves in a hostile environment of wild

33. See map 4, p. 59.
34. In 1929 Paulo Mathenge of Mahiga Mission gave details of two such cases. See his notebook, pp. 7b-8b in 'Barlow Papers'.

animals and other enemies, not to mention the co-operation demanded of them in the task of clearing the giant trees of the primeval forests. This, then, saw the birth of the ancestral land, to which in the course of time the descendants became deeply attached for economic and religious purposes, the latter including the pouring of libations and the propitiation of the ancestors to ensure the well-being of the family. Thus the mode of land acquisition, together with reverence for the ancestors, led to the *mbari* tenure of land as opposed to either communal or individual ownership. The communal rights were only limited to salt-licks, rights of way and the collection of firewood.

There were various basic principles governing *mbari* land tenure, the most important being the provision that all the land belonged to the *mbari* as a whole, and that any member of the *mbari* had the right to utilize any part of it so long as no one else had made prior claim to it and, more important, provided that the head of the *mbari*, the *muramati* (guardian), was informed. Such *mbari* land, *ng'undu* (or *githaka* in Kabete), the clan estate, could be sold, but any sale had to be approved by the whole *mbari*, all such sales being redeemable on repayment of the original payment together with a fee to cover improvements, say for perennial crops such as *ikwa* (yams) and *marigu* (bananas). Non-clan members, the *ahoi* (tenants) or *athoni* (in-laws), were also given occupational rights by the *muramati* so long as they were of good behaviour and provided the consent of the whole *mbari* had been sought beforehand. The *ahoi* could be summarily deprived of their occupational rights for any misdemeanour towards the *mbari*, or for theft, or witchcraft. Otherwise, they paid nothing for the use of the land apart from offering the occasional gift, for example of beer, at the appropriate times. No purchaser of such land, *muguri*, could sell it to a third party without the consent and approval of the vendors, to whom he was required to offer it in the first instance. It was only if they were unable to redeem it that it could be sold to others outside the *mbari*. It seems, therefore, that the principle of outright sale was so circumscribed as to make it impracticable unless there were other extenuating circumstances. It is in fact true to say that until the introduction of European influences and ideas, outright sales of land were unknown between the Kikuyu themselves, the more so since any industrious person could have obtained his own land at the frontier, lack of land being unknown in those days.[35] Thus, under customary law, there were no sales of land in perpetuity. Or as the Kikuyu put it, *githaka ni ngwatira*—land is a loan. Answering the question 'can land be sold outright?', elders from Gaki told the Maxwell Committee that, 'All that is [e]ver conveyed is a temporary and provisional right to reside, to cultivate and to keep stock on a given area or areas. There is always right of redemption.'[36]

The principle that land should never irretrievably pass from the *mbari* was reinforced by the close attention paid to the boundaries separating the territory of one *mbari* from that of another. These were clearly marked by natural features such as rivers, valleys or ravines. Where this was not applicable, trees were planted, stones heaped or human hair buried all along such boundaries. No permanent boundaries were, however, fixed between the *thanju* (strips of land, sing. *ruthanju*) of the same *mbari*. This equally applied to the boundaries separating closely related *mbari*. On the other hand, the rights of the individual families were not left to chance, these were safeguarded by the system of inheritance, the practice being that a pioneer apportioned his land to each of his wives, if he had more than one. His sons had equal rights to all the land cultivated by their respective mothers and on marriage the sons acquired for their wives portions of their mother's cultivated land. But they could clear any unused land that belonged to their father in case of need. All the uncultivated land was reserved for grazing or as woodland and was jointly owned by all the sons. Similarly the grandsons would have equal rights to the land cultivated by their mothers, and on marriage would subdivide the land accordingly. After three or more generations, depending upon its size and the number of occupiers, the land became a patchwork of tiny strips of land of all shapes and sizes scattered all over the ridges. This gradual decrease in the size of holdings could only be arrested by a reduction in the population due to famine or disease, or where some families had no male heirs, in which case their land reverted to their nearest kinsmen. Technically, there was no inheritance through the female line.[37] Girls, for example, could still continue to cultivate portions of their mother's land after marriage but only at their father's or brothers' pleasure. This rule tended to reinforce the principle that the *mbari*

35. 'KHT', pp. 155-6; see, also, the Land Tenure file in the 'Barlow Papers'.
36. Maxwell Committee, op. cit., appendix, p. 7.
37. ibid., appendix, p. 9.

had absolute ownership of land. The *ahoi*, or those given rights of cultivation such as friends and *athoni*, could not inherit such land outright and their continued use of it rested solely with the *mbari* owners who could terminate such rights at will.

While this has generally been accepted as the traditional system of land tenure prevailing in Gaki and Metumi, there has been a great deal of argument as to what system operated in Kabete. One school of thought, and this includes some of the Kikuyu themselves and their supporters, has maintained that the Kabete practised individual land tenure because they had bought their land from the Athi on an individual basis.[38] Their opponents, on the other hand, hold the view which was generally espoused by the Kenya government and the settlers, that the Africans had no value for land *per se* until the corrupting European influences introduced the concept of individual land tenure. In common practice with all the Bantu, so the argument ran, there was at best only communal ownership of land, and all that the Kikuyu actually had were occupation rights, and that this was all they had bought from the Athi. The livestock paid to the Athi was intepreted as being no more than compensation for disturbances for, it was argued, the Athi themselves did not own the land in the first instance.[39] Both views, however, oversimplify a more complicated situation.

The settlement of Kabete was in many ways similar to the situation further north in Metumi and Gaki. In some parts of Gatundu, for example, first clearance of the virgin land was the basis for land acquisition, but the existence of large concentrations of Athi colonies in Kabete led to the adoption of other methods of acquiring land. Basically, this made it necessary to create friendship with the Athi, which was a prerequisite to any land transactions. Once mutual understanding was established, the Athi sold land to the Kikuyu or simply allowed them to occupy it, especially where they were adopted by the Kikuyu. It is in fact very clear that the *mbari* owning large tracts of land acquired it through intermarriage with the Athi. Examples are Waiyaki, who was married to Tiebo (a Mwathi woman), the Mbari ya Gathagu and Marigu.[40] Others, for example

38. M. W. H. Beech; *Kikuyu System of Land Tenure*, pp. 46-59 and 136-44; F. H. McKenrick, J. Henderson and L. S. B. Leakey to Barlow in the Land Tenure File, 'Barlow Papers'; evidence given by the Kabete to the Maxwell Committee, appendix.
39. *KLC*, vol. 1, pp. 28-81.
40. 'KHT', pp. 180 and 190.

Kihara, were lucky to have Athi protégés, who again offered them land for a song.[41] But the story that the Kikuyu paid hundreds of thousands of goats for land is definitely untenable. Rather, land was indeed cheap then—the sale sometimes stipulating only a first instalment of thirty goats for the virgin forest land with perhaps a further thirty to be paid when the land was cleared.[42] As one informant put it: 'In those days land was very cheap: you could have got land in exchange for arrow-roots or sweet potatoes.'[43] Such transactions were in fact rarely completed for a variety of reasons, for example the Athi migrating. The nature of these transactions, moreover, did not anticipate such a quick finalization of the sale; it envisaged an active and continuous personal relationship, the Athi seeking help when they needed it. It was this feature that made the relationship to be compared with marriage transactions. Other Kikuyu acquired their land as compensation for a variety of crimes alleged to have been committed by the Athi, such as murder, the trapping of livestock by their traps, or theft.[44] One person is said to have demanded compensation when a tree hit his house! But sharp practices were limited to a comparatively few people on both sides, and the fate of Bera is a good illustration of this.[45] What is overlooked quite often is that there were many Athi who peaceably settled among the Kikuyu through adoption and intermarriage.

Having acquired land, an individual was normally followed by his relatives, or alternatively he encouraged warriors to settle on the land as *ahoi* to help with defence against possible attacks by the other *mbari* or the Maasai. The *ahoi* would also help in the arduous job of clearing the forest. They readily accepted such an invitation because the *rutere* (frontier) was regarded as the land of opportunity where an industrious person expected, sooner or later, to acquire wealth of his own to enable him to buy his own land. The frontiersman consequently built large *ihingo* capable of accommodating hundreds of people, some of whom were warriors under his patronage. It was the existence of this motley collection

41. ibid., p. 178.
42. Routledge, op. cit., p. 5; 'KHT', pp. 144, 158-9.
43. 'KHT', p. 144.
44. ibid., pp. 142, 144, 169-70 and 183.
45. See evidence to the Land Commission in *KLC*, vol. 7 (original evidence) by A. Muthuri and Lewis Kaberere; 'KHT', pp. 160-2, 178, 188-9 and 190-2.

of diverse elements which led Ainsworth to the conclusion that the Kikuyu had no clans on the eve of the arrival of the British, as these were in the process of evolution.[46] The halting of this expansion by the British government at a time when waves of immigrants were still coming—this influx was going on even after 1900— together with the alienation of some Kikuyu land for white settlement, created a shortage of land very soon after European colonization. The problem had become noticeable as early as 1910, and particularly the plight of the *ahoi* was brought into sharp focus. Land shortage triggered off a re-examination of the traditional land tenure by the land-owning Kikuyu, and these, fearful of the demands of the *ahoi* as much as they feared white infiltration, sought ways to consolidate their hold on land by demanding titles to individual ownership. The *ahoi*'s traditional rights to cultivation and occupancy received a callous blow, and the deteriorating situation was only partly alleviated by the displaced *ahoi* trickling into the farms owned by white settlers to become squatters.[47]

This should have made the colonial government recognize that the existing land tenure was based on individual tenure, but the officials were reluctant to do so because, for one thing, it would have had adverse effects on the white settlement policy, and, secondly, there was a genuine concern by the administrators over the fate of the *ahoi* should such a scheme be embarked upon. It was no secret among the Kabete that their sense of the value of land had been whetted; they were therefore anxious to throw out the *ahoi*, irrespective of the rights that had existed under the traditional land tenure. The *ahoi* were encouraged by the administrators to stake their traditional claims on land as the former did not cherish the idea of the emergence of a small landed aristocracy at the expense of hordes of landless people. The missionaries, useful allies of the Kikuyu at this time, fully supported the landowners and pressed for the granting of titles, hoping thereby to forestall the ever threatening sword of land alienation dangling over the heads of the Kikuyu.

The problem of the *ahoi*, together with the threat posed by more alienation of land for white settlement, culminated in the theory

46. For example, see Ainsworth's memorandum, in the file on Land Tenure in the 'Barlow Papers', following a series of meetings with Kikuyu chiefs and interested parties. Barlow and Arthur acted as interpreters on 6 and 20 July 1920.
47. See the correspondence about land in the 'Barlow Papers'.

which was christened the '*githaka* system', devised to safeguard
Kikuyu land from further alienation.[48] The early inquirers such
as Tate and Beech accepted that the principle of individual tenure
operated before the coming of the British, but what was in doubt
was whether under customary law land was ever sold in perpetuity.
The theory of irredeemable sales was supported by the missionaries
who, in good faith, wished to safeguard their up-and-coming
missionary adherents, who were in many ways handicapped by
the ever likely redemption of land; this applied in particular to
their newly-acquired land, which they could not develop for fear of
being bought out at a future date. The newly-created chiefs were
at the forefront of this demand for individual ownership, as they
were anxious to safeguard their recent acquisitions, some of which
had been acquired by sharp practice, or by the buying out of poor
relatives and neighbours.[49] But while the majority of the Kikuyu
would have objected to the consolidation of a few landowners by
law, and especially the chiefs, if the principle of outright sale of
land was accepted, it was in the interest of perhaps a good majority
to accept it, perhaps reluctantly, for fear of Athi claims. This
applied especially to the recent Kikuyu immigrants who had bought
land from the Athi and to whom the possibility of land redemption
by the latter was a real problem. It is clear, therefore, that it was
the chiefs, supported by like-minded individuals, who deliberately
altered the traditional system of *mbari* ownership of land and the
redemption of land sales to suit their own ends.[50] Dr John Henderson
of Ng'enda Mission ruefully noted in 1924 that

> Land in the Gikuyu reserve appear to belong to one owner but later it is
> found to belong to several. When the mission has been given a piece of
> land for a school later there may appear two or three men with a right
> to the land which was given [and] the kiama as such does not have any
> right over the land.[51]

And Leakey also noted that 'No Githaka or part of the same can
be sold by any of the Ene without the consent of all the joint Ene.'[52]
This view was accepted by those giving evidence to the Maxwell

48. R. L. Buell, *The Native Problem in Africa*, New York, 1928, pp. 308-10
49. Note, for example, Kinyanjui's extravagant claims in KNA/PC/CP/1/4/2,
    pp. 87-188. For the manner in which he acquired land, see 'KHT',
    p. 164. See also evidence given by Ainsworth, Boedecker, Watcham and
    Canon Leakey in *KLC*, vol. 1, pp. 491-508, 694-708, 734-6, 845-73.
50. 'KHT', pp. 149, 155-6, and 159.
51. Henderson to Barlow in 'Barlow Papers' (Land Tenure File).
52. ibid., L. S. B. Leakey to Barlow.

Committee on land tenure of 1929. Indeed, as late as 1936, an administrator noted that 'the principle of redemption has not entirely disappeared in the Kiambu district.'[53] And Barlow was informed, as late as 1941, that 'formerly if a man sold land clandestinely he might be "hung" by the mbari', and that even land acquired in lieu of blood money could still be redeemed by the mbari concerned.[54]

One is led to the conclusion, then, that land and politics among the Kikuyu were not simply problems arising out of a confrontation between the Kikuyu and the white settlers.[55] The resentment of the Kikuyu towards the newcomers was generated as much by changing modes of land tenure within the Kikuyu society itself and prior to the coming of the white man, as it was affected by the alienation of land. The frontal attack on the traditional social fabric by the individualism of western society aggravated a situation which already existed, and as much energy, time and money were expended in interminable land cases amongst the Kikuyu themselves as was spent in the campaign against the settlers. The pressure within the society was only reduced by the emergence of a political leadership which re-orientated this growing resentment from within the society towards the administration and the settler community. Moreover, landlessness was not solely aggravated by the alienation of land, but also by the increase in population attendant on the introduction of modern medicine. Increases in population were taking place at a time when further population expansion along the traditional lines was impossible, and when the cash economy was affecting many aspects of the traditional framework which could have acted as safety valves. It is for this reason that the *ahoi* played a significant part in the political movement once they were mobilized, whether they were squatters on farms owned by white settlers or as landless peasants among their own people.[56]

53. Correspondence by the DC and PC re land, of 24 June 1936 in 'Barlow Papers'. The Maxwell Committee noted that 'any man who attempted to sell land without the knowledge of his *mbari* would have been killed'. See Maxwell Committee, op. cit., appendix, p. 52.
54. Notes of an interview—Wagakari, Kinyanjui Muriu and Samuel Gitau—on land, 13 October 1941, in 'Barlow Papers' (Land Tenure File).
55. For a fuller treatment of this subject, see G. Muriuki, 'Background to Politics and Nationalism in Central Kenya: the Traditional Social and Political Systems of Central Kenya Peoples', *Hadith 4* (Proceedings of the 1971 Annual Conference of the Historical Association of Kenya). Nairobi, 1972.
56. Rosberg and Nottingham, op. cit., pp. 243-4 and 248-59.

Literature on this subject is still scanty. Nevertheless, the existing evidence offers significant clues. Sorrenson, for example, portrays the Mau Mau war as partly a civil war and partly a nationalist struggle.[57] He argues that the conflict over land was a major source of the unrest in Kikuyu reserve itself during the post-war years. Furthermore, it was this unrest which eventually crystallized into a civil war as much as it was a revolt against the colonial government. He concludes:

> It would seem also that the attack on chiefs and headmen, initiated before the Emergency, was directed against them as representatives of the landed gentry as much as for their political position as government servants.[58]

He cites the Lari massacre as a good example to illustrate his views, when he points out that the massacre was 'largely a gruesome conclusion to a long-standing land feud'. It was also clear that those responsible were the previous land owners or their descendants, who had since migrated to the Rift Valley and other parts of Kenya. But Lari was not unique; the District Commissioner, Kiambu, readily admitted that half the murders committed in the district in 1953 had been due to land cases.[59] Further evidence showed that

> On the basis of returns of confiscated land, the Mau Mau activists were to a considerable extent landless or the owners of small areas of land. They were passively supported by the mass of small holders in the reserve and by the Kikuyu repatriated from outside, again mainly landless people. On the other hand the active loyalists were, on the whole, from "the landed and wealthy classes".[60]

57. M. P. K. Sorrenson, *Land Reform in the Kikuyu Country*, chap. VI.
58. ibid., p. 101.
59. ibid., pp. 99-101.
60. ibid., p. 107.

Chapter 4

THE KIKUYU
AND THEIR NEIGHBOURS

PRIOR to the advent of colonial era, East Africa was plagued by famine, disease, slave trading and inter-tribal conflict, each of which had a disruptive effect on the people of this region. For the exponents of the British Empire, as well as the propagandists of the imperial cause all over the world, the chaos that was occasionally brought about by these destructive agents, and especially the last two, was a popular propaganda theme. It was eagerly seized upon to stir the conscience of an otherwise sceptical British public, for instance, into pressuring their government to extend the Empire to East Africa. Lugard, one of the chief exponents of this course, hopefully pleaded:

> Surely people in England will presently begin to realize that the Arab slave-raider is not the only curse of Africa, but is rivalled, as I have elsewhere said, by the awful intolerable tyranny of the dominant tribe. It is from this tyranny, no less than from the slaver, that our administration, and the dawn of an era of law and order is to deliver the more peaceable and industrious agricultural tribes of Africa.[1]

Concerning the inter-tribal conflicts, the attention, if not the wrath, of most observers was directed against the Maasai who, because they 'loved war and slaughter, loot and rapine',[2] were for 'long the terror and scourge of all their neighbours'.[3] They were accused of having spread their terror from the shores of Lake Rudolf to the north, to central Tanzania in the south and from the banks of the Thagana river to the east, to the shores of Lake Victoria in the west. As Low has put it, the 'Masai had two overriding passions—cattle and warfare'; cattle were their pride and source of livelihood while

1. Lugard, op. cit., vol. 1, p. 87.
2. C. Wills, *Who Killed Kenya?* London, 1953, p. 29.
3. C. Eliot, *The East Africa Protectorate*, London, 1905, pp. 133-4 and 239.

warfare was an essential ingredient for a youth's attainment as well as proof of manhood. The aggregate of these factors was seen to be the thing which aroused abject terror in the peaceable and sedentary agriculturalists, such as the Kikuyu, a terror inflicted on the latter by their neighbouring 'lords of the plains'.[4] Commenting on Kikuyu-Maasai relations at the turn of the century, Routledge remarked that 'between the two nations reigned perpetual war'.[5] However, the view that the Maasai were a terror to their neighbours, or that they were constantly at war with them, needs drastic qualification as far as it affects Kikuyu-Maasai relations.

It is true that considerable raiding took place between the two groups, but this state of affairs was tempered by other factors which enhanced mutual understanding. First, their respective modes of life were in some ways complementary; the pastoralist needed some of the agricultural produce, in the same way as the agriculturalist required some animal products. Like most pastoralists in East Africa, the Maasai were particularly vulnerable to famine, because any natural calamity—such as the vagaries of the weather or any epizootic epidemic—was a threat to their chief source of livelihood, the livestock. On such occasions they were heavily dependent upon their agricultural neighbours with whom they had either to trade or else seek refuge to avert starvation. If there had been a rupture of relations beforehand, emissaries were dispatched to explore the possibilities of concluding a peace treaty before trading activities were resumed. Regarding Maasai-Kikuyu peace negotiations, it is apparent that the initiative was mostly taken by the Maasai. Peace negotiations were not lightly undertaken, as the conclusion of a peace treaty (*munyoro*) involved a protracted and elaborate procedure, culminating in a religious ceremony during which both parties took a solemn and binding oath.[6] 'If we ever kill the Maasai,' the Kikuyu declared publicly, 'may we be slaughtered like this [ewe]! If we ever harm them, may we be killed thus!'[7] And very

4. D. A. Low in Oliver and Mathew (eds.), op. cit., p. 301; and in V. Harlow, E. M. Chilver and A. Smith (eds.), *History of East Africa*, vol. 2, Oxford, 1965, pp. 1-2.
5. Routledge, op. cit., p. 13.
6. 'Leakey ms', chap. 13; Unsorted Miscellaneous File in 'Barlow Papers'; 'KHT', pp. 228, 237 and 262.
7. The procedure for the taking of an oath was as follows. An ewe was tied and the elder taking the oath on behalf of the people cut its throat while simultaneously chanting, 'Ithui tungikoraga Ukabi turotuika uguo! Ithui tungikonera Ukabi kirii turotuika uguo!'

serious consequences were believed to befall anyone who broke such a solemn oath; the most serious being either a visitation of natural calamities on the offender as a result of being ritually unclean, or being handed over to the wronged party for the appropriate punishment. That the oath was no idle threat is demonstrated by the fate of a warrior from Kiambu, called Wangai, who was handed over to the Maasai after he had broken a peace treaty in the 1890s.[8] Peaceful coexistence, therefore, was duly recognized as being of prime importance to the well-being of the two communities. Indeed, the experiences of the Maasai in the nineteenth century is a good demonstration of the above observation. The various disasters that overtook them—the cattle epidemic, smallpox and their internecine wars—culminated in a large-scale influx of refugees into Kikuyuland. In fact, this phenomenon was not confined to the Kikuyu alone; throughout the century Maasai refugees are known to have settled among the Taveta, the Chagga, the Arusha and the Luhya.[9] Moreover, an arrangement whereby women and children could be pawned in times of misfortune existed, as it did among the Ashanti and the Dahomey of West Africa.[10] Desperate Maasai families left their children and women in the hands of the Kikuyu in exchange for foodstuffs, hoping to ransom them in better times. No stigma was attached to the pawnship and the system was commonly practised by the Kamba, the Kikuyu and the other Mount Kenya peoples, but it was only practised during famine time. In any case, it fulfilled an important function by ensuring that a family did not starve.[11] Pawnship was certainly not regarded as slavery, indeed it was a stage towards full adoption. Such children became full members of the respective Kikuyu families which had adopted them, until they were ransomed. It seems unlikely that the Maasai would have sought refuge among the Kikuyu, let alone would have pawned their children, if there had been any possibility of their being seriously ill-treated.

Equally, interdependence was mutual. The agriculturalists would

8. *KLC*, vol. 1, pp. 248-9.
9. Oliver and Mathew (eds.), op. cit., p. 307.
10. S. Miers, 'Great Britain and the Brussels Anti-Slave Trade Act of 1890', Ph.D. thesis, University of London, 1969, pp. 151-73.
11. Commenting on twenty-five women and children found among the Kikuyu, Craufurd noted, 'In a great many other instances it transpired that the alleged captives had imposed on themselves captivity; they had in point of fact thrown themselves on the Wakikuyu in order to obtain food, promising future payment in return for this.' *Report*, 20 January 1899, in FO2/189.

also call upon the pastoralists, to some extent, at times of similar adversities. Irrespective of the occasional adversity, however, the importance of trade in its own right was well appreciated for it to stimulate peaceful relations.[12] Undoubtedly, the possibility of experiencing natural calamities mellowed Maasai attitudes towards their neighbours and made them amenable to intercourse. But some of their daily requirements, such as gourds for milk and tobacco, were equally essential to them and these could only be obtained from the agriculturalists. Trade between the Kikuyu and the Maasai was singularly profitable to the former; it was not at all surprising therefore that the Kikuyu normally took the initiative to ensure that trade relations were maintained. The Maasai possessed all that the Kikuyu lacked and desired most—livestock, leather cloaks, hides and skins, and various ornaments, such as beads and cowrie shells, which the Maasai obtained from the coastal traders. It was an accepted axiom that trade was above petty squabbles, and this led to a gentleman's understanding that trade would continue in spite of any hostilities in progress between them. Thomson observed this ambivalence in the Kikuyu-Maasai relations along the south-western border and commented:

> Curiously enough, however, though they are eternally at war to the knife with each other, there is a compact between them not to molest the womenfolk of either party. Hence the curious spectacle is exhibited of Masai women wending their way with impunity to a Kikuyu village, while their relatives are probably engaged in a deadly fight close at hand.[13]

This was to be confirmed by von Höhnel and Teleki a few years later. Not only did they find that women were perfectly safe in spite of Kikuyu-Maasai feuds, but they successfully appointed a Maasai woman to act as their intermediary along the same frontier.[14]

Apart from the spirit of good neighbourliness engendered by mutual economic convenience, good relations between the two appear to have been the norm rather than the exception. Contact between them probably dates back to the first half of the eighteenth century, and the oral traditions of the Kikuyu suggest that there were amicable relations with the Maasai from, at the latest, the beginning of the nineteenth century when they co-operated in driving

12. G. Muriuki, 'Kikuyu Reactions to Traders and the British Administration, 1850-1904' in *Hadith 1* (the Proceedings of the Annual Conference of the Historical Association of Kenya, 1967), Nairobi, 1968. pp. 104-5.
13. Thomson, op. cit., p. 308. See also Fischer, op. cit., pp. 40 and 99.
14. von Höhnel, op. cit., p. 291.

out the Barabiu. As discussed in chapter 3, the Barabiu, presumably assisted by the remnants of the Athi and Gumba, had made an inroad into northern Gaki driving the inhabitants into Mukurue-ini division and the lower extremity of Mathira division. This incursion of the Barabiu into the highland region might have sparked off a spate of disturbances and turmoil in the highlands, which appears to have characterized the period between the end of the eighteenth century and the first quarter of the nineteenth. Subsequent to the expulsion of the Barabiu, ca. 1800-30, there was an era of comparative peace between the Maasai and the Kikuyu, which lasted until the great cattle epidemic of 1889-90.[15] The Kikuyu inhabiting Gaki, for example, aver that it was taboo for them to attack the Burugu (Purko) Maasai, who were considered to be their close kinsmen. It is also widely maintained that it was not until the time of the Ndung'u warriors, who were initiated about 1884-8, that the two groups started to raid each other. This comparatively congenial relationship, however, was not apparently extended to the Laikipiak Maasai with whom the Kikuyu claim to have had particularly strained relations all along.

Other evidence lends credence to this view. It is significant to note in this respect that the Kikuyu word for Maasai is *Ugabi/ Ukabi*, which was not only derived from the word *Wakuavi*, Iloikop, but also synonymous with enemy. It would appear therefore that the Kikuyu in Nyeri, like all the other peoples in and around the highlands of Kenya, had largely to contend with the Iloikop Maasai whose aggression and addiction to raiding, even against the other Maasai tribes, was well known.[16] Nonetheless, Laikipiak-Kikuyu relations, though strained, did not amount to 'perpetual war' either. For one thing, there were extensive intermarriages between the two groups, to the extent that specific Laikipiak families or localities had cordial relations or even close kinship ties with specific Kikuyu families. The Maasai state, for example, that when the Laikipiak were defeated by the Purko, ca. 1870-5, many of them took refuge among the Kikuyu in Nyeri precisely because they had previous relatives among them.[17] Secondly, Krapf recorded an

15. Jacobs, op. cit., p. 96.
16. See, for example, Krapf's Journals for March 1845, December 1847, March/April 1849 in CMS, CA5/016/M1 & M2 and Jacobs, op. cit., pp. 89-91, 104-6.
17. Jacobs, op. cit., pp. 73-83, 97-8 and personal communication; *KLC*, vol. 1, pp. 110 and 527; 'KHT', pp. 11, 27, 249.

interview that he had with five Kikuyu who had come from 'Kizu'[18] in the 'neighbourhood of Mount Kenya' and had accompanied a Kamba caravan to the coast in 1853. He recorded, *inter alia:*

> They also mentioned that a division of Wakuafi was residing in their territory, and that they were on good terms with them, the Wakuafi feeding their herds on their ground.[19]

It was the existence of such peaceful and close relations along the northern frontier which, though erratic, accounts for the extensive intermarriages which took place between the two groups. Furthermore, it underscores some of the factors behind the claim, made by many Kikuyu *mbari*, that either their ancestors were of Maasai origin or alternatively that their *mbari* have Maasai blood. Even today many of them still claim to have many relatives among the Maasai.

The view that the Maasai were 'fierce traditional enemies'[20] of the Kikuyu, or that the two were wont to raid each other, would seem to be largely based on the conditions prevalent in the last decade of the nineteenth century. Their relations worsened in this decade subsequent to the rinderpest epidemic which decimated their livestock. But while most observers comment extensively on Kikuyu-Maasai hostilities, there is surprisingly little comment on the equally fierce raiding between the various Kikuyu localities in the same period. To the north, for example, it appears that the Meru, the Ndia, the Gicugu and the Embu were not so seriously affected by the epidemic as Nyeri was. In the event they became the target of various raids by warriors from some parts of Nyeri, such as Mathira division. But no sooner had some of the Mathira acquired the coveted livestock than they too became the target of raids mounted by their neighbours. In Mathira itself there was a spate of local raids such as the ones between Konyu and Magutu, Iria-ini and Kiri-mukuyu. As late as 1903, Konyu was reported to have robbed Tumutumu and 'Mazeras' of their goats, which they then took to

18. These traders probably came from the vicinity of Kiru in Kangema division, Murang'a district.

19. See Krapf's letter to Baylis in CA5/016/M2, pp. 519-20. In his 1851 journal, Krapf has noted: '... in many localities in that region the Kikuyuans appear to live in companionship with the Wakuafi'. See J. L. Krapf, *Travels, Researches and Missionary Labours During an Eighteen Years' Residence in Eastern Africa*, London, 1860, p. 351.

20. E. Huxley and M. Perham, *Race and Politics in Kenya*, London, 1944, p. 67.

Nyeri town as payment for the hut tax.[21] These internal conflicts, however, did not deter them from uniting to make major raids on their other neighbours. They made a particularly large raid on the Ndia in September 1891.[22] The raid was the brainchild of Wang'ombe Ihura, a man who was closely associated with the Maasai warriors.

Wang'ombe, a Mumbui (pl. Ambui) of Mbari ya Thiukui, had an interesting career. Born at Kamakwa, near Nyeri town, Wang'ombe was probably the son of a Laikipiak woman from Baringo and a Kikuyu father, Ihura Karugu, who made frequent trading expeditions to Maasailand, particularly during the natural calamities which hit the Maasai in the second half of the nineteenth century.[23] It was during such an expedition, accompanied by his young and uninitiated son, that Ihura was killed by the Laikipiak warriors at Ngaring'iru, near Mutara. Young Wang'ombe managed to escape with his life and temporarily sought refuge among his Maasai relatives. However, on returning to Tetu he became extremely unpopular, for people living in his neighbourhood feared that he might betray them to the Maasai. Hearing that some people were secretly hatching a plot to kill him, Wang'ombe fled to Ruthagati, in Mathira, to join his other relatives. But though a refugee, fortune seemed to smile on him. Particularly because of his knowledge of Maasailand, he became an influential warrior who successfully led Kikuyu raiders against the Maasai. He was also able to unite warriors from a large part of Mathira and Tetu. His popularity, however, began to wane, for two reasons. It is said that he quarrelled with the Nuthi warriors—a warrior group in formation from 1898— over spoils of war. Secondly, he was wont to lead Maasai warriors against the Kikuyu, an action which did not endear him to the Kikuyu. Thus ultimately he became distrusted and greatly feared. It appears that finding himself unable to command the loyalty of all the warriors from Mathira, he decided to bolster up one of their sections, which he could trust, with Maasai mercenaries, in order to raid the Ndia for livestock. Several raids were made on the Ndia,

21. See historical notes on Iria-ini and Fort Hall in KNA/PC/CP/1/1/1/; Mackinder, op. cit., pp. 459 and 462.

22. E. Gedge, 'A Recent Exploration under Capt. F. G. Dundas, R. N., up the River Tana to Mount Kenya' in the *Proceedings of the Royal Geographical Society*, vol. 14, 1892, pp. 527-8; 'KHT', pp. 223-9.

23. Interview with Wang'ombe's wife, Wanjuku, on 16 December 1970 and 30 March 1971.

but the 1891 raid appears to have been the largest and most famous of the raids of the period. It is estimated that more than five hundred Maasai and Kikuyu warriors took part. The raid itself was symptomatic of the general deterioration of tranquility throughout the highlands of Kenya as a result of the rinderpest.[24] But the situation was aggravated by Wang'ombe, who was not slow to exploit the situation. Ultimately his tactics made his presence in Mathira insufferable and it was not surprising that he was forced to flee from Mathira to Tetu, despite his Maasai mercenaries. Before this episode, however, he had masterminded yet another major raid, this time against his fellow Kikuyu in Uthaya, Mukurue-ini and the contiguous parts of the Murang'a district. Once again he had enlisted the aid of Maasai mercenaries who, together with the Tetu and Mathira warriors, combed the region from Uthaya division to the banks of the Maragua river. This took place sometime between 1892 and 1894.[25] Incidentally, this was the only occasion when the Maasai are known to have conducted such a big raid in those parts, hitherto, the inhabitants of the region claim, they had only experienced sporadic cases of cattle theft by small groups of Maasai *morans*. Eventually, Wang'ombe turned against his own allies, leading Kikuyu warriors to attack the Maasai and vice versa. In January and February 1902, he is reputed to have attacked the Konyu on three separate occasions assisted by the friendly Maasai warriors.[26]

What was prevailing in the Nyeri district was not an isolated case. To the east of Kikuyuland, Gutu Kibetu, like Wang'ombe, was harrassing his neighbours, while at the same time the Ndia people were raiding their neighbours to the west as well as the Embu. The Meru, too, were attacking the Cuka and the Embu. And to the south-east of Kikuyuland, the inhabitants of Muruka in the Kandara division of Murang'a were in feud with the Kamba.[27]

The situation on the southern frontier was similar to that in the north and here, too, the Kikuyu had not come across the Maasai in any appreciable numbers until the second half of the eighteenth century, when Kikuyu expansion brought them into contact with

24. 'KHT', pp. 223-35.
25. 'KHT', pp. 231-5; Cagnolo, op. cit., pp. 101-3.
26. See historical notes on Iria-ini and Fort Hall in KNA/PC/CP/1/1/1/ and KNA/DC/FH/6/1 respectively.
27. See historical notes on Embu in KNA/PC/CP/1/1/1/; and A. Arkell-Hardwick, op. cit., chaps. III and IV.

the Maasai of the Kaputie plains. And in times of adversity, the Maasai took refuge among the Kabete in the same way as they did to the north. This occurred, for instance, after the great rinderpest epidemic of 1889-90, and again during the outbreak of the small-pox and the famine which followed, as well as during the civil wars between Sendeyo and Lenana, who were the sons of the great Maasai *laibon*, Mbatian.[28] But even among the southern Kikuyu the absorption of Maasai elements pre-dates these disasters, and the Waiyaki family illustrates this. Waiyaki's father, Kumale ole Lemotaka (or Hinga according to the Kikuyu), sought refuge in the home of Gatheca Ngekenya while that family was still at Thare (Kiria) in Kandara division, Murang'a district, and before they had crossed the Southern Cania river to settle in Gatundu. This probably occurred during the second phase of the first Iloikop wars between the Maasai tribes, which took place in the early part of the nineteenth century.[29] The first of the Iloikop wars erupted in Uasin Gishu around 1791 and continued throughout the first decade of the nineteenth century. After a short interval, fighting began again and continued until 1826.[30] There are other Kikuyu and Maasai families which had assimilated Maasai blood, and vice versa, before the rinderpest epidemic. In particular the Anjiru of the Mbari ya Gathirimu, who were noted medicinemen, had very close ties with the Maasai, especially the *laibon* family of Mbatian. There is even a considerable body of evidence which explicitly suggests that Subet (Thubi according to the Kikuyu), the greatest Maasai *laibon*, might have been a descendant of the Mba-ri ya Gathirimu.[31] Indeed, the Maasai respected Kikuyu medicine-men whose help they frequently sought not only in Kabete but also in Nyeri.[32] This was a further important factor which contributed

28. The evidence on the Maasai refugees is quite extensive but the most authoritative account is to be found in the evidence to the Kenya Land Commission of 1932-3 in *KLC*, vol. 1, pp. 167-70, 244-6, 740, 746, 950-2; Reports to the Imperial British East African Company and the diaries of F. C. Hall and J. Ainsworth, in Rhodes House, Oxford; and 'KHT' pp. 239, 245, 247.

29. The word *hinga* (hypocrite or dissembler), was applied to anyone living among the Kikuyu who spoke the Maasai language or who had lived among the latter.

30. Jacobs, op. cit., pp. 55-62.

31. 'KHT', p. 145; Unsorted Miscellaneous File in 'Barlow Papers'; *KLC*, vol. 1, p. 170; 'Leakey MS', chap. 3.

32. In Nyeri the Maasai are reputed to have consulted Njiri from Magutu. See *KLC*, vol. 1, op. cit., p. 527.

towards peaceful relations between the two peoples. In the south, too, joint Maasai-Kikuyu raids were also a familiar feature similar to those observed by Boyes along the northern frontier.[33] Ainsworth reported joint Maasai-Kikuyu raids against the Kamba in 1894, and Kenyatta was informed by his grandfather that this custom was fairly common, joint raids being directed against a section of either the Kikuyu or one of the Maasai tribes.[34] It is also suggested that some of the Kikuyu warriors assisted Lenana during his quarrels with his step-brother Sendeyo.[35]

Similarly, the developments along the northern frontier were echoed in Kabete in the last decade of the nineteenth century— Maasai-Kikuyu relations worsened. Through arbitration, some of these conflicts could have been solved, but the presence of the Imperial British East Africa company in the south radically altered the situation. The company had allowed the Maasai refugees to build their *manyatta* (kraals) within the company's stronghold at Fort Smith, at a time when the Kikuyu were at loggerheads with the company. The Maasai, exploiting the safety offered them, were all too ready to steal foodstuff from the Kikuyu *shambas*, thus invoking the wrath of the Kikuyu. The Maasai also used the situation to harass the neighbouring localities with impunity, but what mainly contributed to a total breakdown of the previously rational, if not amicable, relations between the two tribes was the employment of Maasai warriors by the company as levies, to supplement its troops. The protectorate forces were also to use the Maasai similarly, to carry out the increasingly frequent punitive expeditions against the Kabete,[36] and the latter retaliated by despoiling the Maasai without scruples, a factor that could only lead to a further poisoning of their relations. The situation became so fraught with danger and such a strain on the company administration that Hall was forced to eject the Maasai from the vicinity of Fort Smith to Ngong in June 1894.[37] Thus the peace settlement negotiated at the outbreak of the rinderpest epidemic and the Maasai civil wars became damaged beyond repair.

33. Tetu warriors were rumoured to have threatened to call on their Maasai allies to fight against Boyes. See Boyes, op. cit., p. 110.
34. Ainsworth to IBEAC, 27 March 1894, in FO2/73; and Kenyatta, op. cit., p. 210.
35. 'KHT', p. 244.
36. Hall's diaries; Hall to Col. Hall, 12 February 1894 in 'Hall Papers'; Hall to IBEAC in FO2/73; Hall to IBEAC, 22 August 1898, in FO2/165.
37. Hall's diary for 1894 in 'Hall Papers'.

Yet, the deterioration in the Maasai-Kikuyu relations cannot solely be explained by an inherent hostility between the two peoples. This worsening was indicative of the disruption the two tribes were experiencing, from internal natural calamities on the one hand, and the strains brought to bear on these societies by the outside world. The Kikuyu around the southern border in particular were undergoing rapid change as a result of decades of trade and contact with the coastal people. This process was accelerated further by the establishment of the company posts at Kiawariua (Dagoretti) and, later, at Fort Smith. The demands and requirements of the company, together with the exposure to outside influences, led to a decade of restlessness, and ultimately a section of the Kikuyu, having succumbed to the temptations of personal gain, was ready to co-operate with the new forces. The rise of a pro-company faction led by Kinyanjui Gathirimu, Hall's *fidus Achates*,[38] was a significant pointer to the transformation of social and political attitudes taking place in Kabete. And it is significant that those who were ready to compromise and accommodate themselves to the changing circumstances were nonentities in the traditional society. Kinyanjui and his faction were ready to support the company at all costs in order to bolster up their position and influence outside the traditional structure. But a major consideration was the economic rewards to be got from employment as porters, informers or as soldiers of fortune. Self-interest, and particularly quick gain, were slowly but surely eroding the traditional ideas and norms about the supremacy of the community's welfare over individual interests. This inevitably led to a weakening of the social structure; it is not surprising, therefore, that by the turn of the century, McGregor found the business instincts of the Kabete people astonishingly keen. 'They work fairly well compared to the other East African tribes,' he remarked, 'but unfortunately owing to the many caravans which passed here in the past, the love of the Rupee is getting hold of them in a remarkable degree.'[39] Above all, some of the larger *mbari* were becoming a law unto themselves, as noted in chapter 3. Also, some elements in the migrants into Kabete were criminals who had either fled from justice, or had been disowned by their families and had therefore sought refuge on the southern

38. Hall to Col. Hall, 12 February 1894, in 'Hall Papers'.
39. A. W. McGregor to the CMS dated 24 November 1900 in CMS Archives, G3. A5/no. 7.

frontier. Significantly, it is alleged that Kinyanjui, who was Waiyaki's dependant, migrated to Kabete after being disowned by his relatives in Kiria (Kandara, Murang'a) for misbehaviour.[40] Finally, it should be noted that the vanguard of pioneers was usually joined by a clientele of relatives or *ahoi*, who hoped to make their fortunes eventually at the frontier. The *ahoi* were usually younger men of the warrior group and their main preoccupation was the defence of the frontier, and raiding. It was not unusual for the *ahoi* to be numerically more than the *mbari* members and it sometimes became virtually impossible for the *mbari* members, or the *kiama* (elder's council), to control them. It was this unruly element that periodically made the frontier politically unstable. It is even most likely that it was this group which harrassed the caravans passing by the southern frontier.

It was perhaps a combination of all, or some of these factors, that explains to some extent why some of the Kikuyu were quick to despoil the Maasai or ally themselves with the company, and later the colonial administration, in expectation of economic and other rewards. The victims of the changing traditional structure and values were not only the Maasai refugees, or the Maasai-Kikuyu relations, but also the Kikuyu themselves in the long run. The social changes which had been taking place prior to colonization set the stage for the spirit of individualism that altered the traditional social pattern even further in the twentieth century, with far reaching consequences.

The situation in Gatundu division during the Great Famine of 1898-9 demonstrates what was happening. Imitating the company and government forces, some Kikuyu warriors arrogated to themselves the powers and functions of the traditional council of elders and warriors. Initially, they acted as the traditional and innocuous council of warriors which from time to time had been entrusted with some civil functions, such as the enforcement of the payment of debts, or even the punishment of thieves. But ultimately they mimicked the outward trappings of a *thabari*,[41] but in fact they were no more than an unprincipled band of marauding brigands who terrorized all and sundry. They burnt homes, locked people

---

40. 'KHT', p. 125.
41. These outlaws ((*njangiri*) modelled themselves on the expeditionary forces which they had seen on many occasions, sent against them by the company and government officers. The name *thabari* is derived from the Swahili word, *safari*.

in their houses and then set them on fire, murdered others and confiscated livestock and food at a time when famine was taking its toll. They were akin to the *ruga ruga* bands of Yao and Ngoni elements who terrorized southern Tanzania in the second half of the nineteenth century.[42] The Kikuyu *thabari* is alleged to have confiscated livestock belonging to the Mbari ya Kigamba, to have terrorized herdsmen at Gacoka, and to have been responsible for murdering some members of the Mbari ya Gitau Thube, the Mbari ya Njege, the Mbari ya Ngiricu Mugwe, the Mbari ya Kaburu and the Mbari ya Ihura. There were many such bands but the most notorious ones were in Kiganjo location of Gatundu division. This group ranged far and wide and their extortionate activities were only brought to an end by the death of most of the robbers while on a raid in Ithiru, Murang'a, and by the end of the famine, when other warriors felt strong enough to assert traditional authority. This was a completely foreign phenomenon in the history of the Kikuyu and the ruthlessness of these outlaws has only been outmatched by the behaviour exhibited by both protagonists in the Mau Mau conflict of 1952-61, with which it has been compared.[43]

Another example of the deterioration in the traditional scheme of things was shown by the Kamba. Formerly they had been the foremost middlemen between the Nyika peoples and the ivory-hunting peoples in the interior. In this role, they were important trading partners of the Kikuyu at the heyday of the latter's commercial activities in the first half of the nineteenth century. But by the second half of the same century their activities had deteriorated into robbing and raiding.[44] They specialized in capturing Kikuyu women all along the eastern border of Kikuyuland.

For these reasons, the conditions prevailing towards the end of the nineteenth century were far from typical. Certainly the Maasai and the Kikuyu were not implacable enemies, and there was no chronic tension and confrontation between them. Indeed, their relations do not seem to have been any worse than those existing between the various Kikuyu localities or amongst the Maasai

42. See Oliver and Mathew (eds.), op. cit., pp. 208-11 and chap. 8.
43. 'KHT', pp. 237-43.
44. For a discussion of the Kamba trade in the nineteenth century, see J. E. Lamphear, 'The 19th Century Trade Routes of Mombasa and the Mrima Coast', essay presented for M. A. in Area Studies (Africa), School of Oriental and African Studies, University of London, September 1968; von Höhnel, op. cit., p. 331.

tribes themselves. It is true that war existed, in the form of raiding and counter-raiding which occasionally cooled their relations; but it should be realized that to the warriors this was a sport arousing in the participants an excitement not unlike the mood of the Football Association Cup final—there was no bitterness or hatred. As Orchardson has remarked in discussing the wars between the Kipsigis and the Maasai:

> War with the Masai was looked on as true war, and was carried on under strict rules, as much for glory and the love of fighting as for the acquisition of cattle. It was played almost in the spirit of an adventurous game, the prize of each bout being cattle. There seems to have been little bitterness or hatred and only when one side broke some rule would the other retaliate by some similar deed. Peace was made under oath and was unbreakable without mutual consent and due warning.[45]

Hence warfare was in certain circumstances regarded as sport, a view that is strengthened by the fact that casualties were few. It was this attitude towards warfare that accounts for the various 'jousts and tournaments' that took place between the various Maasai tribes when they were at peace with their neighbours.[46] The Kikuyu, too, had a similar practice, and their 'tournaments' involved the warriors, or even the boys, from the various Kikuyu localities. Thus the popular stories about the hostility and depredations of the Maasai against their neighbours have been very much exaggerated. The alleged bad reputation between the Maasai and Kikuyu can be attributed to the stories spread by the Kamba traders about them. These traders, anxious to retain their monopoly of the interior trade, were quick in spreading weird stories not only of the fierceness of the Maasai, but also of the 'thievish and treacherous' nature of the Kikuyu. They similarly dissuaded their cousins from trading directly with the coastal peoples by spreading negative stories about the Arabs, the Swahili and the Nyika peoples.[47] This chorus was later taken up by the Swahili and the Arab traders in their attempt to keep out other competitors, especially in the last three decades of the nineteenth century, when Europeans were getting interested in the hinterland. Jacobs has convincingly shown that the atrocities attributed to the Maasai in

45. I. Q. Orchardson, *The Kipsigis*, Nairobi, 1961, p. 7; Thomson, op. cit., p. 414; A. C. Hollis: *The Masai*, Oxford, 1905, pp. 321-2.
46. D. A. Low in Oliver and Mathew (eds.), op. cit., p. 303; Thomson, op. cit., p. 414.
47. G. Muriuki, op. cit., pp. 107-8.

general were mostly in fact committed by the Wakuavi, the semi-pastoral Maasai. He has argued that the depiction of the Maasai as 'the all-powerful, ferocious people' cannot be sustained by fact, this picture being the result of a deliberate campaign on the part of the Swahili traders to keep out competitors by playing upon their susceptibilities towards the people of the interior. The attempt to discredit the Maasai was carried a step further by some of the early administrators, particularly Charles Eliot, in order to have an excuse for depriving them of their land and thus make way for white settlement.[48] The evidence called to prove that there existed traditional Kikuyu-Maasai enmity, however, stems largely from the role that the Maasai played during the period of company rule, between 1890 and 1895, and the establishment of the British administration thereafter. The officials of both the company and the government frequently employed the Maasai *morans* as levies to assist the regular forces during the punitive expeditions, some of which took the Maasai where they had never set foot before. By 1898 the Maasai had seen service 'on many occasions in Kikuyu, Ukamba and Eldama [Ravine]',[49] and this occurred even more extensively in the first decade of this century. Hence, to the majority of the Kikuyu, the Maasai gained the reputation of being fierce and war-like enemies mainly because their alliance with the all-powerful *Comba* (Europeans) gave them the opportunity of having the field to themselves. Commenting on the 'abject terror' which the Kikuyu and Kamba were supposed to have for the Maasai, Dundas remarked that this was 'not always a fact', just as the Maasai power was 'much over-rated'. The reputation of the Maasai in this respect, he concluded, rested on 'their unceasing minor raids, which might better be described as robberies', and on the fact that 'they were often employed [by the administrators] to subdue other tribes, and were therefore regarded as in league with the all-powerful European'.[50] In any case, though formidable on the plains, the

48. A. H. Jacobs, 'A Chronology of the Pastoral Maasai' in *Hadith 1*, pp. 24-30 and also in his thesis, pp. 89-91, 104-6.
49. Hall to IBEAC, 22 August 1898 in FO2/165.
50. C. Dundas, 'The Organization and Laws of some Bantu Tribes', *Journal of the Royal Anthropological Society*, vol. 45, 1915, pp. 236-7. See, also, Routledge, op. cit., p. xi. Hobley, another early administrator commented: 'It is probable that the scourge of the Masai was generally much overrated, and that they were as often as not badly beaten by other tribes.' See C. W. Hobley, *Bantu Beliefs and Magic; With Particular Reference to the Kikuyu and Kamba Tribes of Kenya Colony*, London, 1922, p .244.

Maasai were an easy target if they ventured into the forests where their spears and shields were no match for the Kikuyu and Kamba arrows, or for the latter's staked war-pits. The Kikuyu-Maasai contact had far-reaching consequences. As already noted in chapter 3, some of the Kikuyu *mbari* trace their origin to Maasai ancestors, while an even bigger number has absorbed Maasai blood as a result of the extensive inter-marriages that have taken place between the two peoples. It is not surprising therefore that there has been a deep and extensive cultural fusion, especially along the northern and southern frontiers of Kikuyuland. The most easily noticeable influence was the insignia of the Kikuyu and Maasai warriors—the hair style, the shield decorations etc, were identical.[51] Yet these outward signs were merely indicative of a more deeply-rooted cultural exchange dating back to many generations.[52] Linguistically, for example, the Kikuyu language is heavily indebted to Maasai from which it has borrowed nearly all the words relating to cattle, and especially the descriptive ones. Also, certain religious concepts, such as Ngai (God; Maasai, E'Ngai) were borrowed from the Maasai. But the most significant cultural influences were in the fields of initiation and military tactics. With the increase of the *hinga*, that is, those Kikuyu who were of Maasai origin or had lived among the Maasai, these people as well as other non-Kikuyu elements were grouped with their descendants into an all-embracing section, called the Maasai 'guild' for ritual purposes. Their children were initiated following rites similar to the Maasai ones, which were slightly different from those practised by the Kikuyu 'guild'.[53] Initiation in the Maasai 'guild', as indeed with most of their ceremonies, was less elaborate and therefore less expensive than its 'Kikuyu' counterpart. This feature sometimes recommended the simpler ceremonies to the poorer members of the Kikuyu community, who otherwise had no claim to having Maasai blood.[54] Ordinarily, members of the Maasai 'guild' suffered no social or political disabilities, and were only

51.   C. W. Hobley, *Ethnology of the Akamba and Other East African Tribes*, Cambridge, 1910, p. 132; Routledge, op. cit., pp. 15-16, 30; Thomson, op. cit., p. 308.
52.   Eliot, op. cit., pp. 106, 127 and 134; Boyes, op. cit., pp. 110-11, 298-300; Oliver and Mathew (eds.), op. cit., pp. 199, 203 and 207.
53.   Hobley, *Bantu Beliefs and Magic*, chap. 5; L. J. Beecher, *The Kikuyu*, Nairobi, 1944, pp. 5-6.
54.   For the variation in religious rites between the two 'guilds', see M. N. Kabetu, *Kirira kia Ugikuyu*, Nairobi, 1966.

barred from officiating in public rituals or ceremonies. It was not unusual for a family, plagued by misfortunes, to change from one 'guild' to the other in order to break the sequence of bad luck, as it was believed that such a transfer would bring misfortunes to an end. The division of the Kikuyu into two respective 'guilds' was only in vogue to any appreciable extent along the frontiers of Kabete and Gaki, the two places where Maasai impact was both extensive and of long standing. The acceptance of the Maasai initiation rites and the setting up of special 'guilds' to cater for the new cultural elements is a strong testimony of the extent of Maasai influence upon the Kikuyu. This is all the more significant when it is realized that initiation influenced every facet of Kikuyu society, as will be discussed in the next chapter.

But Maasai influence went far beyond the initiation rites and affected the subsequent training of youths into an efficient fighting force. This was particularly so in Gaki, where, it is claimed, their military organization owed its efficiency to the guidance given to them by the Maasai. The latter are said to have instructed the Gaki in such activities as scouting, reconnoitring and recruitment, which enabled them to drive out the Barabiu at the beginning of the nineteenth century, during the Kikuyu-Maasai alliance.[55]

In most parts of Gaki, too, the warrior corps was divided into two main groups. The first batch of initiates to inaugurate the recruitment of a new warrior set after the *muhingo* (closed period) was called a *muricu*. It was also designated *tatane* (right hand, derived from the Maasai, *tatene*), while the subsequent initiates that completed a warrior set were called *mucenge* and regarded as *gitienye* (left hand) or *kedianye* in Maasai. The *muricu* warriors were regarded as, and indeed were, senior and more experienced than *mucenge* warriors; and the name given to the former at initiation was normally the one subsequently adopted by the whole warrior set.[56] Over time, however, these distinctions would blur, especially with subsequent recruitment of other warrior sets. It was

---

55. See historical notes in 'Barlow Papers'.
56. 'Lambert, 1965', p. 11; 'KHT', pp. 193-9. According to Maasai customs, they were divided into two moieties corresponding to the two sides of a cattle-post. When a man married, the first wife built her hut on the right hand side of the gate, the second wife on the left, the third on the right and so on. The 'right hand' was associated with seniority, privilege, strength and worldly things, while the 'left hand' was associated with weakness, misfortune and supernatural things. See Jacobs, op. cit. chap. 4.

perhaps the need to retain the original function and importance of these designations, as well as to avoid the possibility of confusion, that *muricu* and *mucenge* were specifically used to describe the divisions within a warrior set while *tatane* and *gitienye* were ascribed to alternate warrior sets. The former thus retained their initial functional importance, while the latter lost all significance since warriors belonging to either set had equal status.

The promotion of the younger to the rank of senior warriors was another aspect of military organization that was in some respects similar to the Maasai pattern. Generally there was no specific ceremony among the Kikuyu to mark the occasion, but among the Maasai, the handing over of military responsibility for the defence of the country was an elaborate affair. Throughout Kikuyu-land every junior warrior had to pay a fee to his seniors for his promotion. The senior warriors did not, however, relinquish military duties until they were satisfied that the younger ones were capable of carrying out the functions entrusted to the warrior corps. Practice in Gaki, though, seems to have differed and the takeover from one group to another presumably was as important as the *ituika*, with the junior warriors taking over as a body. Although differing in important respects, this promotion of warriors among the Kikuyu had significant parallels with its Maasai counterpart, the *eunoto* ceremony.[57]

Besides the Maasai, the Athi were the other neighbours of the Kikuyu, to be found along the frontiers to the north, the west and the south-west. From their haunts in the Kirinyaga and the Nyandarua forests, they were constantly in touch with the Kikuyu. And like the Maasai, the Athi offered the Kikuyu attractive animal products which were scarce in Kikuyuland. In particular elephant meat was considered to be a delicacy for which the elephant was avidly sought and pursued. The Athi were expert elephant hunters and hence an important source of ivory, which they sold to their neighbours the Kikuyu, the Kamba and the Maasai in exchange for goats, of which they were particularly fond. This was a most lucrative trade for the Kikuyu, because a good ivory tusk, of say, five 'hands',[58] could fetch between fifty and a hundred goats when

57. For the organization of the warriors in Gaki, see 'KHT', pp. 193-205 and 'Lambert, 1965', pp. 10-17. And for the Maasai system, see Jacobs, op. cit., chap. 4.
58. A 'hand' was the length of the arm between the elbow and the finger tips.

sold to the Kamba or the Swahili traders. By the 1840s Kikuyuland was recognized as an important source of ivory, and in these parts the Kamba were initially the principal ivory buyers, as exemplified by Kivoi, the Kamba merchant prince. He told Krapf in 1849 that he had left his ivory in the Athi country as well as at 'Muca' in Kikuyuland. And one of Krapf's bearers, a Mnyika who had travelled extensively in the interior from Chaggaland to Laikipia, mentioned that in 'Mulama'[59] country there was a lot of ivory which was sold to the Kikuyu.[60] That the Kikuyu obtained ivory from the Athi is not questionable, for the former were indifferent hunters, and in any case it was a taboo for a self-respecting Kikuyu to engage in hunting as an occupation, except for the occasional trapping of wild animals in order to protect crops, which was permitted.

Other articles of trade offered by the Athi were equally in demand, as for instance buffalo hides for making shields, ready-made shields, animal horns, rare skins such as colobus monkey skins which were mainly used for making elders' garments and the warriors' insignia, also ligaments for sewing skin garments. Above all they acted as intermediaries between the Kikuyu on one hand and the Maasai or the coastal traders on the other. The Athi colonies at Mianzini and Ndoro acted as very important middlemen, and were largely dependent on this role for their livelihood.[61] Hardly any caravan ever travelled beyond the Kikuyu borders without stopping at Mianzini for provisions, unless it had managed to have direct access to the Kikuyu while camping at Ngong. On the other hand, requisite foodstuffs could be obtained on the northern border but, once again, the caravan had to employ the services of the Athi living in the vicinity of Ndoro, a place that had become an important market. The Athi were equally useful in other roles; quite often they were called upon to be spies, scouts, guides or even menial servants. They were an important link between their agricultural neighours and the pastoralists, and quite often they were able to introduce the landless and needy Kikuyu to those of their people willing to part with their hunting grounds. In Kiambu, most

59. This perhaps refers to an Athi colony in the vicinity of Nanyuki and Mukogodo regions.
60. See Krapf's Journal for November-December 1849 in CMS Archives, CA5/016/M2, pp. 277-81.
61. Fischer, op. cit., pp. 98-9.

of the land was obtained from them in a variety of ways but chiefly in exchange for goats. And as seen in chapter 3, these transactions were still going on towards the end of the nineteenth century.

Despite the much vaunted absence of natural barriers between the Kikuyu and their related Mount Kenya peoples, in contrast to the situation along the Maasai borders, the conditions which existed between them do not seem to have been radically different from those prevalent along the Kikuyu-Maasai frontiers. In any case, the presence of a fringe of forest along the Kiambu and Nyeri border at the end of the nineteenth century was there by accident, rather than by design. Indeed, it was constantly being eaten away by the axe and the fire. Along the northern frontier, cultivation had been extended to the Ruguru location of Mathira in the 1890s, and by 1902 the forest around where Nyeri town now stands was being furiously attacked to make way for cultivation. And in Kiambu, the Kabete had their eyes on the Thogoto area and the destruction of the oft-mentioned forest fringe was only arrested by the arrival of, and interference from, the British administration. The existence of this forest fringe, therefore, should not be given undue importance in any assessment of the relations between the Kikuyu and their neighbours. Oral data makes it quite clear that there were many fratricidal conflicts not only among the Mount Kenya peoples but also among the Kikuyu themselves. The Kabete and the Kamba, for example, were raiding each other occasionally, but the latter were also raiding as far north as Ndia; the Mathira and the Tetu raided the Ndia as well as the Embu, and at times roamed as far away as Meru. Previous internal conflicts, if not actual enmity, rankle up to the present day.

There is no basis, therefore, for the general assumption that the relations between the Kikuyu and their cousins were necessarily more cordial than those between them and the Maasai. Indeed, there was very little between them which would have encouraged cordial relations. All of them were agriculturalists and, except in times of famine, they did not desire, or require, much from one another. Trade between them, for example, was severely restricted, in contrast to the Maasai/Athi trade. Only the Kamba had any important trade relations with the Kikuyu, and that only for a brief period in the middle of the nineteenth century.

By the 1840s the coastal trade north of Pangani was in the hands of the Kamba, who had managed to wrest it from the Swahili and

Nyika peoples.[62] The Kamba were renowned for their prowess as hunters, and it was this feature that stood them well in the commercial activity that they so ably developed as ivory traders. They were, however, chiefly middlemen, and except in a few cases they did not have direct access to the Arab or Swahili traders. Their caravans, sometimes of up to five hundred people, brought ivory to the Nyika peoples, who as go-betweens passed on the goods to the Mombasa traders.[63] At its heyday the Kamba commercial empire was extensive; it spread from Unguu and Usagara in northeastern Tanzania to the Mount Kenya region, Baringo and beyond. The extent and success of the Kamba commercial activity at its apogee is typified by Kivoi of Kitui. His trading activities extended from the foothills of Mount Kilimanjaro to those of Mount Kenya, and further up to Samburu and further north. His caravans, loaded with ivory, had direct access to Mombasa, instead of disposing his goods to the Wanyika, as was the custom. He was personally known to the governor of Mombasa.[64] His village, too, was a hub of trading activities between the Kamba and the Kikuyu, the Embu, the Mbeere, as well as other Mount Kenya peoples.

Several factors account for the Kamba monopoly of the interior trade. First, this ivory trade was suited to their natural hunting ability and knack for commercial exchange. Besides, the Galla and the Wakuavi were a formidable obstacle to the Wanyika, who were in any case actively discouraged by the Kamba with suitably juicy stories of fierce pygmies and cannibals inhabiting the interior who fattened people for slaughter. Krapf aptly noted:

> I conjecture that these stories have been invented by the Wakamba and caravan leaders, in order to deter the inhabitants of the coast from journeying into the interior, so that their monopoly of trade with the interior may not be interfered with.[65]

Similarly, they spun appropriately bone-chilling accounts meant to dissuade the Mount Kenya peoples from venturing to the coast. However, the moment the Wakuavi got defeated, some time in the 1830s, the situation was radically changed and the Kamba monopoly

62. For a description of Kamba trade, see Krapf's journals and letters in CMS Archives; and J. E. Lamphear, op. cit.
63. Rebmann to CMS in CMS Archives, CA5/016/M2, p. 643.
64. Krapf's journal for November/December 1849, pp. 281, 289.
65. ibid.

became challenged by both the coastal traders and the Mount Kenya peoples.[66]

And by the 1860s, Swahili and Arab traders were posing a serious and effective challenge to the Kamba. Realizing the disadvantages of tapping the interior trade through the Kamba route, which was not only in the hands of the Kamba but also vulnerable to Galla attacks, they travelled to the interior via Taita and the Kilimanjaro region.[67] These traders journeyed from Mombasa to the south-western border of Kikuyuland, camping at Ngong, then known as Ngongo Bagas. From there they veered north-westwards to Mianzini and then crossed the Laikipia plateau to Uaso Nyiro, Meru and beyond. Thus they were able to challenge the Kamba monopoly effectively by getting to the very source of the ivory in the environs of Mount Kilimanjaro and Mount Kenya. By the 1870s, the Arabs and the Swahili had the ivory trade firmly in their hands, and this is confirmed by Charles New, who observed:

> The people of Mombasa do a large trade with the interior. Their caravans visit Teita, Chaga, Ukambani and the Masai country, as far west as to the shores of the Victoria Nyanza, north-west to the regions about Lake Baringo and the confines of Samburu.[68]

Northwards they were also sending caravans to Meru and as far as 'Reya', near Marsabit.[69] At the same time the Mount Kenya peoples appear to have got tired of the Kamba monopoly. Hitherto they seem to have resigned themselves to playing second fiddle in the interior trade; they were content to take ivory, tobacco and food to the Kamba villages in exchange for the coastal goods— cowrie shells, beads, salt and cloth, as well as weapons, and particularly poison for their arrows. The Kamba were also famous for their medicines, and these were eagerly sought.[70] Some of the Mount Kenya peoples appear to have been junior partners, quite

66. It is not certain when the Wakuavi were defeated. Krapf, writing on 9 December 1847, noted that this occurred 'some years ago', while Rebmann, in his journal for March/April 1849, wrote that this took place 'in the last 15 years'. Thomson estimated that it was about 1830. See CMS Archives CA5/O16/M2, pp. 102-3, 214, 270; and Thomson op. cit., pp. 414-15.
67. J. Wakefield, 'Routes of Native Caravans from the Coast to the Interior of East Africa', *Journal of the Royal Geographical Society*, vol. 40, 1870, pp. 314-19.
68. Charles New, *Life, Wanderings and Labours in Eastern Africa*, London, 1873, p. 55. One caravan had reached Samburu by 1869. See Fischer, op. cit., p. 98.
69. ibid, p. 460; Wakefield, op. cit.
70. Krapf, *Travels*, pp. 296-7, 311-16.

often being responsible for the buying of ivory in the interior and transporting it to the Kamba villages or alternatively waiting for them to come and collect the purchases themselves. Kivoi, for example, claimed to have left his ivory among the Kikuyu and Athi in 1849.[71] Indeed, the more enterprising traders from Embu, Mbeere and Kikuyu were travelling as far as the coast, albeit accompanying the Kamba caravans.[72] These occasional trips were bound to have significant repercussions in the organization of the Kikuyu-Kamba trade and it was to be expected that other Mount Kenya peoples would eventually want to have direct access to the coastal trade without having to go through the irksome Kamba middlemen. The fate of Kivoi and Krapf in August 1851 seems to indicate this changing attitude.

Krapf met Rumu Gikandi, a Muembu trader who had visited Kivoi's village during one of his trading expeditions, who gave him a lot of tantalizing information about Mount Kenya and the surrounding regions. This stimulated Krapf's interest in a trip up the Thagana river. Kivoi arranged for one, as he, too, wished to go north in order to collect ivory. It was during this journey that Kivoi was killed by robbers in the Mwea plains and Krapf narrowly escaped with his life. In retaliation for Kivoi's murder, a small Embu caravan was attacked and its members murdered, as it was suspected that his death had been master-minded and effected by Embu and Mbeere robbers. This was in fact not an isolated incident; Krapf was told that prior to this incident a Kikuyu caravan had also been put to death in retaliation for a similar offence committed in Kikuyuland against some Kamba traders.[73] These episodes highlight the problem of trade by the Kamba-Embu route. For, while recognizing the necessity of tapping the source of ivory to the north, the Kamba were all the same reluctant to give access to the coast to their northern neighbours. In the event the rest of the Mount Kenya peoples were getting disenchanted with the Kamba monopoly, quarrels ensued and ultimately one lifeline of the Kamba trade was severed. Outmanoeuvred by the Swahili to the south and west, and their trading activities seriously hampered in the Mount Kenya region, and the Galla making it virtually impossible for them to extend their

71. Krapf's journal for November/December 1849. p. 281.
72. Krapf to CMS, 11 September 1852 and 30 August 1853 in CMS Archives, CA5/016/M2, pp. 454-5 and 519-20 respectively.
73. Krapf, *Travels*, op. cit., pp. 311-33.

trade eastwards, the Kamba trade gradually declined and deteriorated
into mere robbery. And by the end of the nineteenth century the
Kamba, in the eyes of the Kikuyu, were only famous for kidnapping
women and children whom they sold to the Arab slave dealers.[74]
The coastal traders had grown so strong since the 1870s that by
the 1890s the Kamba-Embu route had assumed its former importance, and caravans were travelling from Takaungu to Sabakia,
Athi, Ikutha, Kitui, Ndia—then known as Murang'a—Laikipia
and Tharaka. Ainsworth noted in 1895 that this was 'a route
apparently much used' and that 'Merang'a, a district in the Kikuyu
country, is a place from which many slaves come'.[75] He had earlier
reported, in 1893, that Machakos was an old Arab and Swahili
camp for slaves and ordinary trade, the Kamba doing a brisk trade
in selling the Maasai and the Kikuyu.[76] The last two decades of
the nineteenth century were marked by particularly strained relations
between the Kikuyu and the Kamba, and the situation was worsened
by Kamba attempts to kidnap Kikuyu women for sale.

Once again, the relationship between the Kamba and the Kikuyu
cannot be explained in simple terms and in many ways resembled
the Maasai-Kikuyu relations. In spite of their squabbles, a few
Kikuyu colonies were flourishing in the northern and western
parts of the Kamba country.[77] And when the Great Famine broke
out among the Kamba, they flocked into Kikuyuland in large
numbers in search of food. The spreading of the famine to some
parts of Kikuyuland has been partly attributed to the large reserves
of food sold to the starving Kamba in exchange for livestock or the
coastal goods. The Kamba, too, realized that due to their precarious
geographical and climatic conditions, famine was an ever constant
reality and hence they could ill-afford to antagonize the Kikuyu.
And again as with the Maasai, some of the Kikuyu, especially
those along the eastern border, had relatives among the Kamba
through intermarriage, and although this was on a smaller scale

74. This view has been entrenched in Kikuyu traditions by the story of
     Cinji and his sister. The relevant stanza runs:
         Cinji, Cinji! I have often warned you
         That I am constantly spied upon
         By three men from Ikamba.
75. Ainsworth to IBEAC, 31 January and 20 February 1895 in FO2/97.
     'Merang'a' referred to Ndia.
76. Ainsworth's Machakos district report for 1893 in FO2/57.
77. Ainsworth's Kamba report of 1 January 1894 in FO2/73.

in comparison to the Maasai-Kikuyu intermarriage, it was a mitigating factor.

External trade—particularly that with the Kamba and the Maasai—was an important aspect of Kikuyu society. Kikuyu women went to trade as far afield as Lake Naivasha, Narok, Kajiado and Nanyuki.[78] It involved elaborate preparations, and sometimes the participants had to endure untold hardships, ranging from the fierce wild animals to the weather, let alone the enemy or robber lurking in the bushes along the trade routes (*njira cia agendi*). Trade, however, was largely in the hands of women, and was certainly not the sort of job that appealed to a self-respecting warrior or elder. The poorer man who was unworthy of military service due, for example, to physical disability, or those who had no compunctions in engaging in such menial tasks, accompanied the women on these expeditions. They did not receive, however, the comparative immunity women had on these trading expeditions.

The women traders were drawn from the married, middle-aged, but still strong, age group, lest unmarried girls excite the covetousness of the Kamba or the Maasai warriors. A trading expedition was invariably led by a *hinga*, a man who knew the terrain well, or it would have been difficult to locate the Maasai because of their seasonal transhumance. All the *hinga* spoke Maasai well, being either Maasai descendants or having lived among them. The traders to the Kamba and Maasai countries were given hospitality in the villages or *manyattas*, which became centres of their trading activities. Quite often the traders established themselves in the homes of relatives, friends, or acquaintances and in many cases particular Kikuyu localities traded with particular Maasai localities. It was, of course, an added advantage to have relatives among the Maasai, as this not only ensured welcome hospitality but also gave the trader enough assurance of her safety and chances of success. This feature had important repercussions on the relations between the Kikuyu and the Maasai; it enabled relatives on both sides to keep in touch with each other and promoted further co-operation between specific Maasai and Kikuyu localities.

Temporary trading markets were occasionally established at the borders, especially in times of famine, when it became essential to trade on a large scale. To the Maasai and the Kamba, the Kikuyu

78. Fischer, op. cit., pp. 40 and 99; 'KHT', pp. 253-5.

offered a variety of foodstuffs during famine such as *njahi* (*Dolichos lablab*), maize, several varieties of millet flour, dried banana flour, green bananas and sugar cane. The Maasai also bought honey, tobacco, earthenware cooking pots, a variety of calabash containers, spears, swords and red ochre. In normal times the Kamba were mainly after ivory and tobacco and in exchange for these items the Kikuyu obtained beads, brass and iron wire, salt and cowrie shells (which had been obtained from the coast), and livestock. But each group offered special items—the Kamba specialized in poisons, medicines, chains, snuff boxes, bows and arrows and iron ore from the Ithanga hills, while the Maasai were well-known for skins, leather cloaks and livestock.

There was also a considerable internal trade among the Kikuyu themselves. Indeed internal trade was more frequent, extensive and affected a larger population than the external trade. All transactions were in the form of barter, although by the end of the nineteenth century iron pieces, goats and beads were increasingly becoming forms of currency. The internal trade was well organized, and in Murang'a and Nyeri markets were held every fourth day. Among the oldest and best known markets are Gakindu, Gacatha, Karatina, Giitwa and Muthithi. On market days no other functions of any significance took place nearby the market-place and, even if there were feuds or fighting going on between the ridges, these were halted on that particular day. Law and order was kept by a group of warriors whose responsibility it was to supervise the market. A variety of commodities were bartered in these markets; on the one hand were the agricultural products which were bartered for the traditional handicrafts produced by the specialists. And on the other hand were other rare commodities, such as cowrie shells and beads, which the more adventurous members of the community had obtained from the Maasai or the Kamba. Cowries and beads had a high aesthetic value and were only bought by the well-to-do Kikuyu. The market gave those who confined themselves to farming a chance to exchange their foodstuffs for iron implements, salt, red ochre, pottery and leather garments. Some localities specialized in particular commodities. Gaturi and the contiguous areas, for example, were reputed for their poisons, medicines, tobacco and a host of iron goods such as knives, swords, spears and arrows. Gakindu was known for its grinding stones and tobacco. The area around the Nyeri/Murang'a border seems to have been foremost in trading enterprises; not only did it extend its trade to the other parts of Kikuyuland but it had also trading contacts with the Kamba. These people have retained their business acumen up to this day. Inter-district trade was, however, restricted to the exchange of agricultural products and the few items made by the specialists, except in times of famine. Murang'a sold red ochre, pig iron, iron implements and tobacco to Kiambu in exchange for soda, skin garments, beads and cowrie shells which the Kabete obtained from the passing caravans, or the Maasai. A similar pattern of trade existed between Murang'a and Nyeri. To facilitate this trade there were well-kept roads from Nyeri to Kiambu, with bridges at the appropriate places.[79] These trade routes were cleared during the *ituika* in particular.

79.   von Höhnel, op. cit., pp. 334, 336 and 346.

Chapter 5

THE SOCIAL AND POLITICAL
STRUCTURE

BY the end of the nineteenth century, Kikuyu society was patriarchal, uncentralized and highly egalitarian. These features were
primarily based on two things: the family was the fundamental basis
of its social structure, while the recruitment of males into corporate
groups of coevals, through initiation, was the *sine qua non* for
political interaction and organization. Territorial organization,
however, was essentially fluid and *ad hoc* in nature. Consequently,
there were no formalized administrative units until the beginning of
this century, when these were carved out by the British administrators. Equaly, no single group of people was charged with the responsibility of maintaining the social and political institutions as
they existed in the Kikuyu society. Indeed, it was the duty and
responsibility of each individual to safeguard that part of the
society in which he was involved at any given time. Kikuyu society,
therefore, was basically acephalous, with authority and power
being widely diffused throughout its varied components. The
failure of the British administrators to recognize this fact led to
serious administrative difficulties, the more so when a few individuals
were recognized as chiefs where none had hitherto existed. This
action only helped to sour further the already strained relations
between the British and the Kikuyu, and led to further misunderstandings which, in turn, had far-reaching repercussions on their
mutual outlook.

While most informants found it easy to describe the structure of
Kikuyu society as it existed at the turn of the century, they offered
no information of its historical development. The traditional
claim, for instance, that at one time the Kikuyu society was matriarchal and that the menfolk staged a *coup d'etat* which ended the
female rule remains mainly unsubstantiated. Few informants could

say with any degree of confidence when this occurred; the majority admitted they did not know, while the others were tempted to associate this major social upheaval with the Iregi generation. What seems clear is that the transformation of the Kikuyu society from a matriarchal to a patriarchal social system had taken place before they immigrated into Metumi and Gaki. And as it is difficult to establish the chronological sequence of even some of the major landmarks of Kikuyu social and political history, some of the time-references offered in this chapter are tentative.

The intrusion of Kikuyu elements into the Gumba domain was significant because, as we have seen in chapter 3, the Kikuyu might have borrowed some features of the *mariika* system from them. But this intrusion is hard to date. Those informants who offered 'Gumba' and 'Karirau' as names of generations placed them before the Agu and the Tene.[1] And Lambert was told that the Agu generation was associated with expansion.[2] Furthermore, an analysis of the genealogies of the vanguard of Embu pioneers suggests that penetration into Embuland by an appreciable number of pioneers occurred sometime in the fifteenth century. But as shown in chapter 2, archaeological evidence has strongly indicated that early Bantu elements, the Thagicu, had advanced as far west as the Mathira division of Nyeri by the twelfth century. The Gumba, it should be observed, are recalled by the Embu, Mwimbi, Imenti, Muthambi and Igoji. It is probable, therefore, that Thagicu/Gumba contact dates back to at least the twelfth century, if not much earlier. It is also evident that the *mariika* system had taken root in the Kikuyu society by the middle of the seventeenth century. Further-more, in the period up to the Cuma generation in the early eighteenth century, the Kikuyu were still small in numbers and hence it was possible for them to retain very close kinship ties. This was also the era of pioneers. The organization of all males into corporate groups of coevals, however, would have tended to loosen kinship ties, just as the threat posed by the Gumba and Athi demanded unity and co-operation transcending the kinship group. For these reasons, from the beginning of the seventeenth century, forces that cut across kinship ties existed side by side with those that encouraged kinship solidarity. In spite of the need for ethnic solidarity in periods

1. See, for example, Beecher, *A Kikuyu-English Dictionary*, p. 68; 'KHT', pp. 213 and 218.
2. 'Lambert MS', chap. 6.

of threat, the dispersal of the lineage groups towards Gaki and Kabete, particularly during the Ciira generation, made it increasingly difficult to retain close *mbari* solidarity. The Maasai threat in the second half of the eighteenth century (during the Mathathi generation) would have once more fostered inter-*mbari*, co-operation, but real unity came later in the first half of the nineteenth century, when the Kikuyu had to come together to drive the Barabiu out of northern Gaki. Yet, though it can be seen that external threat stimulated unity which cut across the kinship groups, loyalty to the latter remained an important feature of Kikuyu society, and these two competing forces ensured the survival of a series of petty, and virtually independent, groups divided from each other by streams and other physical features.

A pioneer had to endure the elements as well as danger from human foes and wild animals. The clearing of the forest was an arduous task, demanding a high degree of co-operation and industry by each pioneering group. Understandably the picture of the frontiersmen painted by folklore is that of men of courage, resource-fulness and hard work; in short, the type of hero that any good Kikuyu was exhorted to emulate. Thus the pioneers were the focus of esteem which, in time, turned into veneration, particularly because they came to be regarded as the *mbari* founders after several generations. As *mbari* founders and ancestors, they were revered and they finally became the object of prayers and propitiatory sacrifices, important aspects of Kikuyu religious beliefs and worship.[3]

A *mbari* might inhabit a whole *itura*, *mwaki* or even *rugongo*, depending upon its size and circumstances. Where such a situation prevailed, *mbari* solidarity would be particularly strong because these units, and the *itura* in particular, were the focus of social and political interaction. The settling of quarrels and the regulation of local affairs, for example, were carried out on a kinship or *itura* basis, both of which coincided in some cases. For these reasons, the pioneering groups and their immediate descendants developed into very closely-knit communities with a deep sense of communal interest and spirit. Moreover, their isolation from each other (competition or even actual hostility existed between the *mbari* or ridges), as was sometimes the case, deepened a stage further the

3. For a discussion of Kikuyu religious ceremonies and rites, see Kabetu, op. cit.

localism and particularism that have become such pronounced features of the Kikuyu society. The era of small, closely-knit communities is likely to have lasted up to the middle of the eighteenth century.

Still, the *mbari*, or ridge, owed allegiance and loyalty to a much wider community. Each *mbari* traced its origin to one of the ten Kikuyu clans and hence regarded itself a direct descendant of the mythical ancestors of the Kikuyu people, Gikuyu and his wife Mumbi. An individual Kikuyu saw himself as belonging to the wider community of *Ciana cia* or *Mbari ya Mumbi* (the children of, or descendants of Mumbi). But this wider community of Mbari ya Mumbi was of little practical importance in day to day life, and the clan, or a segment of it, was of more significance. The myth of Mbari ya Mumbi was only relevant when it was vital to foster solidarity and unity within the Kikuyu community. This usually occurred in times of deep internal crisis, or when faced by external threats. A good example is the rallying nationalist songs sang just before and during the Mau Mau upheavals. Opinion varies, however, on how many clans there are, and in the published lists they range from nine to thirteen.[4] All the same, a careful study of the extant literature, taken in conjunction with the recently collected data, indicates definitely that there are ten clans. The evidence points to there having been nine originally and these were directly descended from the legendary nine daughters of Gikuyu and Mumbi. At one point in the history of the Kikuyu, an additional clan, the Aicakamuyu, was formed from the descendants of a girl, from one of the clans, who became an unmarried mother. Evidence for this assertion is not so readily forthcoming, but it is widely accepted by the Kikuyu that their clans are *kenda muiyuru*, 'full nine', meaning ten. This designation gained currency from the Kikuyu aversion, for magical reasons, from correctly counting either human beings or livestock, because it was widely believed that such an irresponsible act would be followed by calamity. On request, on the other hand, most informants enumerate ten clans, their beliefs notwithstanding.

4. For example, Kenyatta (pp. 5-6) enumerates nine; S. K. Gathigira (*Miikarire ya Agikuyu*, London, 1952, pp. 1-2), G. Wanjau (*Mihiriga ya Agikuyu*, Nairobi, 1967, pp. 3-5), Kabetu (pp. 1-2) and Benson (p. 158) all enumerate ten; Tate, 1910 (p. 237) enumerates eleven, and Routledge (p. 21) thirteen. The clan names are Anjiru, Aceera, Agaciku, Ambui, Ambura/Akiuru/Ethaga, Angeci/Aithirandu, Angui/Aithiegeni, Angari/Aithekahuno, Airimu/Agathigia and Aicakamuyu.

These ten clans were already in existence at the time of the initial
Kikuyu immigration into the plateau. By the end of the nineteenth
century, they were widely dispersed all over the Kikuyu plateau.
But despite the long distances involved, the Kikuyu attempted to
retain clan/*mbari* solidarity by holding occasional reunions, when
kinsmen from Kabete, Metumi, Gaki and even Ndia were expected
to be present. Each clan appears to have had a particular spiritual
home around the Metumi/Gaki border, where clan/*mbari* reunions
are alleged to have taken place. The last reunion is claimed to have
taken place towards the end of the last century.[5] No single clan was
politically dominant, though some of them were entrusted with
specific public duties on behalf of the community at large. Each
clan, however, was associated with distinctive traits and idiosyn-
cracies and all of them made distinguishing markings on their
beehives and livestock.[6] The Anjiru clan, for example, were reputed
to be expert medicinemen, while the Ethaga were the rain makers
as well as specialists in certain forms of witchcraft. In theory, at
least, and distances notwithstanding, clansmen were supposed to
act as a corporate body, particularly on important occasions such
as initiation, marriage, sale and purchase of land, or on payment
of blood money. Supposedly there was a strong bond linking clansmen, and wherever they met they were expected to assist each
other if necessary. This, however, was very much dependent upon
their size. Some clans were extremely large; the wealthier a clan was
the larger it tended to become because in a polygamous society, or
a section of it, having many sons wielded considerable influence and
such a family normally became relatively rich, wealth in those days
being measured in terms of the number of livestock, wives and offspring that an individual had. A large, wealthy and influential clan—
and the three normally went together—augmented its ranks by acting
as a magnet which attracted non-clan and non-Kikuyu elements,
such as the Maasai and Athi, into their fold. Within a comparatively
short time, such elements were completely absorbed, thereby
considerably enlarging the already substantial clans. This was,
however, not always the case. Some of these elements were never
really absorbed and they remained as *ahoi*, tenants of their host
clans. Then with the increase in population, there was a considerable

5. 'KHT', pp. 52-3, 78.
6. The most comprehensive discussion of the qualities and characteristics
    of the clans is in Wanjau, op. cit.

hiving-off of clan and *mbari* groups, and descendants of the original pioneers—such as the Ambui of Mbari ya Magana or the Mbari ya Marigu—became widely dispersed and tended to lose touch with each other. Owing to the increase in and the subsequent dispersal of the population, the original pattern of settlement was significantly modified in due course. It became no longer true that the descendants of a pioneer or members of a single clan were the sole inhabitants of an *itura* or even a ridge. The presence of the *ahoi* altered the original picture even further as it tended to loosen the *mbari* and kinship ties. For these reasons it became physically impossible to muster all the descendants of a pioneer. In any case some of them had by now developed into fully fledged *mbari* in their own right. Also, even if it had been possible to muster all the clansmen, the gathering would have been too unwieldy for practical purposes. In the long run, therefore, it understandably became impossible to retain even a modicum of cohesion in the larger *mbari*, let alone within a clan. Ultimately the *mbari*, or a part of it, depending upon its size and distribution, became the chief nerve for co-ordinating essential clan affairs. In some parts of Gaki and Metumi the clan, as a social factor, had declined so much, due to fission, that by the beginning of this century when people talked about the *muhiriga* (clan), they were in fact referring to the *mbari*. This is not surprising, since some clans in this area were so widely dispersed that some of them claimed to be related to some of the Kamba and Maasai clans.[7] The Agaciku and the Aceera, for example, are reputed to be descendants of the Akamba, while the Ethaga claim to be descended from the Chagga of Kilimanjaro. Presumably these clans may have had a shared origin, particularly those that are common to both the Kikuyu and the Kamba.

To ensure the smooth running of *mbari* affairs, each family (*nyumba*) was regarded as a social and administrative unit under the headship of the father. In the case of absence or death, his duties devolved upon the eldest son, or the eldest son of the senior wife in an extended family. The head of the *nyumba* was supreme in all family affairs, although if he was the son he would normally consult his brothers or the other close relatives before executing important matters. *Mbari* affairs, on the other hand, were co-ordinated by a *mbari* council comprised of all the initiated males who

7. K. R. Dundas, 'Notes on the Origin and History of the Kikuyu' *Man*, 1908, pp. 136-9; McGregor, op. cit., p. 31; Hobley, *Man*, 1906, p. 120.

had attained elder status. But this rule was quite flexible and sometimes even warriors could participate in the deliberations of the council. Normally the council chose a titular head called a *muramati* (guardian), whose primary duty was to regulate the day to day affairs of the *mbari*, such as mediating or, more important, being its spokesman in intra-*mbari* affairs. It was the *muramati*, too, who administered the *mbari* land as well as called the *mbari* council when the need arose. A *muramati* was normally the eldest son from the senior house line (*githaku*, pl. *ithaku*), although a junior but more capable man from the other *ithaku* could also be appointed.

There were other factors which contributed to wider integration among the Kikuyu, such as the organization of initiation rites and public sacrifices, and prayers that were deemed necessary for the general welfare of the community at various times, for instance sacrifices for rain in times of drought, or the libations poured at the beginning of the planting season and at the harvesting of the first fruits.[8] In the long run, however, neither the sentimental notion of belonging to the Mbari ya Mumbi, nor the external threats, nor even the public co-operation needed during the religious ceremonies, contributed more towards cohesion than the all-embracing and institutionalized *mariika* system that cut across lineage and territorial groupings.

Oral traditions do not give a clear picture of when the Kikuyu began to adopt the *mariika* system. But we have clear evidence that the *mariika* system was a feature of the Kikuyu society by the middle of the seventeenth century and was the most effective counterpoise to the introvert tendencies of the *mbari* and the other fissiparous forces. Above all, it was this aspect of the Kikuyu society that contributed most to the bond that linked up all the Kikuyu and made them feel they were a single people.[9] Its importance cannot, therefore, be overemphasized; and significantly all the students of Kikuyu society have noticed, in varying degrees, the existence and importance of these coeval institutions.[10] However,

8. Kabetu, op. cit., pp. 87-9.

9. For a discussion of the integrative role of the age groups in uncentralized societies, see S. N. Eisenstadt, *From Generation to Generation, Age Groups and Social Structure*, London, 1956; and by the same author, 'African Age Groups: A Comparative Study' in *Africa*, London, 1954, vol. 24, pp. 100-12.

10. For a survey of Kikuyu age system, see A. H. J. Prins, *East African Age-Class System: an Inquiry into Social Order of Galla, Kipsigis and Kikuyu*, Gröningen, Jakarta, 1953, pp. 40-57 and 98-118; H. R. Tate, 'Further

partly because the Kikuyu age system has been inoperative in the twentieth century, there has been considerable divergence of opinion on how it operated. The Kikuyu, like other ethnic groups, ascribed a role, or status, to each individual according to age, for example, *ciana* (children), *mumo* (young initiates), *anake* (warriors), and *athuri* (elders) had each an assigned part to play in society. The males, especially, passed from childhood to old age through a prescribed pattern, but the most significant experience, both socially and politically, was circumcision and the attendant grouping of the initiates into age groups or sets. Each age set was given a name which was distinct and institutionalized and consisted of novices (both girls and boys) initiated at any given time, who remained members of it throughout their lives. Their promotion, too, was by groups and not as individuals, with the exception of their promotion to the elder grade, which depended on other factors as well.

Failure to distinguish that, according to the Kikuyu age system, the word *riika* could refer to four different age groups has led to a considerable confusion, as can be seen in the divergent *mariika* lists published in the past. In its broadest and most general sense, *riika* means a generation. This referred to the tribal moiety charged with the responsibility of running the tribal affairs at any given time and whose term of office began with the conspicuous and distinctive handing over ceremony, the *ituika*. This took place every thirty to forty years, during which one generation handed over to its successor the reins of power to conduct the political, judicial and religious functions. The two moieties were Mwangi and Maina (or Irungu), and members were recruited according to birth. Sons were born into their grandfather's moiety, particularly the first-born sons who, in any case, were named after them. There was, therefore, a linking of grandfathers and grandsons, both of whom regarded each other as classificatory equals and exhibited a deep mutual attachment and affection. The moieties' names, Maina and Mwangi, seem to have been only applicable to the living generations; those which had died off were given a definite

Notes on the Southern Gikuyu', *Journal of African Society*, pp. 285-97; Leakey MS, chap. 18; Dundas, 'Kikuyu Riika' *Man*, pp. 180-2; Routledge, op. cit., pp. 9-11, 154-67; 'Lambert, MS', chaps. 6, 7, 8; McGregor, op. cit., pp. 30-36; Cagnolo, op. cit., pp. 81-95, 120-25, 198-202; Hobley: *Bantu Beliefs and Magic*, chap. 5; Kenyatta, op. cit., chaps. 6 and 9; 'Barlow Papers', and 'KHT', pp. 193-214.

name, specific to them, and which noted the most outstanding
feature of their period or rule.

In its more restricted sense, a *riika* meant an initiation set which
comprised of all those boys, and girls too, who had undergone
circumcision in a given year. Circumcision was the only criterion for
its membership and the set was normally named after the most
outstanding event that had occurred either shortly before or after
their initiation. Several such initiation sets were grouped together
to form a contingent of an army, and for this purpose they were
then given an all-embracing name which may have been the name
of one of the initiation sets—normally the first one to be initiated
—or a totally different one. This army contingent or regiment was
also called a *riika*.

Whereas the boys underwent a *muhingo* (closed period) during
which no initiation took place, it was considered to be ritually
unwise to include the girls in the ban. Girls were hence initiated
every year. If their initiation coincided with that of the boys, as a
rule they associated themselves with and acquired the same *irua*
(circumcision) name as the boys. But on those occasions when
initiation was exclusively female in composition, it was given an
individual name which distinguished it from all the others. Hence
the fourth sense in which the word *riika* could be used was in reference to an exclusively female initiation.

Compared to the various ceremonies that every Kikuyu underwent
from birth to death, none was more significant than initiation.
Its importance was underscored by the fact that it was the basic
prerequisite for the attainment of full, adult, social status.

> The festivals and rites associated with both marriage and death hold but
> a small place in Kikuyu imagination compared to that greatest of all
> ceremonies whereby the boy becomes a man and the girl a woman.[11]

The initiation rites dramatized the transition of an individual from
childhood to adulthood. They also highlighted the symbolic casting
off of childhood values, especially because of their emphasis on the
initiate's complete and symbolic separation from the world of
youth. Hence initiation conferred social status, and the erstwhile
youths became full members of the community. Above all, it was
also at this stage that the neophytes were instructed in tribal lore.
This instruction (*kuumithio*) was considered to be just as important

11.   Routledge, op. cit., p. 154.

as the physical aspects of the initiation rites (*ndemengo*); indeed, any boy or girl who did not participate in the educational aspect of the initiation was not considered to have been fully or properly initiated, and remained an object of ridicule to his *irua* mates throughout his life.

In the absence of any formal centres of instruction, initiation served as one of the main educational channels in Kikuyu society. This education was both practical and theoretical and covered such fields as tribal traditions, religion, folklore, mode of behaviour and the duties of adults, taboos and sex. Also, the initiates were invested with important roles, responsibilities and privileges in the social system. Among themselves, the members of an age set demanded and encouraged co-operation, solidarity and mutual help as a result of which an age group exhibited a strong sense of comradeship and fraternal egalitarianism. Indeed, *riika* mates looked upon each other as actual blood brothers or sisters, depending upon their sex, and behaved accordingly. The spirit of comradeship was so strong among *riika* 'brothers' that it occasionally even led to a sharing of their wives!

As adult members of the community, the initiates were expected to play their part in the maintenance of the *status quo*. In particular, the male initiates became members of the warrior group whose primary duty was the defence of the country. For this purpose, it was essential to have an army, which consisted of the junior and senior warriors together with the remnants of the retired regiment who had not yet been fully absorbed into the elder group and who, by virtue of their experience and knowledge, acted as advisers. The newly initiated youth were in effect a corps of cadets, and the senior warriors did not relinquish their responsibility for the defence of the country or retire from active service until they were satisfied that the junior warriors were experienced enough to take over effectively. It took approximately fourteen years for each warrior group to be completely formed and ready to assume all the responsibilities of the warrior corps. This period of formation consisted of five or nine years of a *muhingo* (closed period), and nine or five years of pupillage as junior warriors respectively, depending upon whether an individual lived in southern or northern Kikuyuland. In practice, the senior warriors did not retire until a new batch of initiates was ready to take over from the junior warriors, who had in the mean time undergone their pupillage.

The closed period, during which no boys were initiated, served two main purposes. On the one hand it ensured that at initiation there were enough mature candidates capable of shouldering the responsibilities that would devolve upon them as a warrior corps. On the other it provided a useful gap during which the previous initiates, now junior warriors, consolidated themselves as an age set while at the same time acquiring the essential experience of their impending political and military functions before being saddled with the responsibility of executing them and ensuring adequate pupillage of the next batch of initiates. However, the retirement of the senior warriors was a gradual process and there was no ceremonial promotion comparable to the Maasai *eunoto*. It was expected, though, that once the junior warriors came of age, the senior ones would marry and retire to a more peaceful life. But there was nothing to stop them continuing with active military service after marriage and many of them did so. Public opinion and family pressure were so strong, however, that it dictated their retirement sooner rather than later.

The promotion of the junior warriors and the simultaneous recruitment of the new initiates to take their place ushered in the closed period. As stated above, its duration depended upon whether one lived in northern or southern Kikuyuland; it was nine years in Gaki and the contiguous parts of Metumi, and five years in the rest of Metumi and Kabete. This was followed by an open period of initiation, which lasted for five years in Gaki and nine in Kabete. All those initiated in the same open period formed a junior warrior set embracing all the annual *irua* sets. In turn, the set formed a contingent of the army with its own distinctive songs and shield emblems.[12]

Apart from military service, the warrior corps formed a reservoir of able-bodied men for performing other public functions. They acted as executive officers to the elders, being entrusted with such activities as policing duties in the markets and during the festivals, the arrest of habitual criminals and the calling of public gatherings such as *ibata*, during which rules and prohibitions were promulgated and other important pronouncements made. When necessary, a *njama ya anake* (warriors' council) scoured the country, each part in turn, punishing habitual criminals and any other offenders. For this reason, their main function was to carry out governmental

12. Kenyatta, op. cit., p. 206.

operations on behalf of the community at large. But the *njama* only acted when the situation had deteriorated to almost unmanageable proportions.

Warriors were also entrusted with the more difficult tasks which were regarded as a man's job. Such duties included the clearing of virgin land and cutting poles for building houses and cattle kraals. They also planted specified crops—such as yams, bananas and sugar cane. Otherwise the warriors were a privileged elité who to a casual observer did nothing else except gorge enormous amounts of food and meat. Their maintenance was in the hands of all the people, and not just their own lineage groups, but this generosity was in appreciation of their service to the community, especially protecting it. This sense of gratitude was pithily expressed in the Kikuyu saying: '*Mwanake ni kienyu kia Ngai*'—the initiate is God's generous portion, in the sense that he is a generous gift from God to the community.

Despite the enormous power and privileges in the hands of the warriors, they were on the whole adequately controlled. Like all the other age groups, they were strictly governed by their own council, which had the overall command of their activities including personal behaviour. The junior warriors had their own council, *njama ya anake a mumo*, and so did their seniors. Within each territorial unit there was a corresponding council of warriors, each with a nominal leader, *muthamaki*. The *muthamaki* acted as the chief spokesman for the territorial warriors, but his main duty was to control and supervise their welfare and activities, to reprimand wrong-doers and also to assemble the warriors when necessary. Promotion from the junior to senior warrior class was a gradual process, and each initiate had to pay an entrance fee to his seniors before he could be admitted to their ranks. There was a rigid code of behaviour within each warrior group, to make sure that a warrior did not bring shame to the *riika*. Privately, each warrior was anxious to defend his honour for this was considered to be the highest tribute that could be bestowed upon a person by the general public, especially when such acclaim was embodied in songs and dances. Accordingly, the age set acted as a very important agent of social control and thereby contributed enormously to social and political stability and cohesion.

Unlike their male counterparts, girls were not organized into regiments. Nevertheless they were divided into junior and senior girls corresponding to the junior and senior warriors, with whom they associated. Junior girls had to pay a fee in order to be admitted to the ranks of the senior girls. It was the duty of the senior girls to instruct their juniors in order to ensure that they did not act in a manner that would disgrace the girls as a group. Such instruction included what was considered to be proper behaviour becoming of girls, relationship between girls and warriors, how to perform tasks specifically entrusted to women such as looking after children, and most important—sex education. Among the women also there was a rigid code of behaviour and culprits were punished by fines or ostracization in extreme cases.

To ensure that there were adequate defence arrangements, a number of steps were taken. Nearly all the *matura* were built on the brows of the ridges, and where possible on hilltops. The homes, especially those along the frontier, were also strongly fortified.[13] The villages along the frontiers were in effect forts (*ihingo*, pl.: sing. *kihingo*), and in many respects these were similar to the Emergency villages built during the Mau Mau war. When the site or a new village was earmarked, the ground was cleared but the larger trees and undergrowth of the primeval forest surrounding the site were left intact. The trees ringing the site were felled in such a way that the trunks were not completely severed from their roots; they were felled outwards where they were left growing in their fallen position. A hedge of tangled branches and trees was thus formed, and after some time the growth was covered with thorny creepers such as *mutanda mbogo* or *Pterolobium stellatum*, making it impregnable. A single clearance was made to form an entrance to the village and this was strongly palisaded with strong poles on either side. On either side of the entrance, deep holes were dug, fitted with sharpened stakes and covered with brushwood. A number of gates were also constructed along the main path leading to the *kihingo*. At nightfall these gates were closed and entrance to the village could only be gained through a secret passage at the back. The latter was particularly useful during attacks, because women, children and livestock could always flee through it, leaving the men to fight. No one could enter through it without being heard, and in any case its existence was only known to the members of the *kihingo*. Sometimes a pit with a wicker drawbridge was

13. 'Leakey MS', chap. 5; Boyes, op. cit., p. 83, and MacDonald, op. cit., p. 110; Gathigira, op. cit., p. 9; 'KHT', pp. 135, 226.

dug at the main entrance. The primeval forest left intact around such *ihingo* concealed them most effectively, and as Hinde noted, 'So well concealed are the Wakikuyu villages that it is possible to pass within a few yards of one without having any idea of its existence'.[14] In contrast to the *ihingo* at the frontier, the villages in the interior of Kikuyuland were not so strongly fortified or enclosed as a single unit. They were largely a collection of individual homesteads built close to each other, lightly fortified.

At the entrance to the *kihingo* there was a guard house (*boi*), where warriors kept watch for enemies. In the interior, guard houses existed on each ridge, and it was there that the warriors held their consultations. In some places it was only the members of the *njama ya ita* (the warrior corps) who were allowed to sleep in the guard houses. If a Maasai raid was imminent a group of warriors were handpicked from each *itura* to man the guard posts at the border.[15] These were called *miriri*, and food was contributed by all the villages and taken to the warriors daily by the girls. Each *miriri* kept watch for as long as four months before being relieved. Evidently there was an elaborate system of defence and it was perhaps for this reason that the Maasai found it usually wise to attack just before dawn, or at night, when they had the chance of a surprise attack. Their attacks, however, were confined to the borders to ensure a quick retreat. The *miriri* arrangement was the closest the Kikuyu came to creating a standing army and probably this only dates back to the beginning of the nineteenth century.

It appears that the perfection of Kikuyu military organization was very closely associated with the degree of external threat. Apart from the Gumba and Athi, the Laikipiak Maasai seem to have been the only group that presented a major threat as far back as the first half of the eighteenth century. This threat had two important consequences: some of the Kikuyu from Gaki migrated towards the southern frontier, where it was more peaceful. Secondly, the Gaki reorganized their warrior groups in order to meet the new menace, and were most likely influenced by the Maasai system. Then there followed a period of peaceful coexistence between the Gaki and Laikipiak which was not broken until early in the nineteenth century, when the Barabiu invaded the highlands.

14. S. L. and H. Hinde, *The Last of the Masai*, London, 1901, p. 21.
15. See notes on warfare in the Unsorted Miscellaneous File in 'Barlow Papers'.

According to Kikuyu traditions it was during the Barabiu raids that the Kikuyu perfected their military tactics under the guidance of their Maasai allies. And when Kikuyu/Maasai hostilities once more broke out in the 1880s, the Kikuyu were well prepared not only to defend themselves but also to mount raids against the Maasai.

The actual organization of the warrior corps was based on the territorial units as well as the *riika*.[16] Each ridge, or *mwaki*, depending upon size, had a military unit which consisted of a junior and senior regiment, and also a *njama*, the latter constituting the leadership of such a military unit. Before setting out for a large raid the warriors from a number of ridges combined to form a single army, but each military unit remained under the command of their particular ridge's *njama*. The chief co-ordinator of all the activities of the warriors was the *njama ya ita*, whose duty was to summon the warriors (*guukiria ita*), to seek the advice of the medicinemen (*kuragura*), to scout, spy and reconnoitre on the disposition of the enemy (*guthigana*). It was their duty, too, to supervise the division of the spoils of war after a successful raid. The *njama* did not act as a body in all situations; some members were entrusted with the reconnoitring and were called *athigani* while others consulted the medicinemen and hence carried the *muthaiga* (medicine for good luck), the *kinandu* (a flask of sacred oil), and the *githitu* (charm). Still others were entrusted with ceremonial functions, such as prayers before a raid, or the performing of any other rites that the medicineman might have instructed to be carried out before the actual attack. Sometimes the medicineman instructed them to make a sacrifice in the plains just before the raids, and normally they would pray before launching the attack. The *njama*, and particularly the *athigani*, had supreme authority over the activities of the rank and file.

The *njama* was normally chosen from the cream of the warriors and only the brave, the experienced and the courageous were admitted into this rank. In some areas only the first-born were admitted, and in effect they were the officer corps. Second in importance and experience was the *gitungati*, the reserve rank. This group consisted of the natural leaders and candidates were well-built, brave, athletic, clever warriors who were also modest

16.   Gathigira, op. cit., pp. 81-3; 'Leakey MS', chap. 25; 'Lambert, 1965' chap. 8; Kenyatta, op. cit., pp. 205-8.

in demeanour and morally upright. They were appointed by virtue of their having demonstrated ability as young warriors. The *gitungati* only fought when other ranks found themselves hard-pressed and unable to rout the enemy. And as their name implies—derived from *tungata*, to take care of—their chief duty was to remain behind and guard the rest of the army against a surprise attack by the enemy during the retreat. Thus they were the rear-guard.

The vanguard was called *ngerewani*, or *thari*. It also consisted of brave and experienced warriors, as they were the chief combatants. Their duty was to capture livestock while at the same time carefully guarding the carriers of the *githitu* and *kinandu*, the insignia of office. It was essential that the carriers were not captured by the enemy, for it would spell doom if the sacred objects were lost. The *ngerewani* included some of the younger and newly initiated warriors who, because of their bravery, merited such honour. It was this younger group who were entrusted with the initial surprise attack and capture of the enemy's livestock. Finally, there were the older generation of warriors, some junior elders, weak warriors or the young and inexperienced initiates. All these belonged to the *murima* or *mbutu* whose main duty was to drive away the captured stock. They also carried provisions or any of the loot, thus leaving the main body of warriors to fight unhampered.

The chief purpose of the raids was to capture livestock. The immediate aim of the *ngerewani* therefore was to kill the herders, capture their stock and then hand the latter over to the *mbutu*, to be driven away as fast as possible and, in any case, before the enemy had had a chance to organize a counter-attack. Hence, surprise was one of the most essential tactics in order to minimize fighting which was neither necessary nor very common, smash-and-grab tactics being the usual manner of attack, unless the livestock chanced to be well guarded. To achieve a quick raid the *athigani* took great pains to recommend attacks only when and if they were satisfied that the livestock was unguarded, and ideal opportunities arose when the Maasai were feasting or performing ritual ceremonies. Besides, bloodthirsty or wanton killing of women and children was strictly forbidden, and it was taboo for a warrior to rape or seduce women prisoners during a raid. It was an accepted practice that prisoners could always be ransomed, failing which they remained in either country to become full members of their captor's family.

Spoils of war were divided by the *njama* following a laid-down procedure. First, the medicineman got his *ndang'uru*, an animal of outstanding features that, either arising from previous information at his disposal, or by foretelling, he had given as a sign of the herd to be captured. That done, the *njama* selected their own spoils, after which the warriors who had acquitted themselves particularly well in battle did the same. The remainder of the loot was then shared according to the number of ridges that had participated in the raid. To each according to his deeds was the guideline in the sharing out. For example, it was not unusual for a sheep or goat to be allocated to two warriors, while those who had killed an enemy got several head of cattle as well as the personal effects of the defeated foe. Moreover, the triumphant warriors were entitled to sing *kaari* (a warrior's song of triumph after killing an enemy) among their relatives, during which the relatives were required by custom to offer them presents in the form of livestock or whatever they could afford. However, not all the raids were so elaborately organized. Sometimes the more daring and adventurous warriors attacked in small groups especially when they discovered that their prospective victims were unprepared.

When the junior warriors came of age, their seniors were expected to terminate active military service and thereafter to marry, which was a necessary qualification for admission to the next stage of their life—the council of elders or *kiama*.[17] This was a social status grade, not an age set, and was divided into two main groups. At the lowest level were junior elders, a group that consisted of all those men who had married and hence ceased to be on active military service. In order to be recognized as junior elders they had to pay a fee of a goat (*mburi*) and a calabash of beer. Even then they were not regarded as full members of the *kiama*, and had more in common with the warriors than the elders. They could, for instance, still go on raiding or be called upon to take up arms against the raiders when necessary. As a result of this they were called *kamatimu*, carriers of spears, or *muranja*. Real assumption of elderhood came when their first child was circumcised, an event which effectively marked their transition from warriorhood to the full status of junior

17.   For the organization of the *ciama*, see Gathigira, op. cit., pp. 63-8; 'Lambert, 1965', chap. 9; Benson, op. cit., pp. 6-7; Prins, op.cit., pp. 40-57; Hobley, *Bantu Beliefs and Magic*, pp. 209-15; 'Barlow Papers'; McGregor, op. cit., p. 34; Kabetu, op. cit., pp. 93-4; Routledge, op. cit. pp. 197-204.

elder. On this occasion it was the custom for every parent to pay a fee of one goat and beer before being allowed to have their children circumcised. It appears, however, that the payment of a fee at the initiation of a first-born child was not strictly a fee paid towards promotion to elderhood, and this argument is reinforced by the fact that the council of the junior elders was called *kiama kia mburi imwe*, the council of one goat. It emphasizes the aspect of elderhood being a social status which a man gradually entered, rather than an age set in which conditions for qualifying were more explicitly set out. What is clear is that a retiring warrior paid two goats before attaining the junior elder status. The junior grade can therefore be conveniently subdivided into two minor groups—the newly married warriors who still continued to participate in raiding and who carried spears and thus earned the epithet *kamatimu*, and those who had had their first-born children circumcised, and had therefore qualified to be called elders (*athuri*). The latter group carried white staffs (*mithigi*, sing. *muthigi*) together with loosely tied *mataathi* (leaves of *Clausena anisata*) as symbols of office. This was also essentially a training grade comparable to the junior warriors. The *kamatimu*, in particular, were not entitled to judge a case, let alone officiate in any ceremonial or ritual activity. They were assistants who often acted as errand 'boys' for their seniors as part of their training. In contrast, the *athuri*, though regarded as junior elders, could in special circumstances hear minor cases which did not involve serious offences.

Depending upon individual circumstances, the junior elders paid a further fee of two goats and beer to mark the end of their period of apprenticeship. They were then admitted into the *kiama* proper and were henceforth regarded as senior elders. As symbols of their office they wore ear-rings and carried blackened staffs and *mataathi*, or *maturanguru* leaves tied with a twisted string. The council of senior elders was known by a variety of names such as *kiama kia mburi igiri* (the council of two goats), *kiama kiria kinene* (the big council), *kiama gia athamaki* (the council of leaders) or simply as the *kiama* (the council). It was the highest authority in the land, vested with legislative, executive and judicial functions. Like its junior counterpart, the *kiama* could be sub-divided into several sections based on its various functions. Some elders, by talent and inclination, were proficient in judicial or religious affairs. Such people tended to be more influential in those spheres than their comrades. The outstanding feature of the *kiama*, however, was an inner core of prominent elders who virtually ran the affairs of the *kiama*.

Special qualifications, too, were necessary before an elder could be permitted to officiate in religious rites. And like the *athigani* among the warriors, these officials formed, in some parts, an inner circle of the *kiama* called *kiama kia maturanguru*, so-called because of the tradition of carrying *maturanguru* leaves as a symbol of office. They were also the only *athuri* permitted to wear earrings where this custom obtained. This appears to have been the case in Kabete, where the designation was *kiama kia ukuru*, the council of old age. No such distinctions seem to have been prevalent in Gaki or Metumi where the religious officials were simply part of the inner circle of the *kiama*. Their duty was to officiate in all public rites and prayers to Ngai on such occasions as praying for rains, at planting or harvesting ceremonies or when conducting cleansing rites in times of adversity.

Each territorial unit had a corresponding *kiama*: at the lowest level was the village council which dealt with village affairs, and above it was the *mwaki*, the ridge or district council. Each of them had a leader or spokesman (*muthamaki*), who acted as the co-ordinator. Not all the elders actively participated in the council affairs and in order to play any significant role in its functions, he had to be a member of the ruling generation, a rule that did not apply to the warrior corps.

The most significant function of these councils was the administration of justice. This was carried out through arbitration by a court of the *kiama* assessors.[18] The primary purpose of the judicial process was to maintain peace and stability in society. Under customary law, there was no imprisonment, compensation being the main method of concluding most litigations. The choice of assessors involved in the hearing of a case depended very much on the type and number of people that it affected. Within the kinship group, the settlement of disputes was the responsibility of the head of the family or *muramati*. Depending upon the seriousness of the offence committed or the number of families involved, a *ndundu ya*

18. For the procedure followed in such cases and the amount of compensation payable, see Tate in the *Journal of African Society*, vol. 9, pp. 238-54; Cagnolo, op. cit., pp. 147-59; Hobley, *Bantu Beliefs and Magic*, pp. 215-19, 230-4; Routledge, op. cit., pp. 204-21; Kenyatta, op. cit., pp. 214-30; Kabetu, op. cit., pp. 94-101.

mucii, mbari or *muhiriga*, the private bench of the family or clan, would be assembled to settle a private dispute. However, matters involving members of different *mbari* were settled by the village council, or a bigger council, depending upon the seriousness of the dispute and the background of the litigants. The latter, however, had an important say in the proceedings, for it was they who requested members of the appropriate *kiama* to take action. Initially the disputants attempted to settle their differences privately, failing which they agreed to refer the case to the elders for arbitration. Their evidence, together with that of any witnesses, was then heard. After this the case was open to general discussion by those present. Normally the hearing was public and anyone could express an opinion on the points raised, or on the issue. Included in the audience were junior elders and even some of the warriors who wished to be acquainted with the legal procedure. Indeed, it was partly through attendance at such hearings that most people acquired experience and knowledge of the customary law. Finally, a smaller group, *ndundu ya kiama*, the inner consultative council, retired to consider judgement. The *ndundu* consisted of the senior elders but excluded anyone who had a direct or indirect interest in the case. Meanwhile, before the case could be heard, each litigant produced a goat as the court's fee and this was duly slaughtered and roasted during the *ndundu* session. The *ndundu* having arrived at a decision, the meat was then eaten and judgement pronounced.

If any of the aggrieved party felt dissatisfied with the verdict, he could appeal and the case was heard all over again. In such circumstances the elders who had heard the case initially co-opted other *athamaki* from other villages or *miaki*, who were requested to attend on an individual basis, there being no distinctions between the elders who constituted the village or ridge council. Obviously the litigant preferred to have his case heard by the senior elders whose knowledge of precedence and impartiality could be relied upon. It was common, therefore, for the famous ones to be in demand at all levels.

After the pronouncement of the judgement, the guilty party was expected to pay compensation within two days. And although the elders did not use power to enforce their judgement, it was common knowledge that they could resort to religious sanctions with dire consequences. Nothing was more feared than a public curse by the elders, some of whom were noted for being the highest ritual and ceremonial personalities in the land. Moreover, a person who persistently flouted the judgements of the elders got ostracized by society or, as an extreme measure, he had all his crops uprooted by angry neighbours. Close relatives of the culprit would also put a lot of moral pressure on the offender to pay compensation and, failing that, they would pay it themselves, other than risk the prospect of a public curse, the efficacy of which was not only expected to affect the culprits and their immediate families, but also their distant kinsmen. It was rarely, therefore, that a culprit deliberately disregarded the judgement of the elders, and in order to at least avoid a curse being pronounced on one, the decisions of these courts were obeyed.[19]

In a situation where the elders could not determine the guilty party, or if one of the parties persistently maintained his innocence, the normal course of action was to resort to trial by ordeal. The litigants would either be made to take an oath, or to lick a red-hot knife, or else the medicineman would use his skill to determine who was guilty. In the more serious cases, such as sorcery, theft and murder, the accused swore their innocence by killing a malegoat, called *kuringa thenge*. The litigants, who were invariably male (women did not take an oath in the Kikuyu traditional society) broke the limbs of a he-goat, at the same time declaring that their limbs, and those of their family, be broken likewise if they were telling lies. The sacrificial animal that was thus killed was not eaten but left in the bush to be devoured by hyenas. As a last measure, they were made to take the dreaded *githathi* oath, using a special stone used for the occasion. The *githathi* was a seven-holed object made of stone or clay. The accused passed several sticks through each hole seven times, while at the same time professing his innocence. Elders present wore *mukengeria* (*Commeline* species) sprigs to protect themselves against the potent *githathi* medicine. The *githathi* was such an object of dread and horror, and its efficacy was so much believed in that the accused would often rather plead guilty than be subjected to such an ordeal.[20] Habitual offenders, particularly if their crimes were of a serious nature, were publicly put to death by the *muingi* or *king'ore*—the people. Before a person could be publicly put to death, however, consent had to be granted

19. See notes on the *kiama* in KNA/PC/CP/1/1/1/.
20. Kenyatta, op. cit., pp. 224-5; Cagnolo, op. cit., pp. 152-3; Hobley, *Ethnology of A-Kamba*, pp. 139-43. Note that seven was a sacred number.

by his close relatives who, in any case, were the first to stone or set him on fire, depending upon the method of punishment. But for the lesser offences customary law decreed the appropriate compensation payable for each offence. Rules of precedence were particularly brought to bear on such cases. Theft was considered to be a serious crime, especially theft of livestock or honey, which for compensation purposes was comparable to causing bodily harm. Injury of a person, or theft of a goat or honey, were compensated for by paying ten goats and a *ngoima* (fatted ram). A much more serious offence was homicide. Compensation for it, however, depended upon the relation between the murderer and his victim, and also the victim's sex. Compensation for murder of a man was a hundred goats paid to the relatives, and ten *ngoima* for the elders, whereas for the murder of a woman it was thirty goats and three *ngoima* respectively. A small and rather interesting detail, no charge was preferred against a person who helped himself to cooked food, or any plants intended for replanting such as sweet potato vines or banana suckers.

It has been frequently mentioned that the various social segments and territorial divisions were under a *muthamaki*. It is time to examine how he was chosen and the extent of his power.[21] First, it cannot be over-emphasized that the *muthamaki* (spokesman) was no more than the chairman of a territorial unit or leader of his *riika*. His powers were very circumscribed and he could only act in accordance with the wishes of his peers who delegated power to him. He was not a chief; the idea of chiefs had no basis in the political institutions of the Kikuyu; indeed chiefs were a creation of the British administrators at the beginning of this century.[22] Dundas pinpointed this when he concluded: 'The history of the institution of these chiefs shows positively that they are mere creations of the Govt.'[23] Equally important was the manner in which a *muthamaki* emerged. There were no formal elections and the Kikuyu believed that *uthamaki nduoyagiruo iguru, uciaraguo na mundu*, a leader is born, not made.

From an early age, some of the boys displayed a flair for leadership. They asserted themselves and became chief organizers of the dances and the other exploits pertaining to young boys. This

21. 'Lambert, 1965,' pp. 100-6.
22. Routledge, op. cit., p. 195; Cagnolo, op. cit., p. 24; Dundas in the *Journal of the Royal Anthropological Institute*, vol. 45, 1915, p. 238.
23. See a review of chiefs and *ciama* by C. C. Dundas, 1912, in KNA/PC/CP 1/4/1/, pp. 61-77.

natural bent would not only be apparent, but recognized, by the time they neared initiation. It was, however, only after becoming junior warriors that their role was publicly acknowledged by being created captains of their army contingents. If they acquitted themselves honourably at this stage, they became the leaders of the senior warriors on their promotion to this grade. As *athamaki* in the warrior corps they wielded a lot of power and a distinguished career led to considerable respect and greatly influenced a man's status on promotion to eldership. This, however, was not always the case; the qualities essential to a war leader were not necessarily applicable to the elder status. In fact, some outstanding warriors failed as elders.

The emergence of and recognition as a *muthamaki* was hence a slow process and no single qualification was decisive—it was the general consensus of opinion that mattered. Self-assertion, courage, self-confidence and diligence were important assets for a warrior, while wisdom, tact, self-control and wide experience were some of the qualities looked for in an elder who aspired to be a *muthamaki*.

As seen above, the elders specialized in particular fields—some became important in judicial matters (*athamaki a cira or aciri*), others in ceremonial rites (*athamaki a kirira*) and still others became general or political leaders (*athamaki a bururi*) with no special responsibility. All of them, nevertheless, were just 'the prominent personalities in a democratic system, and there was nothing hereditary about *uthamaki* . . . '[24] *Athamaki* were consequently neither chiefs nor kings, rather, they were simply the first, or leading, personalities among peers. Moreover, their role was specific and rigidly controlled by the other peers. They were not expected to negotiate or make treaties without the consent of the rest of the elders and the attempt by a few *athamaki* to be and act as chiefs landed them, and their British supporters, into serious trouble. This was the genesis of many of the administrative problems encountered by the early British rulers, who ignored the traditional leaders, and thus aroused resentment and hostility. A more serious blunder, however, was that nonentities, including some who were not even Kikuyu, let alone elders, were created into chiefs simply because they had ingratiated themselves with the British by being porters or presenting them with gifts.[25] Others had acquired 'chits'

24. 'Lambert, 1965', pp. 105-6.
25. A notable example was Kibarabara, a Maasai, who had served the

from a passing and obliging *Mzungu* (European), and this was taken by later arrivals as a sign of friendship to the white man, who reciprocated accordingly. One of the so-called chiefs, Wangu Makeri, was a woman who became a chief simply because Karuri spent his nights at her house on his way to Murang'a, the district headquarters.[26] Mostly such chiefs became extremely unpopular, particularly when they had to enforce unpopular measures. In their turn, they upheld their authority by autocratic and high-handed methods thus creating a lot of misunderstanding and bad blood on both sides. And as the colonial rule gradually entrenched itself, it seemed as if the chiefs had backed the right horse and the Kikuyu, realizing that change was inevitable, grudgingly came to terms with the new order. In so doing some of their traditional values and norms—such as their egalitarian outlook, the emphasis on hard work and self-assertion—stood them in good stead. They gradually adapted themselves and acquired some of the techniques necessary in the reconciliation of the old and the new. It was perhaps some of these traditional features that have made them play such a significant role in the political and economic life of Kenya.

To conclude, social and political interaction among the Kikuyu were based on descent groups and the age system or *mariika*. Or as they put it, *Nyumba na riika itiumagwo*—one cannot contract out of one's family or age set. While the descent group was the primary factor governing social relationships, the age system was of equal importance. The system of age differentiation, and in particular the organization of adult males into age sets, acted as a bridge which enabled individuals to become members of a wider community that surpassed the kinship or territorial relations. Recruitment into a new age set coincided with an individual's transition from child-hood to adulthood. This phenomenon was marked by an important *rite de passage*—circumcision. The initiation rituals dramatized the symbolic 'death' of childhood, and the 'birth' of adulthood. Childhood had tied the young to their family, their lineage or locality; adulthood, on the other hand, flung the adolescents into the willing arms of the community as a whole. Life, thereafter,

government as leader of Maasai levies against the Kikuyu and as an office boy at Fort Hall. See autobiographical notes in KNA/PC/CP/1/1/1.

26. Scorn and malicious rumours were heaped upon Wangu. She was accused of behaving like a man by dancing the *kibata* naked. No doubt her appointment outraged the conservatives.

was a delicate balancing of the demands imposed on an adult by these two sources of allegiance, and civic vigilance ensured that any conflicts therein were reconciled, for the general good of society. Consequently, initiation was not a private concern but a public and communal rite. It was of crucial importance to the community as a whole because it conferred social status upon the initiates. To the Kikuyu, initiation was of fundamental importance. 'It stands', Prins has rightly noted, 'for the whole values embodied in the age-class system with all its "educational, social, moral and religious implications". It is a *conditio sine qua non* for being a real Kikuyu, and the visible and outward sign of adhering to the tribal culture.'[27] It is not surprising, then, that failure to recognize this fact landed the missionaries into a quagmire of recrimination with their adherents, when the converted were demanded to renounce female circumcision or else face excommunication.[28]

The majority of traditional African societies believed in the continuity of life, in life after death and a community of interest between the living, the dead and the generations yet unborn.[29] This fundamental and three dimensional concept gave these communities not only coherence, but also a deep sense of history and tradition. This concept deeply influenced their day-to-day religious, social and political life, and hence the widespread view that each community was founded by an ancestor, or a group of ancestors, from whom the ethnic group derived its possessions and status. Besides, the ancestors were believed to have established the basic pattern of life for all time which could be modified or adapted, but could not be entirely altered lest the ancestors became offended. Consequently, reverence for the ancestors was uniquely important and led, in some cases, to what appear to be ancestor worship. The fear of 'what the ancestors would say' was, therefore, an ever-present consideration as well as a most powerful and effective political sanction among traditional African societies. Seen in this light, the total rejection of female initiation demanded by the missionaries was virtually impossible at the time, for its renunciation would have been tantamount to rejecting the tribe's cultural tradition, or charter of life, which had been handed down from the

27.   Prins, op. cit., p. 102.
28.   C. J. Rosberg and J. Nottingham, op. cit., chap. 4.
29.   Kenyatta, op. cit., dedication (p. v); K. O. Dike and J. F. A. Ajayi, 'African Historiography', in David L. Sills (ed.), *International Encyclopedia of Social Sciences*, New York, 1968, vol. 6, pp. 394-9.

ancestors throughout the generations, in exchange for a dubious Victorian morality and set of values. For this reason alone, renunciation was unthinkable, particularly by the more traditionally-minded Christians. With the ever present and gnawing fear of 'what the ancestors would say' in their minds, it is understandable that there was a major revolt within the ranks of adherents of the Church of Scotland Mission.

There were other considerations too. Circumcision was not merely a mutilation of the body, as the missionaries would have had the adherents believe, but also a vehicle for the transmission and perpetuation of the norms and values of the Kikuyu cultural traditions. Through it individuals gained membership to an age set which provided them with 'a new focus of identification with the society, a new frame of reference through which they relate themselves to the total society and identify themselves with its values and symbols'.[30] Furthermore, the grouping of adult males into age sets provided a system of ranking on the basis of which important duties—such as military, police and judicial—were allocated. This, then, was the only known method in the exercise of authority and the regulation of public affairs; it virtually constituted the Kikuyu system of government, and ensured political organization and interaction with their attendant duties and privileges.

Besides their religious and educational functions, the age sets played another key role. In a society that was uncentralized and highly egalitarian, they had an integrative function. Finally, the generation and age sets were, as Lambert pointed out, 'a series of dynasties with names of which important happenings in the tribal history may be associated. They take the place of reigns and to some extent dates in the histories of literate peoples.'[31] In the event, they serve as a useful guide in the attempt to establish a framework of chronology for the history of the Kikuyu.

30. Eisenstadt, *African Age Groups*, p. 107.
31. Lambert, MS, op. cit., p. 384.

Chapter 6

PRELUDE TO BRITISH RULE

THE course of Kikuyu history was radically altered by the momentous events that took place in the last quarter of the nineteenth century. By the mid-nineteenth century, only a handful of Kikuyu had managed to reach the coast, while others had had a glimpse of the outside world by coming across the white man and the Swahili nearer home in the Kamba villages. This trend of increasing contact with the outside world was one of the chief features of the second half of the nineteenth century and culminated in the colonization of the Kikuyu country by the white man. The Kikuyu were steadily drawn into the orbit of Swahili commercial activity and enterprise, a process that was quickened by the decline of the Kamba commercial empire which had reached its nadir by the 1870s. Hard on the heels of the Swahili commercial intrusion into the hinterland came the Imperial British East Africa Company (hereafter IBEAC), founded by philanthropists, businessmen and empire builders, and which was granted a royal charter in 1888. In turn, the IBEAC paved the way for the subsequent establishment of British administration, from 1895 onwards, and thereby opened the way for all the new forces that were to influence the development of the Kikuyu in this century. Administrators, settlers, traders and missionaries poured into the Kikuyu country bringing with them what was, in the Kikuyu's eyes, a new and strange way of life with its sometimes incomprehensible demands and ideas. Gradually the Kikuyu realized that they had to come to terms with the new order and the period between the last decade of the nineteenth century and the end of the First World War witnessed the attempt, on their part, to adjust themselves to rapidly changing circumstances and environment.

The attitude of the Kikuyu to all the newcomers—the Swahili, the Arabs and the Europeans—was largely influenced by the initial behaviour of the Swahili caravans that had penetrated into Kikuyu-land. Traditionally, the Kikuyu are a hospitable people who believe that '*mugeni ni rui*', a visitor is like a river that passes on. They were particularly hospitable to the coastal traders because of the Kikuyu attitude towards trade. By the time the coastal traders reached the borders of Kikuyuland, the Kikuyu had had a long tradition of trading activities with their neighbours. They were very much aware of the profits that would accrue from having direct trade relations with the coastal traders instead of having to go through the Kamba middlemen.

Cege wa Kibiru, the famous and greatest Kikuyu seer, had apparently forewarned the Kikuyu that strangers would come to Kikuyuland from out of the big water to their east. These would be peculiar people; they would look like the small white frogs because of their oddly-coloured skins, their dress would resemble the wings of butterflies, they would carry sticks that spit fire and that they would also bring an iron snake which would belch out fire and as it travelled to and between the big waters to the east and west. Clearly these were no ordinary people and Kibiru specifically forbade warriors from attacking them because spears and arrows would be no match for the stick that spat fire, nor could they make an impression on the iron snake.[1]

Although it is difficult to assess the significance of these prophecies, it is nevertheless clear that Cege wa Kibiru was a remarkable person and medicineman, a man of undoubted foresight. But it should be remembered that a few intrepid and enterprising Kikuyu traders had journeyed to the coast, accompanying the Kamba, as early as the 1840s. Others had travelled to Kambaland where they had met coastal traders and possibly the white explorer, Krapf.[2] These Kikuyu traders must have talked about their experiences at the coast and in Kambaland, and it is conceivable that Kibiru—who had many clients, was greatly respected and widely travelled in Kikuyuland—must have heard of the activities of the Swahili, the Arabs and, perhaps, the Europeans. It would not have been too difficult for him to foresee what was likely to happen in the near future, for it must

1. Kenyatta, op. cit., pp. 41-4, summary. See also 'KHT', pp. 301-2 for warnings from another seer.
2. Krapf to CMS, 11 September 1852 and 30 August 1853 in CMS Archives, CA5/016/M2, pp. 454-5 and 519-20 respectively. See, also, Krapf's ournal for November/December 1849 in CMS, CA5/016/M2.

be remembered that the coastal traders were beginning to penetrate the interior from Mombasa.

Yet, despite their traditional hospitality and value for trade, and Kibiru's entreaties, they were hostile to traders and did their best to stop them entering their country as early as 1870s. And even accepting that the coastal traders were wont to spread false and alarming stories about the interior people, in order to discourage the Europeans from venturing into the hinterland, it was evident that fighting between the Kikuyu and the foreigners had become common by the 1880s. Thomson, for example, heard stories in 1883 of 'some bitter lessons' that the Kikuyu had been taught by the traders 'in several fearful massacres at Ngongo and other places'.[3] That there were increasing quarrels between the traders and the Kikuyu is borne out, too, by the genuine fear that appears to have been exhibited by the porters as they approached the borders of Kikuyu country. What, then, changed the attitude of the Kikuyu to the newcomers so decisively?

There were many grounds for friction. The truculence of some of the warriors was a contributory factor, in spite of the elders' efforts to control them. On the other hand, the behaviour of the caravans was a major cause of friction—the failure to pay for goods, the propensity to forage for food in the Kikuyu *shambas* (cultivated fields), the tendency to take sides in local affairs, and the attempt to overawe the Kikuyu by the Maxim gun.[4] In any case, the coastal traders were generally noted for their outrageous behaviour in the interior of East Africa as a whole, and one would not expect them to have behaved differently in their dealings with the Kikuyu. But the most damaging factor must have been the wild stories spread by the Kamba, who had for a long time emphasized the hostility and treacherousness, and even cannibalism, of the people of the interior, in their effort to dissuade the coastal traders from up-country travel. The interior people were warned, in turn, that the coastal people—the *Comba*, *Makorobai* or *Thukumu*—were human specimens best left alone. From the outset, therefore, each group was suspicious of the other and tended to behave accordingly. The Kikuyu, in particular, looked upon the white man with curiosity mingled with awe and fear. Indeed, after Teleki and von Höhnel had traversed Kikuyuland, many rams were sacrificed because some

3. Thomson, op. cit., p. 306.
4. 'KHT', p. 271.

believed that these two were gods, and, according to their religion, one had to make a sacrifice if one saw god in person. The early contact between the Kikuyu and the coastal traders was not a happy one, and it grew worse as the nineteenth century drew to a close. The hostility of the Kikuyu to newcomers, however, should not be exaggerated, as much depended on the behaviour of the individual caravans as on the temperament of the local inhabitants. Despite the chorus of the 'inveterate hostility and treachery'[5] of the Kikuyu, it is significant that this did not deter trade between the two, as one would have expected if the situation was as bad as it was painted. Caravans of 1,200 to 1,500 men were a common sight at Ngong, and all of them expected to get their provisions from the Kikuyu.[6] Of greater importance, however, is the fact that a number of the Swahili caravan headmen and guides were ivory traders in their own right and knew the interior very well. Jumbe Kimemeta, Teleki's guide, had frequented the Maasailand and the Kikuyu country in this capacity. Thomson had met him at Mianzini 'fairly well loaded with ivory from regions never before reached by a coast caravan'.[7] And significantly, he did his best to dissuade Thomson from returning to the coast by the Kamba route.[8] It was from him, too, that rumours of impending Kikuyu attacks on Teleki's caravan originated, with devastating effect on the morale of the porters.[9] He had in any case been most sceptical of Teleki and von Höhnel's caravan ever being able to pass through Kikuyu-land.[10] Without wanting to betray his reasons to the Hungarian travellers, Kimemeta tried his best to keep away their caravan from visiting his trading haunts, from where the bulk of his ivory came. He had in fact been to these parts only a few years before, perhaps at the time of Thomson's journey.[11] Certainly the head of Kimemeta's caravan, Kijanja, a man from Tanga, even knew the Kikuyu language,[12] as did Juma Mussa of Teleki's caravan.[13] This seems to suggest that these Swahili traders were frequent

5. Lugard, vol. 1, op. cit., p. 327.
6. Thomson, op. cit., pp. 307, 572.
7. Thomson, op. cit., p. 571.
8. ibid., pp. 572-3.
9. von Höhnel, op. cit., pp. 326-7.
10. ibid., p. 296.
11. G. K. James, 'History ya . . . Athungu Aria Mambire Gukinya Gikuyu-ini Tene' in 'Barlow Papers'.
12. von Höhnel, op. cit., pp. 289-310.
13. ibid., p. 291.

visitors to the borders of Kikuyuland, not only in search of food but also of ivory. It was primarily for this reason that they were not at all keen to see their lucrative trading haunts opened up to potential competitors, and naturally they took up the Kamba chorus of the hostility of wild people in the interior, particularly the Kikuyu and the Maasai, in order to keep out the Europeans.

It is ironical that every European traveller seemed to believe that 'Fischer had had to fight every inch of his way' through Kikuyuland,[14] when in actual fact he never went across Kikuyuland, but based his reports on rumours spread by his own caravanmen. His reports borrowed from the experiences of Krapf in Thagicu.[15]

Newcomers who had close contact with the Kikuyu do not support such stories. Richard Crawshay, who was an administrative official among the Kikuyu, got to the heart of the matter in his conclusion that travellers in 'Kikuyu owe any rough treatment they have to complain of either to their ignorance of "savoir faire" . . . or much more frequently to the secret misconduct of their followers'.[16] A similar conclusion was drawn by von Höhnel and Teleki after traversing the Kikuyu country, despite the bad reputation of the Kikuyu and the fact that they had to fight on three separate occasions. Their fortunes varied from ridge to ridge; in some they met with implacable and hostile opposition, as they had been led to expect, while in others they were amazed by the assistance offered them, especially by the Kikuyu guides such as Mucia Muriithi and Gathu Waruiru. Teleki and von Höhnel were 'always able in Kikuyuland to secure faithful guides who would even warn [them] of the designs of their people against [them]'[17] and the guides' 'honesty and faithfulness to [them] in the midst of their own people struck [von Höhnel and Teleki] as being amongst the most remarkable facts of [their] journey through Kikuyuland'.[18] This view was echoed by Mackinder, who found his guides remarkably loyal to him 'in spite of considerable temptations'.[19] Teleki and von Höhnel did not, however, minimize the difficulties encountered in traversing Kikuyuland, and it is in spite of the

14. von Höhnel, op. cit., p. 287.
15. Fischer, op. cit., p. 98.
16. Crawshay, op. cit., p. 39.
17. von Höhnel, op. cit., p. 319.
18. ibid., p. 338.
19. Mackinder, op. cit., p. 457.

difficulties posed by the Kikuyu and their 'excitable and restless nature' that von Höhnel concluded:

> They were all so very friendly that we could not help thinking that the traders who had had such difficulties in these parts had only themselves to blame, probably because in their nervousness they always fired a few shots with a view to overawing the people before breaking up camp.[20]

To Teleki and von Höhnel, travelling through Kikuyuland did not seem to be fraught with any special danger, nor was it any more dangerous than in any other part of the country. On the contrary, they found the Kikuyu less hostile than they had been led to expect, and in spite of their having had to fight the Kikuyu at Mbari ya Minja in Riara, in Mang'u and just north of North Mathioya river, and perhaps in Gaturi.[21] It did not pass unnoticed that on two occasions warriors who had snatched trade goods from the caravan were caught and publicly flogged on the spot by the Kikuyu themselves.[22]

The overriding factor governing the relations between the Kikuyu and the newcomers was the attitude generated between the two groups. The Kikuyu were understandably suspicious of, and they even feared, the newcomers; while the coastal traders, European travellers included, believed that force was the only language that the Africans understood. Twice Kimemeta advocated that tough measures be taken against the Kikuyu[23] while von Höhnel believed that 'to employ force is the only means of producing the necessary impression' of being feared.[24] It is not at all surprising, then, that the Kikuyu experience of the coastal caravans, led initially by the Swahili and the Arabs, was unpleasant from the outset. Yet, it was on the very people who had acquired such a bad reputation in the eyes of the Kikuyu that the white man depended upon mainly, for guides, spokesmen and porters. If the Kikuyu and the white man approached each other with suspicion, their contact all but proved their worst forebodings about one another. The experiences of Thomson, and surprisingly even of von Höhnel and Teleki, their own conclusions to the contrary not withstanding, reinforced the 'evil reputation' of the Kikuyu as hitherto spread by

20. von Höhnel, op. cit., p. 298.
21. ibid., pp. 318-21, 329-31, 339-43.
22. ibid., pp. 294 and 310.
23. ibid., pp. 320-1, 343.
24. ibid., pp. 336 7.

the coastal traders. In the event, this had a significant and a far-reaching repercussion, for it set the tone of the relationship which was to develop between the Kikuyu and all the other newcomers, white or brown. The Kikuyu came to look upon all newcomers with the greatest suspicion and fear, while the white man saw hostility and treachery written on every Kikuyu face. Gregory, travelling on the northern Mathira border in 1893, was warned by a Kikuyu elder that he would not be allowed to enter Mathira because:

> Some white men came some few harvests back to our friends away there at Karthuri,[25] they stormed the villages, they seized what food they wanted, and then burnt the rest. When the elders asked for payment they were shot, while the young men were taken away as slaves into the land of the Masai, and we have heard of them no more.[26]

The reputation of the Kikuyu as a 'thoroughly bad lot' was, however, clinched by the relations prevailing between them and the IBEAC on the southern frontier after 1890. Three incidents highlight this mood—the evacuation of the Dagoretti Fort by George Wilson, the death of Maktubu, and the arrest of Waiyaki. Buganda was the centre of attraction for the IBEAC and for all practical purposes, Machakos and Dagoretti, established in 1889 and 1890 respectively, were built to provision the caravans bound for Buganda. For the Kikuyu to be harrassed by a passing caravan was one thing, to have a permanent station on their doorstep quite another. Already they had had a foretaste of what was to come from Thomson; the Swahili caravans had taught them some bitter lessons at Ngong; and Teleki and von Höhnel, passing through their country, had given some of them a thorough mauling only three or so years before. These episodes were too fresh in the minds of the Kikuyu for them to have accepted the establishment of a company station in their midst with equanimity. Given a strong administrator capable of controlling the caravans and the ill-disciplined soldiery, the situation might have improved, but none of the company's agents—Wilson, Purkiss or Nelson—was capable of such firmness. Purkiss, young and inexperienced, was only meant to be an assistant, yet he remained in charge until Hall took over.

25. Gaturi in Metumi.
26. Gregory, op. cit., p. 158. This was undoubtedly a reference to Teleki's and von Höhnel's expedition when a fight occurred and Teleki's caravan captured 90 heads of cattle, 1,300 sheep and goats, burnt villages and took 19 prisoners. See von Höhnel, op. cit., pp. 339-43.

And Nelson's brief rule was marked by a mutiny of his garrison in 1892. Lugard had set them a good example by entering into blood brotherhood and making a peace treaty with a number of the Kikuyu along the southern border when he established a fort at Kiawariua, Dagoretti, in 1890. He had also steered clear of being embroiled in local squabbles.[27] His approach could have ensured a good foundation for the future, but no sooner had he left for Uganda than George Wilson, on the advice of Ernest Gedge, withdrew to Machakos on 30 March 1891 after pressure to leave became too much. On his way to the coast Wilson met Leith's caravan at Kikumbuliu, and with fresh reinforcement he returned to Kiawariua only to find the station razed to the ground by the Kikuyu and all his goods, which he had buried, dug up.[28] Thereupon Wilson demanded a daily payment of fifty goats as compensation for the looted goods, free labour of three hundred men to rebuild the destroyed fort, and he also enlisted two hundred porters.[29] However, this only poured oil on the flames and Wilson was once again forced to evacuate Kiawariua on the advice of Eric Smith, who had arrived there on 13 June 1891. Wilson reached Machakos on 19 June 1891.

The sudden change of attitude on the part of the Kikuyu was partly brought about by the rowdy behaviour of the ill-disciplined troops. There had been no amity, however, as the Kikuyu were still aggressively hostile to outside interference with their affairs. Several reasons sparked off Kikuyu-IBEAC hostilities at the end of 1890 and early 1891. According to eye witnesses, the Kikuyu warriors who had been engaged as porters absconded with their luggage *en route*, or disappeared immediately after pay, which appears to have been given in advance sometimes. However, the basic cause of dissatisfaction was that many of them had been recruited by force.[30] The company *askari* (soldiers) attempted to arrest the deserters without much success. On one occasion fighting broke out when the *askari* captured livestock and burnt houses while attempting to arrest Warari Njuni, one of the deserters.[31] This is confirmed by Kinyanjui; he reported to Hall that in attempting to arrest the conscripted warriors the *askari* raided 'Kicheka's' kraal but they

27. M. Perham, *The Diaries of Lord Lugard*, vol. 1, pp. 316-44.
28. 'KHT', pp. 267, 271-2, 279, 280 and 282.
29. Lugard, vol. 2, pp. 535-6.
30. 'KHT', pp. 269, 281 and 304.
31. ibid., p. 271.

were driven off and one of them killed in the struggle. For this, 'Kicheka' had to pay a fine of a hundred goats.[32] The warriors were upset by this and decided to do their best to stop the company's employees from fetching water from the Dagoretti or Nairobi rivers. They adopted unpleasant tactics, such as waylaying them, or besieging the fort, and two *askari* were killed while fetching water. Wilson felt he had no option but to evacuate Kiawariua as he did not have sufficient forces to embark on a punitive expedition.[33]

There were other reasons which made the Kikuyu to feel injured and the behaviour of the *askari* towards local women was a major one. The *askari* are reported to have harassed the women by intimidating them, and even sometimes attempting rape, whereupon the victims would raise the traditional danger-signal (*mbu*) and all the warriors at hand would assemble in full battle array. Such incidents were all too common: Hall reports that two of his men, who were supposed to be herding the company's goats and sheep, tried to rape a woman on 25 October 1892. She resisted and one of them shot her, she died two days later.[34]

Theft, too, was to remain a problem: the soldiers could not resist the temptation of either foraging in the *shambas* or else forcibly taking food. And Kinyanjui recounts another episode involving seven Swahili soldiers who had been sent on an errand to Machakos and who stole Kamwingo's goats. In the fighting that followed five of the looters were killed.[35] Pillaging of the crops in the *shambas* was a sure way of provoking the wrath of the Kikuyu women, who did their best to goad their menfolk into retaliating. As the situation worsened it became the habit for women to raise the danger-signal the moment they saw the soldiers near their *shambas*, as much for their safety as for averting theft of their foodstuffs. Predictably

32. See Kinyanjui's account of George Wilson's occupation of Kiawariua (Dagoretti) in Hall's diary for 1894.
33. G. K. James, op. cit.; 'KHT', p. 271. Compare this with Lugard and MacDonald's accounts in MacDonald, op. cit., chap. 8 and Lugard, vol. 2, pp. 534-7.
34. Hall's diary, 25 October 1892. Hall gave a slightly different version to his father—two *askari*, he wrote, 'went off foraging for sweet potatoes in the natives' land and when a woman remonstrated with them one of them cutely using the other man's rifle shot her and left her for dead'. See Hall to Col. Hall, 22 October 1892. See, also, 'KHT', p. 271.
35. Kinyanjui's account, op. cit.; Gedge's diary quoted by H. B. Thomas in 'George Wilson and Dagoretti Fort', *Uganda Journal*, Kampala, vol. 23, 1959, pp. 173-77.

enough this resulted in fights between the *askari* and the warriors. From February to June 1894, no less than four theft cases were reported to Hall ranging from a seizure of goods or food to the 'levying of black mail' by his interpreter.[36] The behaviour of the soldiers at Dagoretti and Fort Smith was not an isolated case; Jackson's caravan was accused of stealing crops and violating women among the Kamba.[37] Besides, the soldiers got themselves embroiled in local squabbles at the instigation of those Kikuyu who were using the company for their own interest, particularly those living in the vicinity of the fort, who were not slow to seize the opportunity to settle old scores, or to enrich themselves.[38] In this connection Kinyanjui relates that, prior to Wilson's first evacuation of Kiawariua, a certain Kamau persuaded eighty of Wilson's men to accompany him to Ruiru to recover livestock, which he alleged had previously been stolen from him. The expedition, which went under the pretext of buying food, was successful and returned with a lot of stock.[39] There was, therefore, enough tinder that only required a spark to set off a conflagration.

These episodes demonstrate not only the type of soldiers that manned Kiawariua (and Fort Smith later), but also the state of indiscipline tolerated by their superiors. Purkiss and Nelson, for example, were faced by a serious breakdown of their administrative machinery. They had the truculent Kikuyu on the one hand and a mutinous garrison on the other.[40] Drunkenness was and remained a serious problem, something that had even troubled Lugard when he was building the Kiawariua fort in October 1890. It became such a vexing problem that Purkiss had to plead with his superiors to send him ten to twelve Somali soldiers whom he hoped would be able to prevent his men from buying *tembo*, the local beer. As he argued, 'if men obtain it, there generally is trouble either with the Native or Swahilis themselves'.[41] The company was also facing financial difficulties and in 1892 it decreed that Fort Smith and Machakos had to be self-supporting, a policy that was effected by

36. Hall's diary, February to June 1894.
37. Perham (ed.), op. cit., vol. 1, pp. 290, 299-300.
38. 'KHT', pp. 280 and 282.
39. Kinyanjui's account, op. cit.
40. Purkiss to IBEAC's Administrator, 27 December 1892; Sir Gerald Portal to Lord Rosebery, 31 January 1893 in FO2/57.
41. Purkiss to IBEAC's Administrator, 28 February 1893 in FO2/57. Ainsworth also records that his *askari* went to buy food, got drunk and fired on Ndengi and his party. See Ainsworth's diary for 15 October 1898.

a series of punitive expeditions and raids for food or stock. This dealt a death-blow to the Kikuyu-IBEAC relations. Lugard aptly summarized the situation by observing that 'Owing largely, I believe, to the want of discipline in the passing caravans, whose men robbed the crops and otherwise made themselves troublesome, the people became estranged, and presently murdered several porters.'[42]

With the final evacuation of Kiawariua station, the Kikuyu thought that their troubles were now over. They failed to realize that Kikuyuland was too important to the company to be abandoned so easily and they witnessed with dismay the return of Purkiss and Eric Smith towards the end of 1891, who came back with a strong force which defiantly pitched their tents in Waiyaki's *kihingo* at Mbugici, where they stayed until the new fort, on which Captain Smith bestowed his own name, was completed. The fort was built on the site where Lugard had erected his first camp and overlooking Waiyaki's village.[43] The Kikuyu-IBEAC relations deteriorated further, largely because of the machinations of the Kikuyu collaborators and the need for the new station to be self-supporting. It was the interaction of these two factors that led to the death of Maktubu and the subsequent arrest of Waiyaki.

The company was in the habit of dispatching Maktubu to the Kikuyu villages to buy or forage for food. Yet Maktubu, a former slave from Malawi, was in many ways the least suited for this delicate task, as events were to prove. Undoubtedly he was one of the most reliable and experienced *askari* at Fort Smith; he had seen service thrice with Thomson, and once with von Höhnel. He was highly thought of as steadfast, courageous, intelligent and hardworking, but unfortunately he was endowed with 'an utter absence of tact in dealing with the men under him'.[44] He had a violent temperament which made him intolerable to work with.[45] During Thomson's expedition through Maasailand he had several quarrels and on one occasion he had a 'bloodthirsty quarrel' with Martin, whom he almost shot. And on Teleki's expedition he 'quarrelled perpetually'

42. Lugard, vol. 2, op. cit., p. 535.
43. For an authoritative account of subsequent events, see 'The Passing of Waiyaki' by Brig. Gen. H. H. Austin, probably written in 1929. It has not proved possible to find out where it was originally published but a carelessly typed copy is in the hands of Mr. T. M. Waiyaki, to whom I am grateful. See also 'KHT', pp. 267, 272 and 280.
44. Thomson, op. cit., p. 20.
45. von Höhnel, op. cit., pp. 33-4.

with Dualla.[46] He was, for this reason, an unfortunate choice to be entrusted with the food-buying expeditions.

In August 1892, Kamaru Wamagata, one of the Kikuyu collaborators, induced Maktubu to accompany him to Githiga—known to the company as Guruguru—to demand repayment of dowry from Rimui and Kiarii Gathura. Kamaru had married Wanjiku Gathura, who had since left him when their marriage failed and Wanjiru had subsequently married a Kamba. Under the pretext of going to buy food, and against orders as it turned out, Maktubu and Kamaru were accompanied by fifteen soldiers and several Kikuyu. On arrival at Gathura's home they peremptorily demanded repayment of the dowry, otherwise threatening to take the goats by force.[47] Their threat was duly carried out—they seized the goats and a war-cry was sounded and fighting ensued. Outnumbered and far from Fort Smith, all but a few of the group were killed and of those who escaped was an *askari*, Abdulla bin Omar, who took refuge with Wangengi (a vowed friend of the company from the neighbourhood), who provided him with escorts to take him back to Purkiss.[48] Maktubu was not, therefore, murdered while buying food, as Omar reported and as the officials came to believe.[49] Neither was the 'murder' planned by Waiyaki, who knew nothing about it at all. For the alleged outrages, the company administration dispatched an expedition of five companies—under Pringle, Foaker, Austin, MacDonald and Purkiss—to punish the Githunguri people.[50] This took place from 12 to 14 August 1892.

Meantime Waiyaki was nonplussed by the sudden turn of events, and particularly the billeting of the company soldiery on his doorstep. He feared, and not without reason, that he might be punished in retaliation for the sins of the Kikuyu warriors who had had the audacity to ransack and raze down Kiawariua. He was apprehensive, too, lest his livestock be confiscated. To allay some of the likely consequences, he dispersed part of his flocks and herds to an area near Muguga under Githagui, his son, while another lot was sent to the Mbari ya Gikonyo in Githunguri under Munyua,

46. Thomson, op. cit., pp. 284-5, 296; and von Höhnel, op. cit., pp. 201-2.
47. G. K. James, op. cit.; 'KHT', pp. 273, 275, 280-1.
48. Lugard reported that seven out of eleven *askari* were killed and Austin six out of ten. See Perham (ed.), op. cit., vol. 3, pp. 377-80; Lugard, op. cit., vol. 2, p. 537; and Austin, op. cit.
49. MacDonald, op. cit., p. 115; Perham (ed)., op. cit., vol. 3, p. 377.
50. 'KHT', pp. 273-4 and 280-1.

his other son.[51] For a while Waiyaki's forebodings proved quite unwarranted, for Purkiss soon after accepted to help out the Kikuyu when in May 1892 the Maasai launched a large raid and seemed to take all before them. To avoid total defeat, the Kikuyu appealed to Purkiss for help and, reinforced by the Company forces, they were able to launch a counter-attack on 23 May 1892. The Maasai were no match for the guns and consequently were defeated at Gicamu's near Muguga, where they were caught jubilantly carousing their success.[52] This offer of aid contributed more than perhaps anything else, albeit temporarily, to the allaying of Kikuyu fears towards the Company. The Maktubu fiasco less than three months later, therefore, was embarrassing and unfortunate, coming when it did.

Despite the elaborate precautions taken by the company officials to ensure a surprise attack on the Githunguri people, Waiyaki had somehow managed to get the details of the planned punitive expedition. He had no wish to see his livestock impounded together with those of the culprits who had murdered Maktubu, and it is only natural, too, that he should have given a timely warning to Gikonyo Maagu, his *riika* mate and the man who had temporarily harboured his livestock, to the astonishment and exasperation of the punitive expedition. As Austin summed it up later:

> The expedition was disappointing in one respect and that was our failure to capture herds of cattle and flocks of sheep which the Wandorobo were known to possess in large numbers. We secured no cattle and only fifty or sixty goats and sheep. For this we learnt later we had to thank Waiyaki who had by some means obtained news of the impending punitive expedition and sent out warnings hot-foot to his Wandorobo relatives.[53]

The expedition, which was guided by Kinyanjui and Muiruri, discovered that prior to their arrival the Githunguri people had hidden their livestock in the adjoining forests. A captured woman, Nyagitathuru Muriithi, told them that they had been warned by Waiyaki, who had sent a messenger. The company officials had neither the resources nor perhaps the time for a prolonged campaign in the inaccessible forests and where poisoned arrows would have been at their most effective. On the afternoon of the third day,

51. 'KHT', p. 272.
52. ibid., pp. 241, 244, 245, 246, 269 and 272-3.
53. Austin, op. cit., Austin makes reference to Dorobo because Githunguri is one of the areas where they had abandoned hunting and taken to the Kikuyu way of life.

14 August 1892, the expedition returned to Fort Smith, having burnt about 30 villages and 'spoilt all their crops besides shooting every armed man [they] saw'.[54] And on their return to the fort, Waiyaki, who had been drinking beer at Mbari ya Mutiria's, came to Fort Smith apparently on his own initiative.[55] The encounter between Purkiss and Waiyaki did not go well and their tempers quickly wore thin. Waiyaki was drunk and Purkiss furious with him for sabotaging the expedition. A row flared up and a scuffle ensued during which Waiyaki was wounded in the head with his own sword, which he had drawn from its sheath to attack Purkiss. Waiyaki was soon overpowered and 'handcuffed to the flagstaff with a chain around his neck as an additional safeguard and in this state spent the night in the fort square'.[56] On the following day a group of nineteen or twenty 'lesser chiefs' reluctantly agreed to come to the fort to discuss the fate of Waiyaki. They are reported to have concurred with the decision of the company officials to take him to Mombasa to be tried by the Administrator General of the IBEAC. The efforts of Waiyaki's father, Hinga, to have his son released went unheeded, and on 17 August 1892 he was marched towards the coast 'in chains under an escort of Indians with fixed bayonets'.[57] But Waiyaki never reached Mombasa: he died and was buried at Kibwezi *en route* to the coast.

The role of Waiyaki in the events of 1891-2 was very much misunderstood by the company officials, just as it has been misunderstood by the nationalist propagandists in this century. He was neither the 'scheming rogue'—breathing treachery, fire and brimstone—of the company officials, nor was he the martyr of the nationalist cause.[58] His conduct right from the beginning demonstrates that he was genuinely interested in cementing his friendship with the white man. As early as 1887-8, and though more of an

54. Austin, op. cit.
55. It is not entirely clear whether Waiyaki had been summoned by Purkiss or not. My informants alleged that he had been summoned.
56. Austin, op. cit. Oral traditions agree completely with the written sources on the sequence of events at this point. See 'KHT', pp. 267-8, 273-4, 275, 281, 282 and 283.
57. Austin, op. cit.
58. Waiyaki has become a martyr of the nationalist cause and one of the songs composed during the Mau Mau days describes him thus:

Andu aitu Waiyaki niakuire	Countrymen Waiyaki died
Na agitutigira kirumi	And left us a death-bed curse
Ati ithaka ici tutikendie	That we should never sell this land
Na ithui no guciheyana.	But we are giving it away.

elder than a warrior, he had personally supervised the safe passage
of Teleki's caravan through that part of Kabete where he had
influence. Waiyaki also welcomed Lugard with open arms and
allowed him to build a fort on his own land, above all, both had
undergone a ceremony of blood brotherhood, the highest expression
of mutual confidence and friendship known to Kikuyu society.
Lastly, when Wilson returned to Kiawariua, after the brief flight to
Machakos, and again when Purkiss and Smith returned to Mbugici,
Waiyaki spared no effort in his attempts to have the looted goods
returned, a fact that even his bitterest opponents admitted.

   Far from fanning the flames of hostility against the white man,
Waiyaki was a genuine and moderating influence on the Kikuyu
warriors, some of whom were anxious to prove their manhood by
driving away the intruders. Even after his arrest, he categorically
forbade the Kikuyu warriors to fight for his release.[59] It is true
that he was afraid of being killed in the process of the warriors
trying to effect his release forcibly, but he was equally concerned
lest the situation worsened and the warriors were massacred.
His request was respected, and this accounts for the absence of any
fighting on the morning of 17 August 1892, rather than cowardice
on the part of the warriors, as some of the company officials were
inclined to believe. Undoubtedly the warriors were capable of
such a feat, as they were to prove in the following year when they
besieged the fort. In any case, failure by Purkiss to take immediate
action after the death of Maktubu had emboldened and given them
the impression that he was afraid of them.

   In retrospect, conflict between Waiyaki and the company officials
seems to have been inevitable. The officials believed that Waiyaki
was the 'Paramount Chief of the Wakikuyu' and treated him
accordingly. Understandably Waiyaki took no pains to undeceive
them, for he was aware that having the white man on his land
meant he was strategically placed for trading with them, a factor
that might have tempted him to exaggerate his own power and
influence. Of greater consideration, his position locally would be
enhanced, since anyone who wanted to have access to the white
man would have to come through him. Whatever Waiyaki's motives
were, the officials' blunder in assessing his influence proved fatal to
the mutual understanding initiated by Lugard, for it soon became
apparent to them that the Kabete were not at the beck and call

59. 'KHT', pp. 268, 274, and 275.

of any single individual, let alone Waiyaki. He was only one, albeit one of the most influential, among many *athamaki*, as we have seen in chapter 5.

It is true, though, that as the owner of a large *ng'undu* and *kihingo* at the frontier he wielded considerable power. On his own, however, he could neither make a treaty that affected the welfare of the community, nor even control the truculent warriors as he had undertaken to do. His authority was severely curtailed, and whatever agreement he came to with the officials, if it was to be regarded as binding, had willy-nilly to be ratified by the council of elders, if not actually initiated by them. But he does not seem to have consulted his peers before or after making treaties with the company officials; it is not surprising, then, that he later failed to control the warriors. It should have been clear to the newcomers that Waiyaki's power was limited at the time when Teleki was passing through the Kikuyu country. Although he had protected him in his area, he was unable to take Teleki beyond Karura, and Teleki's safe conduct was achieved with considerable trouble even in those areas where he claimed to have been the *muthamaki*.[60]

Ultimately, the after-effects of the Kikuyu-IBEAC conflict rebounded on him and formed the basis of the accusations of treachery levelled against him. The misunderstandings over his power and authority, which as an individual were minimal, led to his being held responsible and regarded as the chief instigator every time something went wrong between the Kikuyu and the company. Waiyaki was, therefore, a victim of circumstances, partly of his own making. On the other hand, Purkiss and Mac-Donald enormously increased their own problems by their refusal to accept the Kikuyu peace overtures. As events later proved, this was an error of judgement on their part. Many accounts confirm that Waiyaki was drunk[61] and hardly in a position to realize the full impact of what he was doing that fateful evening of 14 August. The failure of the officials to pardon him aroused anger in the Kikuyu, who made Purkiss 'practically a prisoner with all his people'.[62] Moreover, this led to a general escalation of the situation and there was continuous fighting up to 1896.[63] This was

60. von Höhnel, op. cit., pp. 298-317.
61. 'KHT', pp. 267, 281 and 282.
62. Portal to Sir Percy Anderson, 22 February 1893 in FO2/60.
63. For the state of Kikuyu in 1893, see G. H. Portal, *The Mission to Uganda*

disastrous for the future: the white man confirmed that the Kikuyu were hostile, treacherous and a 'thoroughly bad lot'. They were given, as Portal concluded, 'a bad name, which sticks to them like a burr, and the stranger arriving within their gates treats them accordingly'. He himself had been advisedly told 'to shoot at sight' the moment he met a Kikuyu.[64] As for the Kikuyu, they could see no difference between the slave dealers from the coast, the European adventurers and the company or government officials. They were men who could not be trusted; men who should be driven away at all costs. Only patient and determined efforts on both sides could have restored confidence in each other but this was not forthcoming.

The arrest and death of Waiyaki exacerbated the situation, with the Kikuyu more determined than ever to drive away the company from Fort Smith. Time and again the Company found itself embroiled in the local affairs and had to mount expedition after expedition, at first against the recalcitrant Kikuyu near the fort, but later as far north as Mang'u, Ruiru, and indeed right up to the southern outskirts of Murang'a district. The situation was complicated further by two elements: some of the collaborators increasingly involved the company in their personal and petty quarrels, and the lure of economic rewards led them to hatch quarrels even where none existed.[65] Already we have seen that this was the cause of the Ruiru expedition led by Kamau and that of Kamaru which resulted in the death of Maktubu. The success of their plots emboldened the 'friendlies' to go directly to the company, or government officials, with a variety of stories all designed to have their enemies punished. Hall's friends—notably Wahero and Kinyanjui—reported in 1893 that their enemies were hatching plots against the company, and that some of their men had been killed because, they alleged, they had assisted Hall.[66] Kamaru, one of Hall's messengers, even 'tried to recover some goats from some old enemy of his own by telling the people that [Hall's] men were coming to fetch these goats [and] if they were not given up there

London, 1894, pp. 89-93; Portal's reports to Lord Rosebery of January and February 1893 in FO2/60; and Hall's diary for 1892-3.

64. Portal, op. cit., pp. 92-3.
65. It was Hall's deliberate policy to split the Kikuyu—'I have been backing up these friendly chiefs on one or two occasions, [and] so cemented their friendship, [and] also split the tribe into two parties, which considerably strengthened my position.' Hall to Col. Hall, 24 November 1893.
66. Hall's diary, 27-8 May and 6 September 1893.

would be war'.[67] By the end of 1894, Hall had come to realize that his 'friendlies' had been telling lies, no doubt because they hoped to share in the loot captured. His own herdsman, Kiragu, alleged on three occasions that his house had been burnt down. By then it had become obvious to Hall that the intention was 'simply a plan to get [him] to go out to fight [and] get goats'.[68] The chief collaborator—Kinyanjui, Hall's *fidus Achates*—had acquired a gun as a reward for his services. He then dispensed with the company soldiery and raided on his own. One of his victims was a well-known elder, Muru wa Mugwe.

But the 'friendlies' were not the only source of trouble; of equal importance, in this respect, were the Maasai refugees. The outbreak of pleuro-pneumonia seriously reduced the Maasai herds, an epidemic of smallpox broke out, followed by a serious famine in the 1890s. As if these misfortunes were not enough, rivalry flared up between Lenana and Sendeyo, the two sons of the Maasai *laibon* (ritual expert), Mbatian. Thus very much reduced, some of the remaining Maasai groups sought refuge in Kiambu, as well as in Nyeri to the north. In Kiambu, Hall acted as an intermediary for Lenana, who sought peace with the Kikuyu and this paved the way for a substantial influx of refugees.[69] It was necessary to make use of Hall's services as an intermediary because the Gicamu war earlier on had strained the relationship with their Kikuyu neighbours. There were some Kikuyu still chafing over this war who were all too anxious to despoil the Maasai of their belongings and it is not strange that the Maasai decidedly preferred to live under the aegis of Hall at Fort Smith.

In January 1894, a group of four hundred to five hundred refugees had built their *manyatta* around Fort Smith and this figure had increased to a thousand by July of the same year. Those others who had settled among the Kikuyu earlier, but who were aggrieved or felt threatened, also decamped and settled in the vicinity of the fort.[70] They soon became a constant cause for quarrels between Hall and the Kikuyu. Cultivating was beneath a full-blooded Maasai

67. Hall's diary, 21 May 1894.
68. ibid., 20 and 24 October 1894. The 'friendlies' had been handsomely rewarded in previous expeditions: for example, after the 'Chamore' [? Kiambu] raid, they received 5 goats each, Kiragu got 20, 'Laroba' 20, Muiruri 20 and Kinyanjui 20, on 26 January 1894.
69. 'KHT', pp. 239, 245, 247 and 262.
70. Hall's diary, 1893–4; Hall's monthly reports to IBEAC Administrator, 13 February and 9 July 1894 in FO2/73.

and the only way of getting food was by foraging in the Kikuyu *shambas*.[71] Hall had recognized that feeding the refugees would be a problem, but he could do nothing to alleviate shortage of food in view of the company's financial predicament. Secondly, Hall used the Maasai *morans* as levies to supplement his *askari* during the punitive expeditions. These two factors did not endear Hall or the Maasai to the already aggrieved Kikuyu and a quarrel between a Maasai and a Kikuyu, and the death of the latter, was enough excuse for a confrontation to take place. The death occurred on 11 June 1894 and was immediately followed by the Kikuyu preparing for war. On 13 June, Hall had to send the Maasai to Ngong to avoid a major clash. Conflict between the Kikuyu, the company and the refugees continued and punitive expeditions became an accepted manner of administration, with the company forces storming Kikuyu villages, burning the houses, spoiling crops and capturing livestock, besides killing all those who opposed them. For example, after Waiyaki's arrest, there was intermittent war until December 1892. In January 1893 the Kikuyu made a determined effort to overrun Fort Smith, and Purkiss, despite the presence of 150 Zanzibari soldiers and armed porters belonging to Martin's caravan, was forced to seek much-needed help from Ainsworth at Machakos on 14 January 1893. However, the fort was besieged completely from 10 to 16 January.[72] On arrival at the fort, Sir Gerald Portal found that

> at Kikuyu the European in charge dare not venture 200 yards from his stockade without an armed escort of at least 30 to 50 men with rifles. He is practically a prisoner with all his people: [and] maintains the Company's influence [and] prestige by sending almost daily looting and raiding parties to burn the surrounding villages [and] to seize the crops and cattle for the use of the company's caravans [and] troops.[73]

Such expeditions were to continue throughout the company rule and beyond. Hall continued with the policy set down by his predecessors until he cracked the resistance of the Kikuyu. In 1893 he mounted two expeditions in which 922 sheep and goats and 5 head of cattle were taken and about ninety Kikuyu killed, casualties among his men being two killed and three wounded. In the following year, he undertook another three major raids in which

71. 'KHT', p. 244.
72. Purkiss to IBEAC's Administrator, 20 January 1893 in FO2/57; Portal to Rosebery, 31 January 1893 in FO2/60.
73. Portal to Anderson, 22 February 1893 in FO2/60; E. L. Bentley to the Foreign Office, 9 February 1893 in FO2/57.

he captured 190 head of cattle and 4,400 sheep and goats and, at the same time, burnt many villages.[74] Lonely and sorely tried, Hall, though temperamentally jovial, became despondent and freely used the sjambok on friend and foe alike. And as for the Kikuyu, he felt that 'There is only one way of improving the Wakikuyu, [and] that is wipe them out; I should be only too delighted to do so, but we have to depend on them for food supplies.'[75] And he threatened that 'unless they took to work like other natives, they would eventually be wiped out [and] better people brought into the country'.[76] There was no significant change of policy even after the British government took over from the company in 1895. Indeed, the government continued to use the same personnel that had served the company and punitive expeditions were regularly mounted in an effort to subdue the Kikuyu and force them to accept British rule.[77]

Eventually, Kikuyu resistance was weakened by a series of natural disasters. Between 1894 and 1899 there were intermittent invasions of locusts which caused extensive damage to the crops. Ainsworth, writing to his superiors in July 1894, commented that a 'very serious state of things exists in [Machakos] district owing to the terrible swarms of locusts which have come in', and 'Kikuyu is in a far worse condition than we are: there is absolutely no food in the country at present'.[78] Swarms of locusts descended on the country again in 1895 and 1896, only to be followed by a severe drought in 1897/8, a cattle plague in 1898, a serious famine in 1898/9 and an outbreak of smallpox simultaneously.[79] The famine was particularly disastrous and was exacerbated by the fact that the Kabete had sold enormous amounts of foodstuffs to the company and the passing caravans at a time when cultivation had significantly decreased due to the disturbed situation in the country at the time. There was a very high mortality and estimates range from 50 to 95 per cent of the population.[80] Some of those who survived took refuge among their relatives to the north, particularly in Metumi,

74. Hall's diary, 1893-4.
75. Hall to Col. Hall, 5 July 1894.
76. ibid., 6 August 1893.
77. 'KHT', p. 276.
78. Ainsworth to IBEAC, 24 and 31 July 1894; Hall's and Ainsworth's reports to IBEAC in FO2/73; 'KHT' pp. 262 and 276.
79. 'KLC', pp. 262 and 283.
80. KLC, vol. 1, pp. 723, 726, 746. Bernard estimated a mortality of 75 per cent, Boyes 95 per cent and Patterson between 50 and 66 per cent. See also 'KHT', pp. 261 and 264.

their original homeland. It was the effects of these disasters that account for the apparently empty land which was alienated for European settlement in 1902-3.

But the effects of the natural disasters were not the only factors that undermined Kikuyu resistance to the establishment of the company and government rule. The emergence among the Kikuyu of a pro-company faction had also begun to corrode their resistance seriously, long before natural disasters struck the final blow. The nurturing of the 'friendlies' owed success to Francis Hall. He came to Fort Smith in October 1892 and, except for brief periods of leave, was the superintendent of the fort from August 1893 until he was transferred to Machakos in 1899. Recruiting collaborators was an easy matter for several reasons. Hall's force of personality, and in particular his bravery, was an important factor which earned him fear and respect. To the Kikuyu he was another brave warrior, but a warrior who, despite his successes in containing the people, was prepared to make peace on certain conditions. This earned him the nickname Wanyahoro, a man of peace. However, the decisive factor was probably the traditional rivalry and enmity between the clans, ridges, or even individuals, inherent in Kikuyu society, and which Hall exploited so effectively. In addition, the presence of the white man on the southern border halted expansion in that direction and a large number of ahoi had no hope of ever owning land of their own, as migration southwards had hitherto implied. The lure of economic rewards was eventually an important factor, as the career of Kinyanjui demonstrates. It is relevant to point out that a good number of those who were to become pioneer mission adherents at Thogoto consisted largely of ahoi or, for one reason or another, displaced people, many of whom attached themselves to the mission during the Great Famine.

The Kabete had virtually been subdued by Hall by the end of 1895. Minor and sporadic punitive expeditions were still undertaken, but there was little determined resistance that was offered by the Kikuyu. The 1894 locust invasion led to a minor famine and many warriors offered their services as porters to Eldama Ravine in exchange for food, goats or cloths. As the 1895 Kedong massacre indicated, hundreds of Kikuyu warriors had swallowed their pride and volunteered as porters, a task they would have abhorred a year or so before. Others became askari and actively helped Hall and others to subdue their fellow Kikuyu to the north, once economic rewards became a reality and whetted their appetite a stage further. Thus Hall was able to build up a clientele of mercenaries which proved very useful as porters or soldiers of fortune. Among his achievements was the fact that there was no significant resistance to the building of the railway. And the Kikuyu not only parted with the land needed for it but also offered themselves as labourers. In this period conflict was isolated and even that occurred only between the coolies and the Kikuyu, a problem easily handled by Hall. The building of the railway, coinciding as it did with the famine, meant that there was no morale for effective opposition to its construction. Hence, by 1897, the Kikuyu along the southern frontier had virtually resigned themselves to the existence of the white man close by. Slowly but surely, moreover, they were ceasing to be a mere source of food and were increasingly becoming servants of the white man.

In spite of these social changes, British jurisdiction was more apparent than real until the turn of the century. The government's influence, let alone effective jurisdiction, hardly went beyond the environs of Fort Smith and further north in Metumi and Gaki, coastal traders of all types, and their European counterparts, were making their presence felt in much the same way as was happening around Fort Smith, and with similar results. No one more clearly symbolized the activities and behaviour of these adventurers than John Boyes. Despite grave warnings from the government officials at Naivasha and the proverbial bad reputation of the Kikuyu, Boyes decided in June 1898 to enter Tuthu in Murang'a district, primarily because with a famine raging in Kabete (the chief source of food for caravans and the railway building party), he saw a good chance of making a fortune by trading in food.[81] He had no cause to regret this decision and was 'highly satisfied' with his first venture. His second trip was such a success and it so pleased the formerly reluctant officials that he was given a contract to supply Naivasha with provisions.[82] Boyes, who was nicknamed Karianjahi (the eater of *Dolichos lablab*) discovered later that trading in ivory, which was ridiculously cheap in the area, especially in Mathira, was even more profitable.[83] Encouraged by this new

81. Boyes, op. cit., pp. 74-5.
82. ibid, pp. 88-9 and 114.
83. Karianjahi bought ivory for 8 to 10 shillings a tusk, or for even less, and sold it at £10 to £15 each.

venture he extended his activities to the Dorobo, who were then living in the Nanyuki-Naro Moru area, in search of ivory.

Karianjahi was lucky to have Karuri Gakure as a chief ally. Karuri saw in Karianjahi a possible source of strength and prestige. Karuri was of lowly birth, the son of a Mwathi who had hitherto earned his living by selling red ochre and by acting as a medicineman in Kabete. During these trading expeditions he had come across Kinyanjui and it was probably the latter who influenced him to make friendship with the white man. In any event, Karuri was introduced to both Hall and Ainsworth, to whom he paid several visits. By 1898 he had already visited Machakos and Fort Smith and even expressed a wish to have a white man at his home.[84] Clearly he was not blind to the prestige attached to wearing the 'amerikani' and the consequences of having the 'stick that spits fire', particularly when pointed at his enemies. Karianjahi found a man after his own heart, and Karuri was not disappointed in his calculations. As his mentor commented:

> As time went on Karuri was to become my friend and right-hand supporter, while I, in turn, was to have an influence over him and his people which was to raise him to the position of a great chief and myself to supreme power in the country—a virtual King of the Kikuyu.[85]

To achieve this position Karianjahi increasingly interfered in local affairs, and Karuri ingratiated himself to Boyes by encouraging him to hammer at his enemies, or those who objected to their joint activities. This happened to Kariara, who objected to Karianjahi's presence in Tuthu and was for this raided on several occasions, as were Karuri's other neighbours.[86] Karianjahi was intent on extending his influence and finally carving out a kingdom for himself. As he readily admits, his aim was to see all the 'chiefs' friendly to one another but, of course, they would remain under his control. With his uniformed private army of Swahili and Kabete askari[87] flying the Union Jack during all his expeditions, he indeed behaved like a king of the Kikuyu; his successes and influence gave him a sense of elation and euphoria. After all, the Kikuyu, who had 'never seen a white

84. Karuri visited Hall on 17 December 1896 and Ainsworth on 8 July 1895 and 15 July 1899. See Hall's and Ainsworth's diaries for 1895 to 1899. See also 'KHT', pp. 289 and 291.
85. Boyes, op. cit., pp. 81-2.
86. ibid, pp. 85-7, 94-5, 110-16.
87. 'KHT', pp. 276 and 291.

man before . . . likened [him] to their god Ngai, as [he] was a great medicine man, and they believed that [he] could make rain'.[88] However, his 'kingdom' did not last for long. His activities and those of the other traders brought turmoil to the country, the whole area was in danger of a major civil war. As McGregor found out, Murang'a district 'was a happy hunting-ground for so-called traders, who seem to have spent their time raiding different parts of the country for the sake of ivory and cattle, setting one district against another, and carrying all before them.'[89] Karianjahi, for example, had taken it upon himself to punish the Cinga people for the murder of a Goan caravan. Meantime, he had allied himself with Gakere and Wang'ombe of Gaki, who now sent several hundred warriors to supplement Karuri and his forces in attacking the Cinga. And 'this army of warriors swept through the Cinga country from one end to the other, destroying the villages and wiping out of existence all who opposed them.'[90] Further adventures of a similar nature were only ended when Karianjahi was arrested by Hall on 19 November 1900, and after the establishment of a government station at Mbiri, later called Fort Hall. By the time of his arrest this 'cheerful rogue'[91] had acquired three Kikuyu wives and had looted cattle, sheep and goats from his opponents on more than six raiding expeditions. The charge prepared against him was that he had 'waged war, set shauris, personated Government, went on six punitive expeditions, and committed dacoity.'[92]

But in fact Karianjahi was not alone in this venture. Gibbons, another freebooter, was to be active in Embu, Gicugu and Ndia later on. With an armed band of thirty Swahili, he, too, was 'collecting hut tax, extorting ivory from the natives and had hoisted the Union Jack to give Government protection to his nefarious actions'. On his arrest, on 16 November 1903, he is reputed to have had fourteen Embu concubines. He was charged with 'illegally collecting hut tax and despoiling the natives'.[93] It was becoming clear that the situation to the north was getting serious and the activities

88. Boyes, op. cit., p. 127.
89. McGregor, annual report in *Proceedings of CMS, 1903/4*, p. 91; 'KHT' pp. 276-8, 289, 290.
90. Boyes, op. cit., p. 232.
91. R. Meinertzhagen's diary, 6 November 1903, in 'Meinertzhagen Papers' in Rhodes House, Oxford.
92. Boyes, op. cit., p. 284.
93. Meinertzhagen's diary for November 1903.

of these adventurers were not calculated to make a government takeover an easy matter, particularly as some of the traders were beginning to sell guns to the Kikuyu. And as McGregor summed it up, 'In the past so-called traders have upset the people, plundering [and] robbing, consequently the people began to think that all white men were fair game for them.'[94]

The establishment of Mbiri station by Hall in November 1900 marked a change of policy in the attitude of the East Africa Protectorate government towards Kikuyuland. The region was no longer regarded as simply a route to, or a provision depot for, caravans going to Uganda. The need for annexing the Mount Kenya region had become apparent to Hall as early as 1896, when he had requested sanctioning of the establishment of a station there. His request was not, however, acceded to, but by 1900 the situation needed an urgent solution because of the activities of the adventurers, who were embarrassing the government by claiming to act in its name. It was essential to end these disruptive activities, and in particular the exploitation of the people, who were nominally under the government's charge. It was felt that failure to do this as soon as was practicable would only store up bigger problems for the administrators in the future. Already a number of incidents had indicated what might follow. As we have seen, a Goan caravan had been murdered in Cinga; Captain Haslam, a government veterinary officer, had met the same fate in Muruka in June 1898; and Mackinder's porters had been murdered by Wang'ombe's people in Mathira in 1899.[95] Evidently friction between the traders and the Kikuyu was on the increase and was resulting in a loss of lives.[96]

Once the decision had been taken, the subjection of Murang'a and Nyeri was relatively swift. And apart from Muruka, Tetu and Mathira, there was no prolonged or bitter struggle between the two contestants. Two factors account for this. Partly it was due to the work of Karianjahi, who had built up Karuri to become an influential friend of the white man. Karuri had a vested interest in the expansion of British rule to this area, and he himself was a good example to other self-seeking Kikuyu; they could easily see the advantages to be gained by associating and supporting the white

94. McGregor to CMS, 22 October 1902 in CMS Archives, G3/A5/016.
95. Mackinder, op. cit., pp. 456, 467-8; *KLC*, vol. 1, p. 705 and vol. 3, p. 3336; Ainsworth's diary for June 1898.
96. 'KHT', pp. 284, 286, 290, 295, 302, 305 and 310.

man. Karuri, once his friend was arrested, was all too ready to throw in his lot with the new power, undoubtedly to reap fresh rewards, just as he had done under the tutelage of Karianjahi.

Karuri, however, was not alone in the quest for the white man's friendship. Several men from Murang'a had requested Hall to establish a station in their area, and others, such as Mbuthia Kaguongo and Wang'ang'a, were frequent visitors to Hall and Ainsworth, whom they presented with gifts to cement their friendship.[97] Such men were sure to have heard stories about the arrest of Waiyaki and the innumerable raids that the Kamba and the Kabete had experienced. They may even have witnessed them at close quarters during their visits to the south. Moreover, the increasing fights between the traders and the Kikuyu drove the lesson home, as Teleki's fight with the Gaturi people seems to indicate. Above all, with the migration of the Kabete back into Murang'a during the famine came stories of their experiences at the hands of the foreigners.

There seems, therefore, to have been a remarkable appraisal of the situation by some people, who thereby decided to side with the white man for a variety of reasons and motives. Men like Karuri, Mbuthia and Wang'ang'a evinced friendship with the white man and acquired 'chits' as a sign of their loyalty. And in Karuri's case, he was such a keen collaborator that he desperately hankered to have a white man of any kind at his home. He was the first person to invite missionaries to enter Murang'a and also the first to send his children to be educated by them.[98] He jealously guarded any access to the white man, as McGregor's correspondence demonstrates, being anxious that everyone else should come through him. His efforts paid dividends; he became extremely influential in official circles and was instrumental in building up most of the other collaborators, both in Nyeri and Murang'a. Most of those who aspired to be made chiefs came to his home with all manner of presents, since they knew that he had the ear of the government. Among his proteges were Wangu Makeri, Wambugu Mathangani, Rukanga, and indeed nearly all the early chiefs from Murang'a and Nyeri. Many of these people played a key role in the government's efforts to subdue the recalcitrant Kikuyu. Karuri played a major role and to the British an indispensable one, in the

97. Hall's and Ainsworth's diaries; Mackinder, op. cit., pp. 456 and 458.
98. McGregor's annual letter for 1902 in CMS Archives, G3/A5/016.

subjugation of the two districts.[99] This accounts for the relatively fewer punitive expeditions undertaken in those areas, especially in Murang'a.

Several minor punitive raids were undertaken in Murang'a. In 1901 Boyes and Captain Wake punished Kariara once again for allegedly murdering the Swahili along the railway line.[100] Around Mbiri, too, the Gaturi people, who may still have been smarting from the mauling they got from Teleki's caravan, presented a modicum of resistance which was easily put down by Hall. Muruka was the only place to show real resistance and that area was not so easily cowed. It got a bad reputation after murdering the leader of a Swahili caravan, Haslam, and his mail runners. Then, Munge Matano's caravan had aroused the wrath of the Muruka people by attacking a man in his *shamba*. In the ensuing fight only two of Matano's people escaped.[101] Muruka had followed this up by killing three porters and a policeman in August 1901, as well as attacking McLellan's camp. A punitive raid was embarked upon under S. L. Hinde and Harrison.[102] In 1902 the Muruka people once again attacked and killed five Indian traders and a European settler. The government could no longer stand this and a strong expedition, consisting of five British officers, 115 *askari*, 300 Maasai levies and Kikuyu warriors, was dispatched under the command of Captain Maycock. With Mbuthia Kaguongo acting as guide, the forces scoured the area from the vicinity of Thika town to Kihumbuini from 2 September to 25 October 1902. The expedition achieved its mission and 200 Kikuyu were killed, 300 heads of cattle and 2,000 sheep and goats captured.[103] The government losses were only one killed and thirteen wounded. As the heavy casualties on the Kikuyu side indicate, this punitive raid was particularly vindictive because of the grisly manner in which the European settler had been killed. On 8 September 1902 Meinertzhagen gave orders that in Kihumbuini 'every living thing except children should be killed without mercy ... Every soul was either shot or bayonetted, ... We burned all the huts and razed the banana plantations to

99.   'KHT', pp.290, 291-2, 300, 306 and 309-11.
100. J. Boyes, *The Company of Adventurers*, London, 1928, p. 130.
101. Hall's diary, November 1896.
102. 'History of Fort Hall, 1888-1944' in KNA/FH/6/1; Meinertzhagen, *Kenya Diary*, pp. 48-53; 'KHT', pp. 284-7.
103. Report on Murang'a by Capt. F. A. Dickson in FO2/450 and 451; H. Moyse-Bartlett: *The King's African Rifles: A Study in the Military History of East and Central Africa, 1890-1945*, Aldershot, 1956, p. 204.

the ground'.[104] This cracked Muruka's intransigence and there was little trouble afterwards.

Towards the end of 1902 it became necessary, too, for the administration to attack Tetu in Nyeri. The immediate reason was to avenge the murder of a Goan caravan that had been murdered at Ithanji, near Kiandongoro. Generally there seems to have been a great dislike of the *Makorobai* (traders) in this region, because of their behaviour. Although it is not precisely clear why this particular caravan got into difficulties with the local people, the quarrel rose from a trade dispute. The Tetu warriors attacked the caravan and the Goans were killed by Ngunju Gakere, Kimamo Kanai and Gacengo. The government thereafter carried out a two-pronged attack on Tetu. Meinertzhagen advanced from Naivasha across the Nyandarua Range, while Barlow, Hemsted and Sub-Commissioner Hinde advanced northwards from Mbiri station accompanied by 200 Maasai levies, policemen and Kikuyu warriors from Kabete and Karuri's. Meinertzhagen reached the outskirts of Tetu on 2 December and had to fight every inch of the way, confiscating livestock and burning houses.[105] On that day alone he captured 665 head of cattle, and many goats and sheep. His party killed twenty Kikuyu, but his casualties were only two killed and five wounded. Fighting continued on the following day when he looted a further sixty head of cattle and 1,000 sheep and goats. On the night of 4 December the Kikuyu warriors launched two daring attacks on Meinertzhagen's camp at Nyeri. Thirty-eight Kikuyu were killed, while the government forces suffered four soldiers and five Maasai killed, with eleven soldiers, fourteen Maasai and seven porters wounded. Meinertzhagen's company thus suffered 'rather heavy casualties' and he felt that reinforcements of a further 200 Maasai levies was necessary. The Tetu people had shown their mettle, and even Meinertzhagen was greatly surprised at their courage. 'I must own', he admitted, 'I never expected the Wakikuyu to fight like this.'[106] However, by 6 December resistance was drawing to an end. When the government forces camped at the site where Nyeri town now stands, 'some friendlies' captured Gakere and one of his sons and handed them over to the officials. In spite of victory, Hinde was

104. Meinertzhagen, *Kenya Diary*, pp. 51-2.
105. Meinertzhagen, *Kenya Diary*, pp. 64-75, 'KHT', pp. 290, 295-6, 302, 305-7 and 310.
106. Meinertzhagen, *Kenya Diary*, p. 67.

anxious to loot more livestock to give him sufficient revenue to build his new station. Consequently, operations were extended towards Mahiga on 16 December where allegedly people had harboured Tetu livestock. The area around Nyeri town, however, shouldered the brunt of official anger. From 16 to 18 December there were mopping-up operations, during which a further 184 head of cattle and 1,200 sheep and goats were captured. Aguthi, too, did not escape unscathed; a raiding party scoured the area capturing sixty-two head of cattle and 6,000 sheep and goats.

On 18 December Kikuyu warriors made a final and desperate effort to dislodge the government forces. They rushed towards the newly-established fort at Nyeri, but they were ambushed and fifty of them were killed. Further resistance seemed hopeless in the face of superior arms and the fighting came to an end. The campaign over, Gakere was deported to Kismayu, but was soon afterwards repatriated to Mbiri in 1905 where he died shortly afterwards, still defiantly against the invaders. Meantime on 20 December, a group of about sixty elders from Tetu sued for peace, guaranteeing security to travellers and agreeing to make a road to Naivasha. By the end of 1902, therefore, open hostilities had come to an end. A moat was dug round the new fort and because of it Nyeri town was nicknamed 'Mukaro' (the trench).

The Mathira people were not perturbed by what was happening elsewhere. Raiding amongst themselves and against their neighbours, especially those to their east, and attacks on the *Makorobai*, still continued. In 1899 they had killed Mackinder's porters who had gone to look for food;[107] in May 1903 the Iria-ini cut up a caravan of six Somali and ten porters; and in November 1903 a party of 200 warriors had stopped McClure, a Collector, from counting huts in Githi, Mukurue-ini division.[108] Besides, a few mercenaries who were anxious to curry favour in order to be made chiefs like their counterparts elsewhere, reported that the Mathira were defiantly vowing that they would never be ruled by the white man, people who dressed like women. Obviously these people were in no mood to submit to the new administration at Nyeri.[109] They did not escape without punishment for these threatening and insulting messages that they allegedly sent to Hinde, and for their defiant

107.   Mackinder, op. cit., pp. 467-8.
108.   See historical notes on Iria-ini in KNA/PC/CP/1/1/1.
109.   'KHT', pp. 291 and 296.

posture. In any case, the subjection of Mathira was just a question of time, threats or no threats. Punishment to quell arrogance was a good pretext that taught a lesson to both the collaborators and the remaining pockets of resistance. The lesson was clear and simple—the white man meant business, and his word was law.

It was in this spirit that the military men approached their Mathira assignment, and since the 'chiefs of Mathira were of doubtful loyalty', Meinertzhagen declared, 'a punitive expedition was necessary to put them in the right frame of mind and to "show them the flag".'[110] A three-pronged attack was undertaken in February and March 1904 under the command of Captain Dickson. Meinertzhagen and Humphrey led one column of sixty soldiers and 250 Maasai levies from Mbiri station to Thiba river, and from the latter they scoured Ndia from Kutus to Kabari, where they camped. From Kabari they were able to comb Ndia and Gicugu right up to the Mount Kenya forest to the north, and the Embu border to the east. The other two columns under Brancker advanced from Nyeri town; one marched via Mukurue-ini and camped at Icaka-hanya, while the other crossed the Thagana river by the Muru wa Hiuhu ford and camped at Ruthagati. Brancker's total force consisted of 100 soldiers and 200 Maasai levies. These two combed Mathira thoroughly, particularly Konyu and Iria-ini, before advancing towards Ndia to join up with the other main column from Mbiri.[111] Hundreds of livestock were looted, many warriors were killed and homes were razed down. For example, Meinertzhagen's column captured over 782 head of cattle, 2,150 sheep and goats and killed 796 Kikuyu. At Icakahanya, now Ngunguru village, Brancker's contingent collected firewood from the surrounding homesteads and lit a huge fire to roast some of the 300 cattle and 6,000 sheep and goats he had captured. Heavier casualties were apparently inflicted on the Ndia and the Gicugu but Brancker and Dickson do not mention the number of enemy killed. It is clear, though, that the casualties inflicted upon the Kikuyu group during this punitive raid were so heavy that none of the officials dared to report the exact number. The official report put them at 400, but Meinertzhagen estimated 1,500 to be a modest figure. It is not surprising then, that there was a furore in the Foreign Office.

The Mathira, having lost the day and realizing that spears and

110. Meinertzhagen, *Kenya Diary*, p. 108.
111. 'KHT', pp. 296-7, 299-300.

poisoned arrows were of no avail in the face of superior arms, collected livestock and ivory, these they sent to the government officials as a token of their genuine desire for peace.[112] Thus military operations came to an end.

112. Meinertzhagen, *Kenya Diary*, pp. 138-52; 'KHT', p. 297.

Chapter 7

CONCLUSION

B Y the end of 1904 the East Africa Protectorate government
had made an all out effort to bring Kikuyuland under *Pax
Britannica*. In the following years minor expeditions were undertaken to contain the remaining few pockets still resisting the new
rule. Spears and arrows had proved no match for guns, and the
Kikuyu quickly submitted. Gradually, they learnt to conform with,
and even accept, British rule, but theirs remained a bitter lesson, one
never to be forgotten. Conquest, however, was hardly the end to
government's problems. The immediate concern was to establish a
viable administration, but there was no visible traditional authority
with which to work, and existing administrative personnel was also
in short supply. Faced with this problem, the administrative officers
turned to the motley crowd of mercenaries who had served them
as porters, guides or *askari*, and created them chiefs. The officials
assumed that chiefs had existed in the traditional society and thus
some of the *athamaki*, or any bold spirits who exaggerated their
own importance, were made into chiefs as well. The so-called chiefs
soon became local 'tin gods' and a law unto themselves, more so
because very little control was exercised over them. According to
all accounts, the hammering that the Kikuyu had experienced at
the hands of the punitive expeditions was nothing compared to
the constant harassment inflicted upon them by the mercenaries
now christened 'chiefs'.[1] Many of these local rulers used their
new power to enrich themselves, while their hangers-on, the
njama, flouted the traditional code of behaviour by harassing all
and sundry, and in particular the girls who had to sleep in the newly
established *bomas*. Some, like Karuri, bent the traditional social
organization to serve their mercenary ends; Karuri decreed that
before the traditional *muhingo* could be lifted any prospective

1. 'KHT', pp. 281, 285, 292, 293-4, 303-5 and 311.

initiate had to pay him a rupee, an idea that the others emulated.[2] Any person who refused to obey the chief and his *njama* was severely beaten, had his home burnt down or livestock looted; and there was no appeal to a higher authority. No one had a better chance to observe this class of people at close quarters than McGregor, who gives a graphic description of their behaviour in 1906–7. He describes their activities thus:

> Under the present arrangements, the njama consists of all the rogues of an enormous district who have the chief's permission to enter. It is an engine of oppression, because by means of it the Government headman can punish any district which does not, as he thinks, listen to him viz. allow his young men to do as they like there. The *njama* entering a district divide themselves up, and each decides upon the village where he will make his home for the time being. During the time he condescends to remain there, he is like the owner of the village; the owner himself is but his servant, and is condemned to sit up and watch that the fire does not go down while his lordship is sleeping smugly in his bed. If the fire goes down the poor man has to pay a fine of a sheep or is beaten by the whole band in the morning. The women of the village become for the time being the property of the visitor. Everyday a sheep has to be killed, and the *njama* live like kings.[3]

McGregor knew of no less than six people who were murdered on trumped-up charges of witchcraft. And one of them, he noted, was killed because he had refused to give up his *shamba* to a chief who coveted it. McGregor was not alone in his condemnation of the chiefs and their hangers-on. Dundas, too, noted that 'it had become a heinous crime to dispute the authority of the so-called chief', and that 'their authority was only sustained through the fear of the Government'. At the same time, 'their chief aim was to enrich themselves and to secure their newly invented authority'. This is supported by many of my informants. As one keen observer said:

> They [the chief's hangers-on] had no official salary and consequently had to live on people. Wherever they went, they commandeered whatever they fancied—food or livestock. They even ordered girls to sleep with them. They went to the extent of killing people and if anyone protested, their village would suffer.[4]

And the chiefs themselves were no better:

> The chiefs overreached themselves and took other people's wives and

2. 'KHT', pp. 292, 293-4.
3. McGregor, *Proceedings of the CMS, 1906/7*, vol. 52, p. 73.
4. 'KHT', p. 303.

property by force to teach them *kutii sheria* (to obey the law). People
had to cultivate in their fields without pay and if they refused they were
in trouble. The behaviour of the chiefs and their hangers-on were the
first complaints voiced by the early politicians. Quite a number of
them were dismissed as a result of this, including court elders who took
bribes.[5]

Clearly most of the early chiefs were opportunists, a feature
that was noted in Kikuyuland, Embu and amongst the Kamba.
In Embu, for example, the newly-created chiefs were so notorious
for beating those who rejected them and their orders that they
were called *nthungu*, small Europeans.[6] They therefore became
extremely unpopular, particularly when they had to enforce dis-
agreeable measures. This did not stop the chiefs from getting
increasingly autocratic and high-handed in executing their duties
on behalf of the new rulers. It is not surprising, then, that by 1912,
they were the 'least in touch with their people'.[7] The hostility and
resentment engendered by the newly-established administration
ultimately gave birth to some of the issues that eventually crystallized into the nationalist struggle against the chiefs and their
mentors. Predictably, the chief became the political and emotional
target of the anti-colonialist activity. He was not only a symbol of
the colonial oppressor but also a constant reminder that the
traditional political structure had either been ignored or rudely
dismantled. And so the wound of defeat in the battlefield went on
festering with added virulence. The conquerors, however, either
forgot that it had ever been inflicted, or chose to see a superficial
scar.

As well as the suffering and humiliation they were experiencing
from the chiefs, the Kikuyu were finding it difficult to adjust
themselves to other factors. Soon after subjection they were forced
to pay a hut tax. The efficiency of a chief appears to have been
measured by the amount of hut tax collected, and anxious to curry
favour with their masters, the 'tin gods' forced their unwilling
subjects to pay the tax under the pain of having their stock
confiscated. In any case, they had to part with their precious livestock
in the absence of any money, and herds had already been depleted
by the punitive expeditions. This was a bitter pill to swallow, but

5. 'KHT', p. 304.
6. H. S. Mwaniki, 'The Impact of the British Rule in Embu, 1906 to 1923',
   B.A. dissertation, University of Nairobi, 1968, pp. 39-60.
7. C. C. Dundas on review of *Ciama* in KNA/PC/CP/1/1/1.

having lost the argument in the battlefield they had, reluctantly, to obey or else face the consequences of official displeasure. But even more disturbing demands were to follow.

In 1896 Francis Hall welcomed three European families— Boedecker, Wallace and MacQueen—to settle around Fort Smith and amongst the Kikuyu. This initiated yet another development that had far-reaching repercussions for the Kikuyu people and their relationship with the government and the European community as a whole. The problem of land alienation and its subsequent interplay on politics cannot be discussed adequately here. But a few salient comments should be made. The construction of the Uganda Railway from Mombasa to Kisumu cost slightly over £5 million. Right from the start it was operating at a loss for lack of traffic, and its running costs had to be met by grants-in-aid from a close-fisted British Treasury. The protectorate lacked mineral resources and hence it was essential for agricultural production to be stimulated. Anxious to reduce the deficit, Sir Charles Eliot, the evil genius behind land alienation, proposed that if white settlers were brought into the seemingly empty land they would, within a comparatively short time, make the railway pay. The railway would be assured of adequate traffic resulting from the increased agricultural productivity in the Kenya highlands. Eliot saw his task as that of creating a white man's country not dissimilar to what had taken place in New Zealand or Australia. The acceptance of this policy by the British government was ratified by a series of land laws designed to facilitate land alienation to the Europeans, which gained momentum in 1903 with the arrival of prospective settlers, mainly from South Africa, but also from Britain and elsewhere.[8]

During the second half of the nineteenth century the Kikuyu had been expanding their territory for about thirty years at the expense of the weakened Maasai. This brought them closer to the plains and, although the area was not very suitable for agricultural purposes, conflict over rights to land was imminent. This was forestalled by the presence of the IBEAC and the government personnel at the southern and northern frontiers in 1890 and 1902 respectively. In Kiambu district, the Kikuyu had barely penetrated beyond the Nyongera river when the IBEAC established its fort at Kiawariua

8. For a detailed examination of European settlement, see M.P.K. Sorrenson, *Origins of European Settlement in Kenya.*

in 1890. Indeed, apart from grazing, Kikuyu cultivation had only extended as far as the vicinity of Mugumo-ini (Fort Smith) by that time. Waiyaki, who was at the vanguard of expansion along this area, had built his *kihingo* at Mbugici after 1887, since von Höhnel and Teleki found him at Mukui (Karura) on their journey across Kikuyuland.[9] The frontier was ringed by a line of fortified villages, and their siting could be regarded as roughly delineating the fullest extent of effective occupation by the Kikuyu. At the frontier several well-remembered individuals had their *ihingo* at several points; Muru wa Mugwe was at Muthaiga, Gatama and Kiarii Ndemengo at the confluence of the Karura and Gitathuru rivers, Waihumbu and Thairu at Kogoge, Mugi at Kabete, Mukiri and Waiyaki at Mbugici, Wamagata at Kinoo, Ngware at Gitaru (Kanjeru), Gatonye at Muguga, Ngeca at Ngeca, Njiriri, Cege and Kiragu at Rungai (the Kabuku/Tigoni area), Kiratu at Limuru and Nding'uri and Nduti at Uplands.[10] Beyond Uplands there were only a few *ihingo* at Korio, otherwise the rest of the area was an unoccupied forest except for Turuthi, a Dorobo, who lived there. And along the eastern border there was a no-man's-land chiefly used for grazing because the land was relatively poor for agricultural purposes. The boundary along the eastern edge, therefore, closely followed the Kikuyu plateau and the Kaputie plains and more or less followed the present-day large coffee farms that skirt Kiambu on the eastern edge. The boundary along the eastern edge of Murang'a district also followed the present coffee farms, or it ran more or less along the Nairobi-Nyeri road.[11] But the frontier was shifting all the time.

Along the northern frontier the Kikuyu had not expanded beyond the Thagana river in Mathira and the North Cania river in Tetu by the turn of the century. In July 1892 Gregory, who had journeyed from Mount Kenya towards the hinterland of Mathira, found that cultivation had only reached Gathuini salt-lick, and the Rui Ruiru 'formed the frontier of the inhabited district'. Kagati was at that time unoccupied.[12] Mackinder (in 1899) and Karianjahi (in 1900) saw no sign of habitation beyond the Thagana river, and

9. 'KHT', pp. 270 and 279.
10. ibid., pp. 152-3, 169, 170, 175-7 and 184.
11. ibid., pp. 119 and 235. See also map 5, p. 172.
12. Gregory, op. cit., p. 190, and also pp. 157-8 and 192.

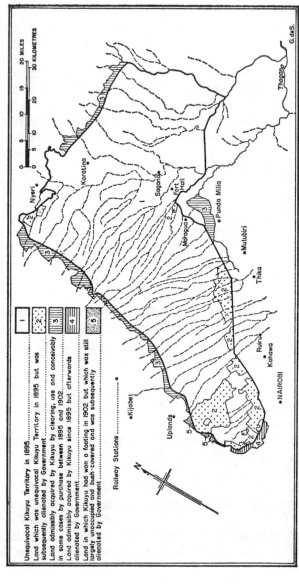

Unequivocal Kikuyu Territory in 1895 ....

Land which was unequivocal Kikuyu Territory in 1895 but was
subsequently alienated by Government ....

Land admissibly acquired by Kikuyu by clearing, use and conceivably
in some cases by purchase between 1895 and 1902 ....

Land admissibly acquired by Kikuyu since 1895 but afterwards
alienated by Government ....

Land in which Kikuyu had won a footing in 1902 but which was still
largely unoccupied and bush-covered and was subsequently
alienated by Government ....

Railway Stations .... •

1
2
3
4
5

0 5 10 15 20 MILES
0 5 10 20 30 KILOMETRES

•Kijabe
Uplands•
•NAIROBI
Kahawa
Ruiru•
•Thika
•Mutubiri
•Punda Milia
Fort Hall
Sagana•
•Maragua
•Karatina
Nyeri•
Thagana
G. deS.

Map 5—Kikuyu plateau: land alienation.

the nearest homes were at Itiati and the Kiamuceru hills.[13] The Kikuyu themselves readily admit that cultivation across the Rui Ruiru was only started after the cattle epidemic in the 1880s.[14] And in Tetu expansion had only reached the banks of the North Cania river when the British government established Nyeri station in 1902. Descriptions given by Routledge, Meinertzhagen and Karianjahi confirm this.

In the light of this evidence, there is no doubt that the hardest-hit victims of land alienation were the Maasai and not the Kikuyu, the latter's clamour notwithstanding. It is true that the Kikuyu lost some land, but their loss should be seen in the right perspective. There is no doubt that in Kiambu, north of the Nyongera river, the incredibly high mortality due to disease and famine had considerably depleted the newly arrived occupants, leaving the land practically vacant at the very time when the first lot of white settlers was about to arrive in search of suitable land for alienation, egged on, no doubt, by an over-zealous government.[15] There is ample evidence to show that a number of families and *mbari* were actually moved from their land during the demarcation of the forest line or to make way for white settlement. The greater source of dissatisfaction, however, arose from the method followed by the settlers in acquiring land. As Hausburg, who acquired land around Punda Milia in 1904, explained, that owing to the absence of a land office in the area the procedure followed was that 'You drew a sketch plan of a river and a tree, and whatever struck your fancy, and you drew a square round the particular bit of land and sent that in for approval'.[16] In effect little attention was paid to the rights of the *mbari*. In most cases, though, the Kikuyu owners were for a time allowed to stay on in the alienated land, where they became squatters and a valuable source of labour, but otherwise life continued much in the same way as it had done. But in due course the white settler found them to be a nuisance, or he wanted to make use of the land that they were occupying. Whenever this happened he had them removed and by 1910 these dispossessed and displaced families had become a big administrative problem. Many of them,

13. See description of their journeys on the northern border in Boyes, *King of Wakikuyu*, pp. 163-78, 180-99; and Mackinder, op. cit., pp. 462-3, and map.
14. 'KHT', pp. 2-3, 12-13, 15 and 36.
15. See map 5.
16. *KLC*, vol. 1, p. 394.

including the *ahoi*, found life intolerable under either their European master or the oppressive and autocratic chief and his *njama*. With official encouragement, they migrated to the Rift Valley to become labourers and squatters in the newly established farms where, for a time, they found life less irksome. Yet the plight of these families was not solely the result of government policy; there were many Kikuyu opportunists, too, who profited by selling their own *mbari* or even other people's land without the latter's knowledge or consent. Others disregarded the customary law regarding the status of the *ahoi* and drove them away as they began to realize the value of land. Kinyanjui Nugu was without doubt the most notorious offender in this respect, but there were many others. He was able to sell other people's land with impunity in the early stages of land alienation, because he could threaten them with punishment from the government, and the unfortunate people still vividly remembered what this implied. He had no land of his own to sell or give, as he was initially a very poor man who at one time had lived on hunting wild animals. It is even alleged that he had been disowned by his family for waywardness while at Kiria (Kandara), after which he attached himself to Waiyaki, a distant relation.[17] He had become Waiyaki's *njaguti* (servant) until the arrival of the IBEAC when his fortunes suddenly changed for the better. As the main company and government collaborator, particularly Hall's, in their struggle with the Kikuyu, and for his association and identification with the European cause, he was handsomely recompensed and was eventually made a paramount chief of the Kikuyu, the sole incumbent of that post.

With the company and government forces behind him, he had nothing to fear and could do much as he liked. On 8 June 1894, he signed a memorandum giving the company some land, land which obviously belonged to Kiarii Muriithi. And in 1896 when the first settlers arrived, his main chance of enriching himself presented itself. He sold land to Boedecker for five cows, three bales of *amerikani*, four sixty-pound loads of beads and four loads of wire.[18] In 1899 he gave P. E. Watcham sixty acres of land at Westlands, and it transpired later that in fact the land belonged to Muya Kingi.[19] In time, even the government officials realized what

17. 'KHT', p. 125.
18. Dr. H. A. Boedecker's evidence, *KLC*, vol. 1, p. 695.
19. P. E. Watcham's evidence, *KLC*, vol. 1, p. 735.

Kinyanjui had been up to all along. In 1912 Beech observed:

> It appears that nearly all the present *ithaka* owners south of [Nyongera]
> river, were compelled in the days of Mr. Hall to pay for their land to
> Kinanjui who is stated to have given out that all the land had been given
> him by the *Serkali*.[20] This may account for Kinanjui's wealth.[21]

Other chiefs followed suit, and many of the early ones acquired
large tracts of land, resorting to any means. Even today, it is dis-
cernible that some of the early chiefly families are among the largest
landowners.

The government was anxious to create the chiefs into an establishment and as long as the British junior officers could hide from their
superiors the extortion that was taking place among the chiefs,
they hoodwinked this social injustice. It should be realized that
the chiefs had enormous power, even of life and death, which they
abused for personal gain. Peculation became rife and as Low
has observed, 'Abuses were rife; numerous headmen were broken
reeds'.[22] Hence there was real and genuine fear of the whole administrative machinery and in particular of the officials: 'We are afraid,'
Beech was told in 1912, because 'we think all white men must
think alike.'[23] Or as the Kikuyu laconically put it, '*Gutiri muthungu
na mubia*'—there is no difference between the white settler and the
priest (or missionary). On the other hand, there were some few
mbari which invited, or welcomed, the white settlers in order to
protect themselves against the excesses of the mercenaries, or the
abuse of power by the chiefs. Others thought that the settlers were
birds of passage, a new breed of *ahoi* who needed hospitality and
accommodation but who would be gone soon. The gifts of 'amerikani' cloth and beads were seen as cementing the friendship between
the new arrivals and their hosts, yet another evidence that when
the time came for it to be gently hinted that the visitors had over-
extended their stay, they would leave in peace. Some individuals
sold land without the consent of the *mbari* in the hope that when
the need arose, it could be redeemed, following the traditional
methods of such a transaction.

The hardest hit, however, were the *ahoi*, who were squeezed out
by both the new European landowners and their brothers, the

20. Swahili word for government, correctly spelt *serikali*.
21. Notes by Beech re Dagoretti in KNA/PC/1/1/1.
22. Harlow, Chilver and Smith (eds.), op. cit., p. 47. See, also, 'KHT', p. 304.
23. Beech re Dagoretti, in KNA/PC/CP/1/1/1.

Kikuyu. They lost the protection offered in traditional land tenure and became squatters on European farms, where they were joined by all those who had been dispossessed of their land due to alienation, as well as those who had miscalculated and had either sold land to the settler in the hope of redeeming it in the future, or those who had welcomed them in order to protect themselves from the draconian rule of the new chiefs.

Compared to Kiambu, Murang'a and Nyeri lost even less land. On the eastern border of Murang'a there was a fringe of no-man's-land between the Metumi, the Maasai and the Kamba. This area had been neglected largely because it was of marginal agricultural value that was only seasonally suitable for grazing.[24] This was the land alienated to the white settlers, although some Kikuyu families were removed from the slopes of Nyandarua during the demarcation of the forest line. The situation in Nyeri was, however, slightly different; claim to 'lost land' here was based on a spate of expansion which took place between 1902-10, immediately after the establishment of the British administration and after the subsequent removal of the Maasai from Laikipia and Nanyuki in 1904, to make way for European settlement. It was during this period that a number of families crossed the Thagana and North Cania rivers into the Nyeri plains. Nderi Wang'ombe, for example, migrated to Kamaha between Nyeri and Mweiga in 1903, soon after his family had fled from Mathira. Another prominent collaborator, Wambugu Mathangani, migrated to Gatitu from Gikondi after 1902.[25] Others followed suit, until this expansion was halted in 1910, when all the Kikuyu beyond the North Cania and Thagana rivers were repatriated to the Nyeri district. Simultaneous with the northward expansion was a vigorous clearing of the forests towards Kirinyaga and Nyandarua. This group was also moved back to Nyeri during the forest demarcation. In the region of Nyeri hill, Kabage and Kiandongoro, the local chief, Ndiyuini, burnt 'well over 100 huts in this area when the [forest] line was marked about 1910, and the people inside the line were turned out.'[26] Similar measures were taken along the Gura and Ragati valleys and the borders of Konyu and Magutu locations where about 600 to 800 people were moved back to Nyeri. In appreciation of their

24. 'KHT', pp. 106-27.
25. KLC, vol. 1, pp. 82-110, 520-39; 'KHT', p. 306; KNA/PC/CP/1/1/1.
26. KLC, vol. 1, p. 517.

services, many of the chiefs (called headmen at that time), and notably Ndiyuini, were permitted to continue grazing their livestock in the forests. Ndiyuini was eventually stopped from grazing in 1926.

It is evident, therefore, that land alienation initially affected a comparatively small group of people in Murang'a and Nyeri. The main source of complaint here centred on the behaviour of the newly-installed chiefs and their *njama*, whose first assignment on behalf of the British administration was to recruit unpaid labour gangs to make roads and build *bomas*. This was followed by the imposition of the hut tax, a payment which was inexplicable to the Kikuyu. Demands to pay the hut tax coincided with forced recruitment of labour for the settler farms. Some Kikuyu, who had known the security of being the rightful inheritors of ancestral lands, became a mere reservoir of cheap labour just as they had been a source of food for the passing caravans in earlier decades. Thus there was a marriage of interest between the new administration and the settlers. The government officials imposed a tax on the conquered people, and the only source of money was the settlers. And as settler needs for greater output increased, so did their demands on the government to press the unwilling Kikuyu into working for them get louder and, in the end, the administration seemed a mere handmaid of the white farmers in the eyes of the Kikuyu. In the chiefs the government had perfect tools for meeting settler demands: a chief proved his loyalty by the success with which he recruited labour, and anyone who refused to pay the hut tax, or to be recruited for work on the farms, was either flogged or fined a goat. Soon it became clear to the Kikuyu that it was inadvisable to disobey the chief, however foreign that institution.

The Kikuyu, in common with other African peoples, finally submitted to the superior strength of the imperial powers. Colonization, however, would not have had such long-lasting effects if the confrontation between the rulers and the ruled had limited itself to a simple display of physical might. After conquest, a new element manifested itself, and this was to leave an indelible mark on the minds of the subjected people. The British administration's declared *raison d'être* after the period under discussion was that theirs was a 'civilizing mission' to the erstwhile benighted Africans; a vague, convenient, but terribly reassuring attitude of mind, which could be used to explain away glaring injustices to the few people in the metropolitan who were anxious of the black man's welfare, as well as to quell the doubts voiced by future African generations, who questioned the validity of the colonizer's presence in their land.

The achievements (and these were many) and the failures of the Christian missionary endeavour, especially in the field of education, can only be properly studied against this overall background of the 'civilizing mission'. This, however, is outside the field of the present study, but a few words on the initial spread of missionary activity in the Kikuyu highlands is an appropriate point at which to close this account.

The East African Scottish Industrial Mission, which had hitherto operated from its base at Kibwezi, moved camp in 1898 and established itself among the Kikuyu at Baraniki, near Dagoretti. Arrival at this point was most opportune for, with famine and disease ranging in the land, the missionaries carried out a vital service in organizing famine relief and caring for the sick. This earned them a good name, and lasting gratitude, among the destitute Kikuyu. It paved the way for a successful evangelizing enterprise and when the Reverend Thomas Watson moved to a 3,000-acre site at Thogoto (Kikuyu), he attracted hundreds of the sick and hungry, amongst whom emerged future stalwarts of the missionary cause. In 1909 the Scottish missionaries spread further north to Nyeri, where Arthur Barlow founded a station at Tumutumu. Before long, an increasing band of mission adherents learned the three 'Rs' and a variety of skills which qualified them as 'readers', who spread the Gospel, manned clinics and taught basic literacy in the 'bush schools'. The mission schools became the government's source of supply of the artisans and clerks needed to run the lower reaches of the administration—the former warriors in the end became paid hands, or servants, of the white man.

The Scotsmen were not the only ones in the field. In 1900 McGregor arrived at Fort Smith and the following year he founded a station for the Church Missionary Society at Kihuruko.[27] In the wake of British rule further north, he hastened to Murang'a at the invitation of Karuri, where he founded a number of mission stations, with centres at Weithaga (1903) and Kahuhia.[28] Murang'a was to remain a stronghold of the Church Missionary Society,

27. R. Oliver, *The Missionary Factor in East Africa*, London, 1952, chap. 4.
28. *Proceedings of the CMS, 1900-7.*

and after consolidating there, a mission was established at Mahiga in Nyeri district in 1909.[29]

In 1901, The Africa Inland Mission founded a station at Kijabe and the following year the Roman Catholic priests established a station at Kiambu, then at Limuru in 1903 and at Mang'u in 1906. The Catholics also took the advantage of Karuri's desire to have white men at Tuthu and in June 1902 a mission was established there, followed by others at Mugoiri in Murang'a, and at Gikondi, Karima and Mathari in Nyeri.[30]

The end of 1904 marked the eventual defeat of the determined pockets of Kikuyu resistance to the establishment of British rule. By that date the elements that were to affect the development of the Kikuyu society in the twentieth century were beginning to emerge. This modernization weakened their traditional religion, beliefs and habits and culminated in a social upheaval. In the face of an onslaught of western ideas, a rapid social regrouping and a new class of leaders emerged. Medical facilities reduced the high loss of life due to epidemics and child mortality, and the resultant rapid increase in population brought about problems which could not be solved by depending on the attenuated powers of the traditional Kikuyu society, which was in any case disintegrating rapidly. Futhermore, the formalization of provincial and district borders halted the expansion of the Kikuyu, it also isolated them from their cousins and their Maasai relatives and neighbours, bringing to an end the Maasai-Kikuyu cultural fusion that had been taking place for hundreds of years. The manner in which the Kikuyu adjusted themselves to the problems and challenges of the new system of government, economy, religion and education were to become the key issues of their modern history.

29. McGregor in *Church Missionary Review*, vol. 60, January 1909, p. 35.
30. Cagnolo, op. cit., pp. 269-70, 272.

BIBLIOGRAPHY

A. PRIMARY SOURCES

SOURCES OF KIKUYU TRADITIONS

Unpublished

'Barlow Papers', The Library, University of Nairobi.
These include most of his research notes covering a wide-ranging field. Barlow was in close contact with the Kikuyu for about four decades.

Leakey, L. S. B., 'The Southern Kikuyu Studies', 1938.
Basically this is an ethnographical survey but it has excellent chapters on warfare, *mariika* and traditional history.

Muriuki, G., 'Kikuyu Historical Texts'.
This is a collection of oral traditions covering the three Kikuyu districts. These were collected during fieldwork undertaken from September 1967 to August 1968. The texts have been translated into English and duly annotated. However, the original scripts, in Kikuyu, have been preserved and are available for consultation.

Published

Beech, M. W. H., 'Pre-Bantu Occupants of East Africa', *Man*, vol. 15, 24, 1915, pp. 40-1.

Boyes, J., *John Boyes, King of Wakikuyu*, edited by G. W. L. Bulpett, London, 1911.

British Government, *Kenya Land Commission: Evidence and Memoranda*, 3 volumes and *Report*. London, 1934.

Dundas, K. R., 'Notes on the Origin and History of the Kikuyu and Dorobo Tribes', *Man*, vol. 8, 76, 1908, pp. 136-9.

Gathigira, S. K., *Miikarire ya Agikuyu*, London, 1952.

Hobley, C. W., 'Notes on the Dorobo People and Other Tribes; Gathered from Chief Karuri and Others', *Man*, vol. 6, 78, 1906, pp. 119-20.

Kabetu, M. N., *Kirira kia Ugikuyu*, Nairobi, 1966.
McGregor, A. W., 'Kikuyu and Its People', *Church Missionary Review*, vol. 60, 1909, pp. 30-6.
Routledge, W. S. and K., *With a Prehistoric People: The Kikuyu of British East Africa*, London, 1910.
Tate, H. R., 'Further Notes on the Southern Gikuyu of British East Africa', *Journal of African Society*, vol. 10, 1911, pp. 285-97.
—'The Native Law of Southern Gikuyu of British East Africa', *Journal of African Society*, vol. 9, 1910, pp. 233-54.
Wanjau, G., *Mihiriga ya Agikuyu*, Nairobi, 1967.

UNPUBLISHED DOCUMENTARY SOURCES
Official

Kenya National Archives, Nairobi.
   The Archives contain a valuable collection of the early district and provincial records.
The Foreign Office Archives (Public Record Office), London.
   FO2 (Africa series), particularly volumes FO2/57, 60, 73 and 97. This collection contains the correspondence between the IBEAC officials and the Foreign Office, Sir Gerald Portal's reports to the Foreign Office on the state of the company stations and the monthly reports by the company officials in the field to the Administrator. Hall and Ainsworth's reports are indispensable.

Unofficial

'Ainsworth Papers' Rhodes House, Oxford.
   Diaries relating to Machakos and Fort Smith stations.
Church Missionary Society Archives, London.
J. L. Krapf—his original journals and correspondence with CMS.
A. W. McGregor—his journals and correspondence with CMS.
Journals and correspondence of the other missionaries, for instance Rebmann.
'Hall Papers', Rhodes House, Oxford.
   Diaries, 1892-1901. Letters to his father, Colonel Hall.
'Meinertzhagen Papers', Rhodes House, Oxford.
   The original diaries contain more details than the published ones.

Theses and Other Sources.

Austin, H. H., 'The Passing of Waiyaki'.
Jacobs, A. H., 'The Traditional Political Organization of the Pastoral Masai', Ph.D. thesis, Oxford, 1965.

Lambert, H. E., 'The Social and Political Institutions of the Tribes of the Kikuyu Land Unit of Kenya'.

Lamphear, J. E., 'The 19th Century Trade Routes of Mombasa and the Mrima Coast', essay presented for an M.A. degree in Area Studies (Africa), School of Oriental and African Studies, University of London, 1968.

Miers, S., 'Great Britain and the Brussels Anti-Slave Trade Act of 1890', Ph.D. thesis, London, August, 1969.

PUBLISHED PRIMARY SOURCES

Arkell-Hardwick, A., *An Ivory Trader in North Kenia*, London, 1903.

Beech, M. W. H., 'Kikuyu System of Land Tenure', *Journal of African Society*, vol. 17, 65, 1917, pp. 46-59 and vol. 17, 1918, pp. 136-44.

Cagnolo, C., *The Akikuyu: Their Customs, Traditions, and Folklore*, Nyeri, 1933.

Champion, A. M., 'The Atharaka', *Journal of the Royal Anthropological Institute*, vol. 42, 1912, pp. 68-90.

Dundas, C., 'The Organization and Laws of Some Bantu Tribes in East Africa (Kamba, Kikuyu, Tharaka)', *Journal of the Royal Anthropological Institute*, vol. 45, 1915, pp. 234-306.

Dundas, K. R., 'Kikuyu Calendar', *Man*, vol. 9, 1909, pp. 37-8.
—'Kikuyu Rika', *Man*, vol. 8, 101, 1908, pp. 180-2.

Fischer, G. A., *Das Masai Land*, Hamburg, 1885.

Gregory, J. W., *The Great Rift Valley*, London, 1896.

Hobley, C. W., *Bantu Beliefs and Magic: With Particular Reference to the Kikuyu and Kamba Tribes of Kenya Colony*, London, 1922.
—*Ethnology of A-Kamba and Other East African Tribes*, Cambridge, 1910.
—'Further Notes on the El Dorobo or Oggiek', *Man*, vol. 5, 21. 1905, pp. 39-44.
—'Notes Concerning the Eldorobo of Mau, British East Africa', *Man*, vol. 3, 17, 1903, pp. 33-4.

Hollis, A. C., *The Masai*, Oxford, 1905.

Kenyatta, J., *Facing Mount Kenya*, London, 1938.

Krapf, J. L., *Travels, Researches and Missionary Labours During an Eighteen Years' Residence in Eastern Africa*, London, 1860.

Lugard, F. D., *The Rise of Our East African Empire*, 2 vols., Edinburgh, 1893.

MacDonald, J. R. L., *Soldiering and Surveying in British East Africa, 1891-1894*, London, 1897.

Mackinder, H. J., 'A Journey to the Summit of Mount Kenya', *Geographical Journal*, vol. 15, 1900, pp. 453-86.

Meinertzhagen, R., *Kenya Diary, 1902-6*, London, 1957.

New, C., *Life, Wanderings and Labours in Eastern Africa*, London, 1873.

Orde-Browne, G. St. J., 'Mount Kenya and Its People: Some Notes on the Chuka Tribe', *Journal of African Society*, vol. 15, 59, 1916, pp. 225-31.

—*The Vanishing Tribes of Kenya*, London, 1925.

Perham, M. (ed.), *The Diaries of Lord Lugard*, 4 vols. London, 1959.

Portal, G. H., *The Mission to Uganda*, London, 1894.

Shackleton, E. R., 'The Njuwe', *Man*, vol. 30, 1930, pp. 201-2.

Stoneham, H. F., 'Notes on the Dorobo and Other Tribes', *Kenya Land Commission: Evidence and Memoranda*, vol. 2, pp. 2061-2.

Tate, H. R., 'Notes on the Kikuyu and Kamba Tribes of British East Africa', *Journal of the Royal Anthropological Institute*, vol. 34, 1904, pp. 130-48.

Thomson, J., *Through Masailand*, London, 1885.

von Höhnel, L., *The Discovery of Lakes Rudolf and Stefanie*, 2 vols., London, 1894.

Wakefield, T., 'Routes of Native Caravans from the Coast to the Interior of East Africa', *Journal of the Royal Geographical Society*, vol. 40, 1870, pp. 303-39.

B. SECONDARY SOURCES

Barlow, A. R., 'Kikuyu Land Tenure an Inheritance', *Journal of the East African and Uganda Natural History*, no. 45-6, 1932, pp. 56-66.

Beecher, L. J., *The Kikuyu*, Nairobi, 1944.

Beecher, L. J. and S. B., *A Kikuyu-English Dictionary*, Kahuhia, Fort Hall, 1935.

Benson, T. G. (ed.), *Kikuyu-English Dictionary*, Oxford, 1964.

Bloch, M., *The Historian's Craft*, Manchester, 1954.

Boyes, J., *The Company of Adventurers*, London, 1928.

British Government, *A Handbook of Kenya Colony and Protectorate*, London, 1920.

—*Report of the East Africa Royal Commission, 1953-5*, London, 1961.

Buell, R. L., *The Native Problem in Africa*, New York, 1928.

Crawshay, R., 'Kikuyu: Notes on the Country, People, Fauna and Flora', *Geographical Journal*, vol. 20, 1902, pp. 24-49.

Dickson, B., 'The Eastern Borderland of Kikuyu', *Geographical Journal*, vol. 21, 1903, pp. 36-9.

Ehret, C., *Southern Nilotic History: Linguistic Approaches to the Study of the Past*, Northwestern University Press, Illinois, 1971.

Eisenstadt, S. N., 'African Age Groups: A Comparative Study',

Africa, vol. 24, 1954, pp. 100-12.
—*From Generation to Generation: Age Groups and Social Structure*, London, 1956.

Eliot, C., *The East Africa Protectorate*, London, 1905.

Fisher, J., *The Anatomy of Kikuyu Domesticity and Husbandry*, London, 1964.

Gedge, E., 'A Recent Exploration under Capt. F. G. Dundas, R. N., up the River Tana to Mount Kenya', *Proceedings of the Geographical Society*, vol. 14, 1892, pp. 513-33.

Gray, J. M., 'Mutesa of Buganda', *Uganda Journal*, vol. 1, 1934, pp. 22-49.

Haberland, E., *Galla Sud-Athiopiens*, Stuttgart, 1963.

Harlow, V., **Chilver, E. M.** and **Smith, A.** (eds.), *History of East Africa*, vol. 2, Oxford, 1965.

Hinde, S. L. and **H.**, *The Last of the Masai*, London, 1901.

Huxley, E. and **Perham, M.**, *Race and Politics in Kenya*, London, 1944.

Kenya Government, *Atlas of Kenya*, Nairobi, 1962.
—*Kenya Population Census, 1962, Advance Report*, Nairobi, 1964.
—*Kenya Population Census, 1969*, vol. I, Nairobi, 1970.
—*Native Land Tenure in Kikuyu Province, Report of Committee and Appendix* (Chairman G. V. Maxwell), Nairobi, 1929.
—*Statistical Abstracts*, Nairobi, 1967.

Lambert, H. E., 'Kikuyu Social and Political Institutions', London, 1965.
—'The Systems of Land Tenure in the Kikuyu Land Unit', *Communications from the School of African Studies, University of Cape Town*, 1950.

Leakey, L. S. B., 'Land Tenure in the Native Reserves', *East African Standard*, Nairobi, 8 and 15 September 1939.

Macpherson, R., *Muthomere wa Gikuyu: Ng'ano*, Nairobi, 1944.

Middleton, J. and **Kershaw, G.**, *The Kikuyu and Kamba, Ethnographic Survey of Africa*, London, 1965.

Moyse-Bartlett, H., *The King's African Rifles: A Study in the Military History of East and Central Africa, 1890-1945*, Aldershot, 1956.

Mungeam, G. H., *British Rule in Kenya, 1895-1912: The Establishment of Administration in the East Africa Protectorate*, Oxford, 1966.

Munro, J. F., 'Migration of the Bantu-speaking Peoples of Eastern Kenya Highlands: A Reappraisal,' *Journal of African History*, vol. 8, 1967, pp. 25-8.

Muriuki, G., 'Kikuyu Reaction to Traders and the British

Administration, 1850-1904', *Hadith 1* (The Proceedings of the Annual Conference of the Historical Association of Kenya, 1967), Nairobi, 1968.

'Background to Politics and Nationalism in Central Kenya: the Traditional, Social and Political systems of Central Kenya Peoples', *Hadith 4*, Nairobi, 1972.

Ogot, B. A., *History of the Southern Luo: Migration and Settlement*, Nairobi, 1967.

Oliver, R. A., *African History for the Outside World* (an inaugural lecture delivered on 13 May 1964), London, 1964.

—(ed.), *The Middle Age of African History*, London, 1967.

—*The Missionary Factor in East Africa*, London, 1952.

Oliver, R. A. and **Mathew, G.** (eds.), *History of East Africa*, vol. 1, Oxford, 1963.

Orchardson, I. Q., *The Kipsigis*, Nairobi, 1961.

Prins, A. H. J., *East African Age-Class Systems: An Inquiry into the Social Order of Galla, Kipsigis and Kikuyu*, Gröningen, 1953.

Posnansky, M., *Prelude to East African History* (papers read to the First East African Vacation School in Pre-European History and Archaeology, December 1962), London, 1966.

Rosberg, C. S. and **Nottingham, J.**, *The Myth of 'Mau Mau': Nationalism in Kenya*, Stanford, 1966.

Saberwal, S. C., 'Historical Notes on the Embu of Central Kenya', *Journal of African History*, vol. 8, 1967, pp. 29-38.

Sorrenson, M. P. K., *Land Reform in the Kikuyu Country*, Nairobi, 1967.

—*Origins of European Settlement in Kenya*, Nairobi, 1968.

Thomas, H. B, 'George Wilson and Dagoretti Fort', *Uganda Journal*, vol. 23, 1959, pp. 173-7.

Vansina, J., *Oral Traditions: A Study in Historical Methodology*, London, 1965.

Vansina, J., Mauny, R. and **Thomas, L. V.** (eds.), *The Historian in Tropical Africa: Studies Presented and Discussed at the Fourth International Seminar at the University of Dakar, 1961*, London, 1964.

Weiss, P., *History: Lived and Written*, Illinois, 1962.

Were, G. S., *A History of the Abaluyia of Western Kenya, c. 1500—1930*, Nairobi, 1967.

Wills, C., *Who Killed Kenya?* London, 1953.

INDEX

acephalous societies, 3
adventurers, activities of, 158–60
African: historiography 3; history, 1, 2, 4; peoples, 2
Africanists, 1
age sets: Boro, 22; Gitau, 72; Gucu Nduike, 16, 22; Kamau, 22; Kianjagi, 22; Kienjeku, 16, 22; Manguca, 15; Mbira Itimu, 22; Mbugua, 22, 69; Mburu, 20, 22; Mungai, 15, 17, 69, 72; Mutung'u, 19, 20, 22; Ndigirigi, 65; Ndungu, 22, 87; Ngigi, 19, 20, 72; Njenga, 19–22; Njihia, 49; Nuthi, 22, 89; Ruhonge, 22; Uhere, 19–20; Wainaina, 72; functions of, 119–22, 135
age system (mariika), 39, 117, 133–4, 135
Aguthi, 54, 64, 68, 164
ahoi (tenants), 35, 75, 77–9, 81, 94, 114–15, 156, 174–5
Ainsworth, J., 79, 92, 154, 155, 158, 161
askari (soldiers), behaviour of, 143–6, 152–5
Athi (Dorobo), 11, 29, 33–4, 37–41, 43, 46–7, 60, 63–71, 74, 77–8, 80, 87, 100–102, 111, 114, 158
Austin, H. H., 147–8

Babito, 46
Baci, 56, 57
Bacwezi, 46
Bantu, north-eastern, 25
Barabiu, 46, 63, 65, 87, 99, 112, 123, 124
Barlow, A. R., 5, 6, 22, 23, 58, 81, 178
Beech, M. W. H., 20, 37, 80, 175
Bennett, P. R., 51
Bera, 78
Boyes, J. (Karianjahi), 37, 67, 92, 157–61, 162, 173

Boyo river, 68
British administration, 5
British rule, establishment of, 7; in Murang'a and Nyeri, 157–66
Buganda, 4, 142
Burugu, see Purko Maasai

Cagnolo, C., 5, 22
Cania river, 26, 28, 68, 69, 72, 91, 171, 173, 176
Cege wa Kibiru (seer), 137, 138
Central Province, 25
centralized societies, 3, 4
centres of dispersal: Igaironi (Kagairo), 60; Igambang'ombe, 51, 55, 56; Ithanga, 47, 51, 56–8, 60; Kiambeere hill, 51, 56; Mukurue wa Gathanga, 47, 56, 58, 62; Mwene Ndega's grove, 51, 56; Ntugi forest, 51, 55
Chagicho (Thagicu), 52. See, also, Shagishu
Champion, A. M., 22
chiefs, 132–3, 161, 167–70, 174–5, 176–7
CiaMbandi, 51
CiaNgoi, 51
CiaNthiga, 51
Cinga, 159, 160
clans, 113–15: Aceera, 57, 115; Agaciku, 57, 115; Aicakamuyu, 113; Airimu, 113n; Aithiegeni, 68, 74, 113n; Ambui, 115; Angari, 113n; Angeci, 113n; Anjiru, 114; Ethaga, 114, 115; system, 44
collaborators, 147, 152–3, 156–7, 158–9, 160–62, 164, 174–5
colonial: era, 1, 2, 10, 11, 26, 83; history, 1
Cuka, 38, 41, 44, 47–9, 51–2, 55–7, 60, 68; migration of, 51, 55–6

Dagoretti Fort (Kiawariua), 19, 73, 93, 142, 143, 144, 170
defence, methods of, 65–6, 98, 122–4

Digiri, 37. *See, also,* Endigiri, Il Tikirri
Dorobo, *see* Athi
Dualla (Qualla), 19, 147
Dundas, C., 97, 168
Dundas, K. R., 5, 6, 38, 41, 52, 57

economy, 34–5
education: traditional, 8, 9, 112, 122; missionary, 178
Ehret, C., 52, 64
Embu, 29, 38, 41, 44, 48–9, 51–2, 55–8, 60, 88, 111, 169; clans, Igamuturi, 56, Kina, 56; migration of, 51, 56
Endigiri (or Muisi), 38, 41. *See, also,* Digiri, Il Tikirri
Ethiopians, 56
European: caravans, 33; history, 1
eponyms: Ithiegeni, 74; Kamoko, 68; Kiambuu, 71, 74; Njiku, 74; Njiru, 74; Unjiru, 74; Wamagana, 68; Weithaga, 69, 178

Fort Smith, 19, 92–3, 145, 152–4, 157, 171
frontiers, 170–73

Gakere, 159, 163, 164
Gaki, 5, 7, 10, 12, 15, 17–18, 20, 22, 25, 29, 38–40, 43, 45, 56, 62, 67, 69, 70, 71, 87, 99, 111, 112, 114–15, 120, 123, 157, 176
Gakuyu, 58
Galla, 39, 40, 48
Gatama, 73
Gatanga, 68, 72
Gathagana; battle at, 45, 63, 65; natural bridge, 63, 65.
Gathanga, 57
gathano, see seasons
Gatheca Ngekenya, 91
Gathu-ini (salt-lick), 67, 171
Gathuki-ini, 62, 69
Gatonye Munene, 71, 72
Gatundu, 77
Gatung'ang'a (iron age site), 52–4
Gaturi, 62, 63
generation sets: Agu, 23, 24, 49, 111; Ciira, 24, 64, 68, 112; Cuma, 48, 55, 62, 64, 68–9, 111; Iregi, 15, 24, 46, 63–5, 111; Irungu, 23, 117; Maina, 22, 64, 117; Manduti, 23, 24, 48, 55; Manjiri, 23, 24; Mathathi, 24, 48, 57, 64, 69, 112; Mwangi, 22–4, 64, 117; Ndemi, 17, 24, 48, 64; Tene, 23–4, 111; mode of formation of, 15, 17, 18–20, 22–4

Gibbons, 159
Gicamu raid, 20
Giitwa, 45
Gikondi, 68
Gikuyu, 47, 62, 113
Gitene, 68
Githi, 62, 164
Gitiha 74
Gregory, J. W., 67, 142, 171
Gumba, 23, 37–42, 44–6, 48, 54, 57–8, 60, 63–5, 68, 87, 111
Gura, 26, 28, 45, 63, 68
Gutu Kibetu, 90

Hall, F. (Wanyahoro), 142–4, 145, 152–7, 158, 160, 161, 162, 170
Harrison, 162
Henderson, 80
Hinde, S. L., 162, 163
Hobley, C. W., 5

Icakahanya, 165
Igembe, 44, 47, 49, 51–2, 55, 57–8, 61
Igoji, 38, 52, 58, 61
Iguku, 72
Iloikop (semi-pastoral Maasai), 29, 87, 91, 97, 103
Il Tikirri, 41, 54, 57, 64. *See, also,* Digiri, Endigiri
Imenti, 38, 52, 55, 58, 61
Imperial British East Africa Company (IBEAC), 20, 92, 97, 136, 142–3, 146, 170, 174
initiation, 9, 44, 65, 98–9, 114, 118–19, 120, 133–5
Iria-ini, 67, 88, 164, 165
iron work, 34, 39, 53
Ithemukima, 54
Itiati, 171
ituika (handing over ceremony), 18, 22, 23, 100, 109, 117

Juma Mussa, 139

Kabete, 7–8, 10, 15, 17, 19–20, 22, 25, 33–4, 39–40, 43, 46, 62, 64, 66, 69–70, 72, 77, 93, 99, 112, 114, 120, 128, 150, 157, 176
Kahuhia, 54, 69, 178
Kamaru Wamagata, 147, 152
Kamba, 29, 47, 49, 52, 57, 64, 85, 90, 95, 105, 115, 136–8, 169, 176
Kambaire, 54, 68, 74
Kangima, 54
Kanja, 54
Karinjahi, *see* Boyes
Kariara, 158, 162
Karima, 68
Karirau, 23, 45, 68

Karura, 67, 72, 73
Karuri Gakure, 133, 158–62, 163, 167
Kedong massacre, 156
Kembu, 51
Kenyatta, 5, 92
Kershaw, G., 5
kiama (council of elders), 126–8.
    See, also, Kikuyu judicial system
Kiambaa, 53, 72
Kiambu district, *see* Kabete
Kiamuceru, 67, 173
Kianjege, 63
Kiawariua, *see* Dagoretti Fort
Kihara, 70, 78
kihingo (fortified village), 72–3, 78,
    122–3, 171
Kihumbuini, 162–3
Kijanja (Nyanja), 19, 139
Kikuyu: administrative system, 115–
    16; ancestry, 56–8, 64, 66, 67–8,
    70, 77, 78, 88, 91, 98; calendar,
    14–15, 32; evolution of, 58, 62–4;
    history, 5, 14, 24, 55, 95, 136;
    judicial system, 128–31; land
    tenure, 74–81; language, 64; life,
    9, 43; migration, 6–7, 29–30, 44,
    45, 47–8, 55, 57–8, 60, 62–4, 68–73;
    myths of origin, 46–7; neighbours,
    29; people, 5–8, 10–11, 15, 19,
    20, 24–6, 28–9, 33–5, 37–45, 49, 52,
    54, 56–8, 62–3, 66–7, 70–71, 74,
    138–40, 152, 170; pioneers, 33,
    37, 39, 40, 41, 44, 48, 56, 60, 112;
    plateau, 26, 28, 30, 34, 45, 46, 54,
    114, 171; political structure, 110–
    35; relations with IBEAC, 142–57,
    Kamba, 90, 92, 95, 102, 103, 106,
    Maasai, 7, 28–9, 40, 66, 84–8, 91–9,
    107, 124, 179, Ndia, 89; resistance,
    decline of, 156–7; response to
    colonialism, 7, 169–70, 177–8, 179;
    society, 5–6, 8, 35, 81, 99, 110–35,
    150, 179; study of, 4; traditions,
    6, 8–9, 12–13, 23, 39, 41, 45, 48,
    55, 58, 124, 135; unifying factors,
    113–22, 135
Kikuyuland, 5–8, 10–11, 18, 26, 29,
    30, 32–4, 40, 52, 85, 119–20, 137,
    146, 160, 167, 169; early in-
    habitants of, 37–46, 53–5
Kimemeta, Jumbe, 139, 141
kimera kia mwere, see seasons
kimera kia njahi, see seasons
Kinale forest, 40, 44
Kinyanjui Gathirimu (or Nugu), 72,
    93–4, 143–5, 148, 152–3, 174–5
Kiratu, 73
Kirima, 54
Kirimukuyu, 54, 67, 88
Kirinyaga (Mount Kenya), 26, 28,
    32, 56
Kirumwa, 68
Kivoi, 101, 105
Knight, 20
Konyu, 19, 67, 88, 89
Krapf, 87, 101, 103, 105, 137, 140
Kwale ware, 53, *see, also,* migration

Laikipia, 28, 53, 176
Laikipikiak: Maasai, 28, 67, 87, 123;
    wars, 66–7
Lambert, H. E., 5, 20, 38, 51, 111
land, 6–7, 11, 34–5, 38–40, 47–8, 54,
    170, 174–6; acquisition, 11, 34,
    54, 70–71, 73–5, 77–8, 80; loss,
    173–7; ownership, 11, 34–5, 63, 74,
    77, 79, 81; tenure, 74–81
leaders (*athamaki*), 121, 131–2, 157
Leakey, L.S.B., 5, 20, 80
Lenana, 91, 92, 153
Limuru, 73
Lugard, F. D., 84, 143, 145, 146, 150

Maara river, 55, 56
Maasai, 7, 17, 18–19, 22, 24, 28–9,
    33, 37, 39–40, 43, 47, 60, 64–9, 72,
    78, 83, 85, 90, 112, 114–15, 123,
    148, 153, 173, 176, 179; influence
    on the Kikuyu, 98–100; refugees,
    153–4
MacDonald, J. R. L., 147, 151
McGregor, A. W., 5, 24, 38, 52, 93,
    159, 160, 161, 168, 178–9
MacKinder, H. J., 67, 140, 160, 164,
    171
Magana, 54, 68, 74
Magumoni, 51, 56
Magutu, 67, 88
Mahiga, 54, 68
Maigua, 68
Maitho or Maitha a Ciana, 37, 38,
    39
Maktubu, 142, 146–7, 148, 150, 152
Manda island, 60
Maragua, 26, 90
Maranga, 56
mariika, see age system
Mathioya, 26, 68
Mathioya river, North, 63
Mathira, 18–19, 46, 52, 54, 62–8,
    87–8, 157, 164–5, 171
Matiiri, 55
matriarchy, 44
Mau Mau, 7, 10, 82, 95, 113, 122
Mavuria, 52, 56
'Mazeras' (Mathira), 52
mbari (sub-clans), 8–9, 12–13, 34–6,
    39, 42–3, 47–9, 54, 57, 66, 70, 74–5,
    77, 88, 93, 112–13, 115–16, 173,
    175; founders, 43, 54; Gathirimu,

91; Gathagu 72, 77; Gicamu, 19; Kihara, 78; Magana, 115; Marigu, 77, 115; Mbuu, 71; Mumbi, 113, 116; Muniu, 70; Muya, 71, 72; Munyori (or Thumbi), 71; Thiukui, 89; Wahothi, 73
Mbatian, 91, 153
Mbeere, 29, 44, 47–9, 51–2, 55–8, 60; migration of the, 51, 56
Mbeti, 56
Mbuthia Kaguongo, 161, 162
Mbwa, 49, 60
Meinertzhagen, R., 162, 163, 165, 173
Meru, 29, 45, 46–9, 52, 54, 57, 60–61; migration of the, 48, 60; moieties, 61; traditions, 6, 41, 48
methodology, 5–14
Metumi, 7–8, 15, 17–18, 20, 22, 25, 38–9, 43, 45–6, 51, 56, 62, 70, 77, 111, 114–15, 120, 157, 176
Mianzini, 40, 100–101, 104, 139
Middleton, J., 5
migration: archaeological evidence of, 52–4; archaeological sites at Chyulu hills, 53, Don Dol, 53, Gatare Forest Station, 53, Gatung'ang'a, 52–4, Kantana, 53, Karen, 53, Kathpat Estate, 53, Kilomba, 53, Kisima, 53, Kyambondo, 53, Ngungani, 53, Njiiri's School, 53, Pare hills, 53, Usangi Hospital, 53; causes, 29–30, 32–3, 47–9, 55, 62; linguistic evidence of, 51–2, 64; oral traditions affecting, 51; mode of, 34
military sets, see age sets
missions, 178–9
Miutini, 61
Mount Kenya peoples, 6, 37, 51, 58, 85, 102–5; migration of, 6, 49, 54–61, 62–4
Mucene Cege, 73
Muguga, 72
muhingo (closed period), 17–18, 20, 22, 99, 118–19, 167
muhoi, see ahoi
Mukurue-ini division, 46, 54, 62, 63, 65, 87, 90, 165
Mukurue wa Gathanga, see centres of dispersal
Mumbi, 47, 62, 113
Mungeam, G., 7
muramati, 35, 75, 116
Murang'a, see Metumi
Muruka, 69, 72, 160, 162–3
muthamaki, see leaders
Muthambi, 38, 52, 55, 58, 61
Muthithi, 69

Muthondu Nduru, 73
Mutonga river, 55, 56, 60
Mwea, 51, 56
Mwea plains, 29, 105
Mwimbi, 38, 41, 44, 52, 55, 58, 61

Nairobi river, 72, 73, 144
Nanyuki, 29
natural disasters, 49, 85, 88, 91, 92, 153, 155–6, 173, 178
Ndia, 29, 45, 47, 49, 56, 58, 60, 62, 63, 67, 68, 88, 114
Ndiyuini, 176, 177
Ndoro, 40, 101
Nduguti, 54
Nelson, 142–3, 145
Ngaa, 60, 61
Ngai, 68
Ngaring'iru, 89
Ngeca, 72
Ngembe, see Igembe
Nginda, 56
Nguo Ntune, 60
Northcote, 39
Nottingham, J., 7
Nthawa, 56
Nvuvoori, 56
Nyandarua (Aberdares) Range, 26, 28, 29, 32, 53
Nyanja, see Kijanja
Nyanjugu, 54
Nyeri, see Gaki
Nyongera river, 170, 173

obsidian industry, 53
Okiek, 41, 46
oral traditions, 2–4, 6, 8, 14, 38, 40, 46, 54, 60, 86, 102, 116
Orde-Browne, G. St. J., 60

Portal, G. H., 152, 154
pottery finds, 53, 54
pre-colonial history of East Africa, 5
proto-Kikuyu, 42, 44, 47, 48, 58, 62
punitive expeditions against: Kiambu, 147, 148–9, 152, 154–5; Murang'a, 162–3; Nyeri, 163–6
Purkiss, 142, 145, 146, 147–9, 150, 151, 154
Purko: Maasai, 28, 87; wars, 66, 67

Rendille, 56
riika, see age system
Rosberg, C. S., 7
Routledge, W. S. and K., 5, 6, 38, 39, 45, 57, 84, 173
Ruara, see Dualla
Ruaraka, see Rui rua Aka
Ruguti river, 55, 56
Rui rua Aka, 28, 69, 71

190   A HISTORY OF THE KIKUYU

Rui Ruiru, 67, 171, 173
Ruiru, 28
Rukanga, 161
Ruthagati, 67, 89
Rwanda, 4

Sagana station, 63
seasons, 14, 15, 17, 32
Segeju, 52
Sendeyo, 91, 92, 153
settlement: Kikuyu, 7, 26, 32, 34, 35, 37, 43, 48, 54; white, 7, 170, 173-4
Shagishu (Thagicu), 52, 57
Shungwaya, 6, 49-51
Siiriänen, A., 53
Smith, E., 143, 146, 150
Somali, 65
Sonjo, 52
Sorrenson, M. P. K., 82
Stoneham, H. F., 37

Tambaya, 68
Tanga, 52
Tate, H. R., 5, 6, 20, 47, 80
Teleki, 19, 138, 140-42, 150, 151, 161, 162, 171
territorial and political divisions: *bururi*, 36; *itura*, 36, 112, 115, 122, 123; *mbari*, 35; *mucii*, 35-6; *muhiriga*, 35; *mwaki*, 36, 112, 124; *nyumba*, 35, 36, 115; *rugongo*, 36, 112
Tetu, 18, 65, 66, 89, 163, 164, 171, 173
thabari, 94-5
Thagana river, 26, 28, 45, 51, 55-8, 60, 63, 67, 165, 171, 176
Thagicu, 47, 51-2, 54-5, 57-8, 60, 64, 111, 140. See, also, Shagicu and Chagicho
Tharaka, 29, 38, 44, 47-9, 51-2, 55, 57-8, 60, 61
Tharia, 51, 55

Thika town, 26, 72
Thimbigua, 71
Thingithu river, 55
Thogoto, 73, 178
Thomson, J., 138, 139, 141, 142, 146
Thuci river, 51, 55
Thuita, 22
Thuthuni, 54
Tiebo, 77
Tigania, 41, 44, 49, 51, 52, 55, 57, 61
trade external, 86, 102-5, 107-8; internal, 108-9; with Athi, 33, 100-101, coast traders, 104-6, 139-40, 142, 163, Kamba, 96, 100-101, 102-6, Maasai, 33, 86
traders, conflict with, 136-42, 160
tribalism, 1
Tumutumu, 88
Turkana, 57

uncentralized societies, 3
Uasin Gishu, 91
Uganda Railway, 170
Uthaya, 54, 64, 68, 90

Von Höhnel, L., 19, 138, 140-2, 146, 171

Waiyaki Hinga, 19, 71, 72, 77, 142, 146-52, 154, 171, 174
Wakuavi, *see* Iloikop
Wamagana, 68
Wambugu Mathangani, 161, 176
Wang'endo, 71
Wang'ombe Ihura, 18, 89, 90, 159, 160
Wangu Makeri, 133, 161
warfare: internal, 71, 88-90, 94-5; inter-tribal, 84-94, 95, 102
warriors, organization of, 9, 117, 124-6
Weithaga, 69, 178
Werimba, 51
Wilson, 142-4, 150